STUDIES IN CHURCH HISTORY
VOL. I.

MATTHEW SPINKA
ROBERT HASTINGS NICHOLS
Editors

A *History of*
CHRISTIANITY IN THE BALKANS

A STUDY IN THE SPREAD OF BYZANTINE CULTURE AMONG THE SLAVS

By MATTHEW SPINKA
THE CHICAGO THEOLOGICAL SEMINARY

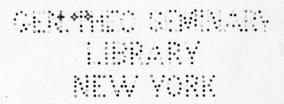
THE AMERICAN SOCIETY OF CHURCH HISTORY
CHICAGO, ILL.

Copyright 1933
by The American Society of Church History
All rights reserved

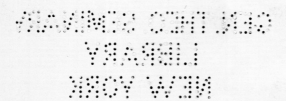

Printed in the United States of America

TABLE OF CONTENTS

❖ ❖ ❖ ❖

PREFACE

No one can be more conscious of the limitations of this work than the author himself. He was constantly impressed with the fact that all too little attention has been paid hitherto to the subject even by scholars of the Balkan nations, not to speak of non-Slavic historians; consequently, much preliminary pioneering work had to be done. Much yet remains to be accomplished; but the restricted scope of this undertaking as well as the paucity of source material pertaining to the early history of the Balkan peninsula combined to make the treatment actually adopted expedient. In gathering his material, the author spent some time during the summer of 1931 in the Balkans. When he came to write the work, he concluded that he must be content with a more modest delimitation of his task than as originally conceived, as a necessary preliminary to further and more detailed studies of the field to be carried on either by himself or others. It was because of the unsatisfactory state of the sources for the Turkish period that he decided to terminate this study with the Turkish conquest of the Balkans.

Special thanks are due, in this connection, to Professors Wilhelm Pauck of the Chicago Theological Seminary, Harold R. Willoughby of the University of Chicago, Kenneth S. Latourette of Yale University, and Robert Hastings Nichols of Auburn Theological Seminary, who read the work in manuscript and made valuable suggestions toward its improvement.

MATTHEW SPINKA

THE RUIN OF GRAECO-ROMAN AND THE RISE OF SLAVIC CHRISTIANITY

It is a matter of no mean pride to the Balkan Christian churches that the beginnings of Christianity in the Balkan peninsula can indubitably be traced to the earliest apostolic times, and that it was none other than the great Apostle of the Gentiles himself who labored there. When St. Paul saw his vision of the man who besought him "to come over into Macedonia and help us"[1] and resolved not to be disobedient to that heavenly vision, the evangelization of Europe, so far as history preserves a record of it, had its inception. Paul himself informs us that he preached the gospel "even unto Illyricum"[2] and that Titus left him to go to Dalmatia, while Demas went to Thessalonica[3]. The apostle did not foresee the development of his labors as we view it in retrospect, or else that knowledge would have given him much sorrow. Who can balance the wrongs and injustice, the crass cupidity, the hunger for land and power which, parading under the fair name of Christianity, again and again submerged the scenes of Paul's missionary zeal in sorrow and misery, against the spiritual blessings of Christianity enjoyed by humble and learned alike, and pronounce with confidence which side tips the scale? But it is probably well that Paul, in his confident belief that the Lord's parousia was near and with his appearance the end of the present age would come, did not dream of the stupendous and far-reaching results consequent upon his hearking to that Macedonian call! The humble laborers who entered upon Paul's work and carried it on remain nameless as far as history is concerned. Yet it was due to them that the spread of Christianity among the Illyrian, Thracian, and Hellenic population, although slow, was not entirely negligible. The new message early penetrated the cities of the southern and western littoral, and such centers as Corinth

---

1. *Acts* 16:9.
2. *Rom.* 15:19.
3. *II Tim.* 4:10.

in Achaia, Thessalonica in Macedonia, Larissa in Thessaly, Salona in Dalmatia, Sardica in Dacia, Heraclea and Anchialus in Thracia, and Sirmium in Pannonia Secunda, became important foci of missionary activity which soon penetrated the interior of the peninsula. Nevertheless, the growth of the new religion was confined generally to urban communities.

The strength of Christianity in the Roman Danubian provinces may be judged from the number of martyrs who fell victim during the Diocletian persecution at the beginning of the fourth century. This outburst of zeal in behalf of moribund paganism claimed the lives of a group of devoted Christians in Sirmium (modern Mitrovitsa) where bishop Irenaeus suffered martyrdom, in Singidunum (modern Belgrade), and in other cities of the Danubian provinces. A serious persecution likewise wrought havoc among the Christians of Salona in Dalmatia, those martyred including even the local bishop, Domnio, and probably his predecessor, Venantius. A similar persecution raged in Durostorum in Moesia Inferior. Also the fact that three councils of the fourth century were held in these regions— that of Sardica (343-44), and the Arian councils of Sirmium (358) and of Singidunum (366)—bears witness to the strength and importance of these sees. Besides, the Balkan provinces produced a number of outstanding Christian leaders, such as Jerome who was born on the confines of Dalmatia and Pannonia, Bishop Nicetas of Remesiana in Dacia Mediterraneum, and the Arian bishops Auxentius of Durostorum, Palladius of Ratiara in Dacia Ripensis, and Ursacius of Singidunum. It must not be forgotten that Emperors Constantine the Great, Jovian, Gratian, and the Valentinians were likewise natives of the Danubian provinces.

But Balkan Christianity was not destined to enjoy a peaceful development. In the first place, its territory was to become the battle-ground between the various invading barbarian hordes and the Roman armies. Had the Danube been retained as the boundary of the Pannonian-Moesian provinces, the western half would have most likely developed a civilization not unlike that of Italy, while the eastern half would have possibly been predominantly Hellenized. But in the struggles between the Romans and the barbarians the latter were ultimately victorious, and after having all but ruined the civilization they had found in the newly won territories, they were in turn conquered by its superior force. In the second place, when the new masters of the peninsula began to feel the seductive influence of the civilization of the Empire, the conflict between the Latin and the Hellenistic cultures for the dominant sway over them proved by no means helpful to the spread of Christianity among them, but rather greatly retarded it. That struggle produced lasting effects upon the cultural history of the Balkan Slavs from that time to the present day, inasmuch as it divided the essentially homogeneous Slavic tribes which settled there into two cultural groups, the westernized Croatians-Slovenes, and the Byzantinized Serbo-Bulgarians.

The ruin of the Graeco-Roman civilization in the Balkans began with the invasion of a million Visigoths who, with the permission of Emperor Valens, settled south of the Danube (376). But in consequence of the galling and oppressive treatment they had received at the hands of imperial officials, they rose up in revolt, and in 378 gained a crushing victory over Valens' army in the battle of Hadrianople. The emperor himself perished in the struggle. Despite the fact that afterwards Emperor Theodosius I had taken them into the service of the Roman army, the Visigoths, dissatisfied with the treatment they had received and seeking new homes, overran the peninsula as far south as Achaia, pillaging the cities and murdering the inhabitants. The greater part of the Balkans was soon in the hands of their leader Alaric. Four years later, they were induced to leave the country and to invade Italy.

The Dalmatian littoral with its hinterland was conquered, in 493, by the Ostrogoths under Theodoric, and was held by them for the next forty years. But in spite of their Arianism, they left the social and religious organizations largely as they had found them. The archbishopric of Salona continued to exercise authority over the territory, and during the Ostrogothic rule two new bishoprics were organized, bringing the total up to six. But in 535 Emperor Justinian determined to reassert the imperial authority over these regions, and for the next twenty years waged battle with the Ostrogoths, who in 548 apparently allied themselves with the barbarian tribes of Slavs, living beyond the

Danube, in an effort to withstand Justinian's armies. Nevertheless, the latter were victorious and the Roman sway was temporarily reestablished.

Besides, new and more formidable enemies loomed upon the horizon. The wild and cruel Huns who had organized their state in the plains of Hungary during the fifth century (it was dissolved in 454), and the no less destructive Turkish Avars who had appeared in Pannonia in 568 and from there dominated extensive regions, wrought havoc by their periodic plundering expeditions into the Balkans. It was in connection with these invasions and as allies of the fierce Avars that a mention of Slavs first occurs in the Byzantine annals.

The original home of the Slavs is the territory which, roughly speaking, may be delimited on the west by the river Vistula, on the south by the Carpathian mountains and the upper reaches of the rivers Bug and Dniester, on the east by the rivers Dnieper and Desna, and on the north by the basin of the Pripet. It seems highly probable that the tribes living nearest the Carpathian mountains began a southward movement into the Danube basin as early as the first century after Christ. The reason for the migration is undoubtedly to be sought in the pressure exerted upon them by other ethnic groups, especially the Goths, who were pushing them southward out of their ancestral homes. The Slavs were thereafter found in considerable numbers in the Roman provinces of Dacia and Moesia Inferior. It even appears probable that they penetrated south of the Danube and the Save rivers during the fifth century, although they founded no considerable settlements there. But beginning with the reign of Emperor Justin (518-527) as Niederle has proved,[4] the Slavic invasions became a formidable menace to the Empire. During Justinian's reign (527-565) the attacks of the Slavs and the related Antae, remote ancestors of the modern Ukrainians, became frequent and serious; both these groups operated in conjunction with the Huns and later with the Avars. In 548 the Slavs for the first time penetrated into the Roman provinces of Illyricum and of Dalmatia as far as Epidamnus. The next year they invaded Thrace beyond Hadrianople and laid the whole region waste. In 550, a large body of Slavs, "such as never before

---

4.   Niederle, L., *Slovanské starožitnosti*, Praha, 1906, V. II, part 1, p. 190 ff.

was known," as Procopius reports[5], invaded the valley of
the Margus (Morava) river, intending to conquer Naissus
(Nish), which Jordanes calls "the first city of Illyricum"[6]
and then to attack Thessalonica. But having learned that
the famous imperial general Germanus, who had defeated
them several times during Justin's reign, had been sent
against them, they retreated. But after Germanus' death,
the Slavs again invaded the Balkans, "overrunning the
Roman domain with complete freedom . . . and wrought
irreparable damage in all Europe, not merely plundering
the country by sudden raids, but actually spending the win-
ter as if in their own land and having no fear of the enemy."[7]
These various invasions greatly depopulated the Danubian
provinces. Procopius reports that Illyricum and Thrace,
from the Ionian Gulf to the suburbs of Constantinople, were
overrun almost every year since Justinian's accession by
Huns, Slavs and Antae, who dealt most cruelly with the
inhabitants. "In each of these incursions, I should say,
more than two hundred thousand Romans were slain or
enslaved, so that all this country became a desert like that
of Scythia."[8] Strong words, these, even though they must
be taken with a spoonful of salt; for in the same chapter
Procopius asserts that Justinian "killed a trillion people"!
When in 568 the Lombards left their seats in the Pannonian
lowlands and the eastern Alps to move into northern Italy,
the Avars along with Slavic tribes occupied these regions[9].
The Slavs then penetrated the basins of the great rivers,
Mur, Drave, and Save. The same process of infiltration
was going on in respect to the Balkan peninsula.

The first permanent occupation of the Balkans by the
Slavs is recorded by John of Ephesus[10]; he relates that in
581, while Emperor Tiberius was busy with the Persian
war, "the accursed people called Slavonians" penetrated into Achaia, Thessaly, and Thrace, and even approached the

5. Procopius of Caesarea, *History of the Wars*, tr. by H. B. Dewing, in Loeb
Classical Library. v. V, Book 7, x1, 2.
6. Jordanes, *Romana et Getica, MGH.*, V; also *The Origin and Deeds of the
Goths*, tr. by C. C. Mierow, Princeton, 1908, p. 91.
7. Procopius, *op. cit.*, v. V, book 7, x1, 32-34.
8. Procopius, *Secret History*, tr. by Richard Atwater, Chicago, 1927, ch. XVIII,
p. 181.
9. Paul the Deacon, *Historia Longobardorum, MGH., Script. rerum Longob.;*
also *History of the Langobards*, tr. by W. J. Foulke, Philadelphia, 1907, p. 62.
10. John, Bishop of Ephesus, *The Third Part of Ecclesiastical History*, tr. by
R. Payne Smith, Oxford, 1860, *VI*, 25, p. 432.

very walls of Constantinople, burning and plundering fearlessly. For four years they had a free hand there, spreading terrible devastation wherever they moved: "they live at ease in the land, and dwell in it, and spread themselves far and wide as far as God permits them," the historian complains. Even after the emperor's return they continued to hold the occupied lands and the plunder they had taken, for "they have grown rich in gold and silver, and herds of horses, and have learned to fight better than the Romans." The situation was not improved under Emperor Maurice (582-602). During his reign, the Slavs invaded Dalmatia, Moesia, Macedonia, and Achaia. The bishop of Thessalonica, Maximus, complained to Pope Gregory the Great of the "vehement afflictions" which his diocese had suffered from the fierce Slavic invaders. The process of Slavicization of the entire peninsula was immensely accelerated during the reign of Heraclius (610-41). By the first half of the seventh century the territory south of the Danube to the Gulf of Corinth and from the Aegean and the Black Seas to the Adriatic, as well as north of the Save River to the boundaries of present-day Austria, was settled predominantly by Slavs. Considering the unnumbered thousands who must have lost their lives during the frequent invasions of the previous centuries, the numbers of the settlers required to occupy and retain the vast depopulated regions of the peninsula must have been immense. That such was the case may be inferred from the fact that the Slavs have not lost their own language and have not amalgamated with the native population they had found in the Balkans to such an extent as was true of the Lombards in northern Italy, the Franks in Gaul, the Visigoths in Spain, and the "Varangians" (whoever they were) in Russia.

The new settlers, "all exceptionally tall and stalwart men"[11], virile, energetic, freedom-loving, hardy, were of course pagan barbarians who invaded the territory not as an organized, compact national unit under the leadership of a commonly-acknowledged prince, but as separate tribes each led independently by its own chieftain. Only upon rare occasions, as for instance in case of an important military undertaking, are their independent tribal units known to have cooperated for the time being. At other times, "they

---

11.   Procopius, *op. cit.*, v. IV, book 7, sec. xiv, 27.

have lived from of old under a democracy, and consequently everything which involves their welfare, whether for good or for ill, is referred to the people," as Procopius reports.[12] This lack of unity also explains why groups less numerous than the Slavs but possessing a superior military or political organization, as the Avars or later the Bulgars, were able to subjugate them. Yet, in course of time they formed a number of more or less closely integrated groups, some of which developed a centralized government and a sense of nationhood—although the Macedonian and Greek groups never developed either. Thus there came to be differentiated among the various tribes the Slovenes, the Serbo-Croatians who in spite of their common ethnic and linguistic character organized themselves into a number of separate political units, the Macedonian Slavs, and the South-Eastern Slavs who, when they had assimilated their conquerors, the Bulgarians, assumed their name, as in like circumstances the Russians were to do later. The theory based upon the report of Emperor Constantine Porphyrogenitus[13] to the effect that the Croatians and the Serbs had been called by Emperor Heraclius from their ancient home to their Balkan seats, although still repeated by some historians, has long ago been exploded as unhistorical by Slavic authorities such as Rački and Jagić.[14] The Serbo-Croatians are known to have been settled on the Save and the Drave rivers for several centuries prior to the reign of Heraclius and to have penetrated deep into the Roman provinces of Dalmatia, Moesia Superior, Dardania, and Praevalitana during the sixth century. By the beginning of the seventh century they were already firmly established in their historic homes.

The uncivilized Slavs put an end to the Graeco-Roman civilization, both secular and religious, which they had found in the Balkans. Since the cities had been ruined in the fierce struggles of the previous centuries, and city-life was foreign to the simple pastoral and rustic Slavs, they settled largely in the open country and for a long time made no effort to rebuild the cities. It was only later that those centers which had escaped total destruction were occupied

12. *Ibid.*, sec. xiv, 22.
13. Constantine Porphyrogenitus, *De administrando imperio*, chp. 30-33; edited by J. B. Bury, *The Early History of Slavonic Settlements*, London, 1920.
14. Cf. the exhaustive discussion of the whole question by Niederle, L., *Původ a počátky Slovanů jižních*, sv. I, Praha, 1906, p. 250ff.

by the Slavs. Thus from a Graeco-Roman cultural domain
the Balkan peninsula rapidly declined into a relatively primitive barbarism, and Slavic paganism with its unsophisticated rude mode of life became dominant. The Latin-speak-
ing population was totally submerged among the new settlers, although it reappeared later as the Wallachians. The
only regions where the Slavs, in spite of their large numbers, have not assimilated the natives, were Achaia and the
craggy, inhospitable Albania.

As for their religious development, Slavs remained on
a comparatively low level. In general, they did not pass
beyond the stage of animism, ancestor worship, and rudi-
mentary polytheism. Moreover, this development was not
uniform: certain Slavic groups never passed beyond the two
first-mentioned stages throughout their pre-Christian history, while others, as the Elbe and the Baltic Slavs, developed fairly high religious concepts and practices. The
earliest description of the religion of the southern Slavs
is found in Procopius, who writes[15]: "They believe that one
god, the maker of the lightning, is alone lord of all things,
and they sacrifice to him cattle and all other victims; but as
for fate, they neither know it nor do they in any wise admit
it has any power among men, but whenever death stands
close before them, either stricken with sickness or beginning
a war, they make a promise that, if they escape, they will
straightway make a sacrifice to the god in return for their
life; and if they escape, they sacrifice just what they had
promised, and consider that their safety has been bought
with this same sacrifice. They reverence, however, both
rivers and nymphs and some other spirits, and they sacrifice
to all these also, and they make their divinations in connection with these sacrifices."

Thus the Slavs poetically conceived the realm of nature
as permeated by personified spiritual forces. The major
objects of worship, such as the sun and fire, were personified
and deified as Perun (referred to by Procopius as the god
of lightning) and Svarog, while the importance of flocks in
the economy of the ancient Slavs is attested by the worship
of the divine guardian of flocks, Veles or Volos. But besides
these major divinities, all nature was poetically regarded

15. Procopius, *op. cit.*, VII, xiv, 23-28; v. IV, p. 271.

as being permeated by personified spiritual beings who partook considerably of human traits—having been originally human—both good and bad, and were capable of intermarrying with mankind, just like the Olympian deities of the ancient Greeks. Forests, rivers, mountains, and even trees and stones, were personified in various fairies, nymphs, dryads and other field-spirits, water-spirits, vily and navky. Worship of ancestors likewise played a very important part in the religion of the Slavs, and they generally venerated household gods—*děd, dědek,* or *děduška domovoy*—a Slavic counterpart of the Latin *penates.* The spirit of the departed ancestor was the genius of the household who was believed to render actual services, such as protection of the house during the night, and whose presence and good-will were absolutely necessary for the well-being of the family.

The Slavs possessed no official priestly class and as a rule built no special temples for their deities beyond providing a more or less permanent altar for the burning of sacrifices. An exception to these statements is found chiefly among the Elbe and the Baltic Slavs, whose various temples —as those of Svantovit, Radegast, and Triglav—became famous, and whose priesthood formed a most powerful class. Otherwise the sacrifices were offered by the heads of families, tribal chieftains, and princes. Religion as such had for its object making the gods and the spirits propitious toward the worshipper by granting him the object of his desire. This result could be gained either by compelling the god or the spirit by means of magic, or gaining his favor by means of offerings. The sacrifices consisted of poultry —especially a black cock or hen—sheep, pigs, and cattle. Occasionally, even human beings were killed as on offering to the gods.

Even if the priestly class were not developed among all Slavic tribes, the class of magic-workers and diviners— a species of shamans or medicine men, known as *volkhvi*— held the most important place in the social life of all Slavs. They combined the practice of magic for the purpose of compelling reluctant or unwilling nature to yield to the suppliant the desired benefits, with the art of healing. Indeed, the modern Russian word for a physician—*vrach*— is derived from the ancient designation for the magic-worker. The *volkhvi,* because of their power over the people, be-

came the chief opponents of Christianity, when this religion
was introduced among the Slavs.

When these primitive and unsophisticated nature-wor-
shippers came into close contact with the high civilization
of the Graeco-Roman world, especially along the coasts of
the Adriatic and the Aegean seas, or along the main
thoroughfares, they readily succumbed to these more
potent cultural forces and not only became Christianized but
in many instances denationalized. But where the Slavs settled in compact masses, not exposed to outside influence to
quite the same degree, their pagan mores remained relatively unaffected. The process of Christianization was not then
a conflict of one culture with another, but rather a gradual
assimilation of the primitive by the higher culture. Thus
the acceptance of Christianity became an integral part of
the process of assimilation of the Slavic barbarians by the
Byzantino-Latin culture. In course of time, this process
has profoundly and radically changed the life of the Slavs,
although they in turn have not left that culture without an
impress of their own. By stamping it with their own genius, they transformed it into what may be called the By-
zantino-Slavic culture.

That being the case, it may readily be understood why
the Slavic tribes, which by political or social exigencies
were exposed to the powerful influences of the Graeco-
Latin culture, found many reasons for resisting them. Not
only the natural inertia or loyalty to the customs of their
fathers, and the self-interest of the *volkhvi* whose existence
as a powerful professional caste was threatened, militated
against the acceptance of the foreign folkways and thought-
forms, but the Slavs soon perceived that the new culture
threatened them with subtle forces of disintegration. Its
dominant expression, the superstitious and considerably
paganized Christianity of the day, was preached to them in
a foreign language. Acceptance of it entailed in many instances a break-up of the solidarity of the Slavic social
group, and consequently resulted in a weakening of its
power of resistance against disintegrating processes. The
Slavic pack soon found that for purposes of self-preservation
they must stand together; and since the closest tie of every
human society is the acceptance of the common customs and
mores, anything which threatened to loosen these bonds

rightly came to be looked upon as inimical to the life of the whole group. Such has always been the case where two cultures were in conflict, as may be witnessed today in the opposition of India's nationalist leaders to western, particularly English, cultural penetration.

Besides the danger of the loss of tribal or national solidarity, there were political dangers. Acceptance of Christianity implied reception of the legal and political concepts of Christian culture which were Byzantine or Latin. Many Slavic tribes found that the process of Christianization inevitably led to the imposition of a foreign political yoke. Thus the perilous period before the foreign cult of Christianity could be nationalized and made politically safe was characterized by a determined opposition to it on the part of those who feared the dangers implicit in such transition.

Furthermore, there were those who out of loyalty or of unfeigned attachment to the poetic lore of their forefathers were determined to reject highly speculative and confusingly involved dogmas of a foreign cult which was bent upon the ruthless uprooting of their own customs and folkways. Even if they did accept Christianity on account of some material advantages, it was in many instances but baptized paganism. Their ancient gods were converted into Christian saints: Veles became St. Blasius and continued to guard the flocks of the Christianized Slavs; Perun became Elijah and continued to drive his thunderous car over the clouds and to wield the thunderbolts of the sky; the household gods were retained as family saints, and the belief in fairies and dryads and other members of that delightful ilk persisted without any apology or camouflage. Most of the sacred days and religious customs of the pagan Slavs were likewise retained, having been but slightly changed or adapted. Thus for instance, the worship of ancestors is still observed in the so-called "slava" celebration, when the Serbian peasants bring food and drink to the graves of their dead.

But if the Slavs were none too ready to exchange their own immemorial religious and social customs for a set foreign to them, the former masters of the peninsula chose to view it as their sacred duty to bring them to the saving knowledge of the gospel. The emperors at Constantinople did not admit that the Balkan provinces had been irrevocably and utterly lost: they held tenaciously to the comforting theory that these fertile lands were still a part of the Empire, only temporarily occupied by a pack of barbarians unfortunately not yet fully subjugated to the imperial sway. Hence, the Slavs were looked upon not as conquerors but as interlopers. The emperors therefore continued to occupy themselves with plans to reassert their authority over the severed provinces. Consequently it was a part of their anxious concern to Christianize the potential subjects and thus make them amenable to their sway.

Hence the territory of the pagan Slavic invaders once more came to be regarded as a missionary field. The ecclesiastical system of the territory had of course broken down as completely as had the imperial administration. Nevertheless, the church was equally loath to relinquish its claim to or give up hope for the reconquest of the region.

The division of ecclesiastical jurisdiction over the Balkan peninsula as set up during the Roman domination proved a potent obstacle in the way of rapid evangelization of the Slavic tribes. Ecclesiastically, the territory had been ruled by both Rome and Constantinople. The division went back to Constantine's delimitation of the respective spheres of the two patriarchates, for he made the boundary of the prefectures of Illyricum and Orient serve that purpose. In 379 Emperor Gratian had detached from the West the dioceses of Dacia and Macedonia, which then became a part of Theodosius' Eastern Empire; thus the boundary was pushed farther west, so that the prefecture of Illyricum was divided into Western and Eastern sections, the line of division running from modern Kotor to a point west of present Belgrade. The provinces of Dalmatia and of Pannonia Secunda formed then the eastern boundary of the western half of the Empire and were placed under the authority of the Praetorian Prefect of Italy, Illyricum (western), and Africa, whose residence was located at Sirmium. But in 437 the province of Pannonia was transferred to the jurisdiction of the Eastern Empire, and came then under the authority of the Praetorian Prefect of Eastern Illyricum, who at first resided at Sirmium, but after the Hunnish invasions under Attila, transferred his seat to Thessalonica. Nevertheless, although politically Illyricum became a part of the Eastern Empire, ecclesiastically it remained under the jurisdiction of Rome. From 437, when Pope Sixtus III appointed

Bishop Anastasius of Thessalonica his vicar,[16] his successors in office acted as papal vicars and ruled the territory in
behalf of their master. Although their authority was a
delegated one, it was to all purposes patriarchal.

It was this discrepancy between the political and the
ecclesiastical jurisdiction over Illyricum which gave rise to
the age-long struggle between the rival patriarchal sees.
Since the territory was politically a part of the Eastern Empire, the Constantinopolitan patriarchate sought to effect
its transfer from the Roman to its own jurisdiction. These
aspirations received a certain measure of support from the
emperors. Thus Justinian, under the pretense of wishing
to enhance the importance of the city nearest his birthplace,
Scupi (modern Skoplye), greatly enlarged and beautified it,
and made it the capital of the prefecture by transferring to
it the residence of the Praetorian Prefect from Thessalonica.
In 535 (by Novella XI) he raised it to the rank of an autocephalous archbishopric, to which he gave the name of
Justiniana Prima. To this new see he granted great privileges and subjected to it the diocese of Dacia consisting of
the provinces of Dacia Mediterranea and Dacia Ripensis,
Moesia Superior, Dardania, Praevalis, Macedonia Secunda,
and as much as remained of Pannonia Secunda[17].

But since the new archbishopric had been founded without papal consent, Justinian's action roused the papacy to a
vigorous protest. Pope Agapetus I (535-536) accomplished
nothing in the matter, but his successor, Pope Vigilius
(537-55) was able to extort from Justinian favorable conces-
sions: the metropolitan of Justiniana Prima was to remain
autocephalous, but was nevertheless to act as papal vicar.
Thus Illyricum boasted of two papal vicariates: one in
Thessalonica, another in Justiniana Prima. This arrangement received the sanction of the fathers of the Fifth
Ecumenical Council in 553.

But the new see was not destined to survive long; for it
appears that an invasion of the Slavs put an end to it. At
any rate, since 602 no mention is made of it in the sources.
Apparently, it no longer existed. For a time the Thessaloni-
can vicariate remained in sole—although only nominal—

---

16. Cf. Thalloczy et al., *Acta et diplomata res Albaniae*, Vienna, 1913, I, No. 15.
17. Zachariae v. Lingenthal: *Imp. Justiniani Novellae*, Leipzig, 1881, p. 130-33.
Thalloczy, *op. cit.*, vol. I, No. 32, 33.

possession of the field, since the barbarian invasions had reduced practically all its sees to the status of "in partibus infidelium." But finally in 732 Emperor Leo III the Isaurian, in pursuance of his iconoclastic policies which were boldly opposed by the Roman West, and furious at the insult offered him by the Roman council which had been held by Pope Gregory III in 731, which had threatened to excommunicate all who should defile, destroy or profane icons, took a decisive step. Leo's iconoclastic legislation committed him to a policy of breaking with the West. He sent a fleet against the Italians, but it was wrecked in the Adriatic. Thereupon, the emperor decided to revenge himself by reducing the papal revenue—a truly vulnerable spot! He withdrew Illyricum as well as Sicily and Calabria from the jurisdiction of the Holy See, attaching these territories to the patriarchate of Constantinople. Besides, Leo confiscated the papal patrimonies in Sicily, Calabria, and possibly Naples. The loss of these regions, especially of Illyricum, was from the financial point of view a very serious one. By these means, the ecclesiastical jurisdiction of Constantinople was extended over the entire territory of the Eastern Empire in the Balkans, and the future of the Slavic states yet unborn was bound up with the Byzantine culture and the Orthodox creed. Thus the iconoclastic controversy with which the Slavs had nothing whatever to do nevertheless exercised a potent influence upon their destiny. From that time the papal policy was directed to the single end of regaining the lost jurisdiction and patrimonies. Amid the colorful vicissitudes of new conditions created by the settlement of the Slavic tribes in the Balkans, the Roman determination to regain the lost authority runs like a red thread through the otherwise disconnected events. In his correspondence with Charlemagne, Pope Hadrian gave expression to this policy by threatening to pronounce the emperor of Constantinople a heretic unless the lost jurisdiction and patrimonies be restored to him[18].

By the time Christianization of the Slavs gained momentum, differentiation among their groups attained the stage which justifies a separate treatment of each resulting national unit. Roughly speaking, these comprised Slovenes, Croatians, Serbs, and Bulgarians.

---

18. Mansi, *Sacrorum conciliorum collectio*, XIII, c. 808-809.

The Slovenes who were seated in Carinthia and Carniola, appear on the stage of history quite early, as far back as the first century after Christ, but began to attract greater attention to themselves as confederates of the Avars. During the reign of Samo (623-658) the founder of the first Slavic realm which temporarily consolidated the Sorb, the Czech, and the Slovene tribes, the Slavic armies gained a victory over their Avar masters[19] which for some decades enabled the Slovenes to enjoy a measure of freedom. But in 745 the Avars attempted to reassert their domination over them. Feeling their own strength insufficient to withstand the Avar hordes, their Carinthian Duke Borut appealed for help to the Bavarians[20]. These latter, after having freed the Slovenes from their Avar foes, asserted their own sway not only over Carinthia but over Carniola as well. When in 788 Bavaria passed under the domination of Charlemagne, the allegiance of the Slovene native dukes was transferred to him as a matter of course.

Christianity began to penetrate among the Slovenes as a concomitant of the Bavarian overlordship. Borut's son and successor, Cacatius, as well as the duke's nephew, were baptized and brought up in the Christian way of life. But even prior to this time there had been attempts at Christianization of the Slovenes. St. Columbanus intended to extend his evangelizing mission to the Slovenes (between 612-13), but his plan was not carried out [21]. St. Amandus from Utrecht came to work among them but with insignificant results. St. Rupert was more successful, as was Bishop Virgilius of Salzburg, who at the request of the Christian Slovene dukes Gorazd and Hostimir sent to their people a number of German missionaries (after 750) under the leadership of Bishop Modestus, who had the right to ordain priests on the field. He founded a number of churches, as the famous one at Maria-Saal, where he was buried. Virgilius' successor, Archbishop Arno, continued this missionary work, sending a considerable number of priests to the coun-

---

19. Krusch, Bruno, ed., *Fredegarii et aliorum chronica*, Hanover, 1888, IV, 48, p. 154-55.

20. *Monumenta Germaniae historica, Scriptorum tom.* XI, Conversio Bagoariorum et Carantanorum, sec. 4.

21. Mabillon, *Acta Sanctorum*, II, Vita S. Columbani, 56. Cf. Hodgkin, T., *Italy and Her Invaders*, London, 1895, v. VI, p. 129, where the author recounts a picturesque legend to the effect that Columbanus saw a vision of an angel who showed him a map of the world and pointed to Italy as the future scene of the saint's labors.

try; finally, in spite of repeated revolts and stout resistance to the work carried on in a language unintelligible to the people and closely associated with a policy of Bavarian political domination, the missionaries succeeded in baptizing a considerable portion of the Slovene population. Toward the end of the eighth century the struggle was terminated with the victory of the new faith.

When the Slovenes passed under Charlemagne's sceptre, the project of their conversion to Christianity was naturally furthered. The great Charles believed in the policy of extending his frontiers by means of missionary work. During his reign there were two foci of missionary work for the Slovenes: the archbishopric of Salzburg and the patriarchate of Aquilea. The chief rôle, however, in the Christianization of the Slovenes without a doubt was played by Salzburg. When in 791 and in 795-96 Charlemagne defeated the Avars and cleared Pannonia as well as the region between the rivers Danube and Theiss of them, these almost totally depopulated regions—the *Avarorum solitudines*—were populated by the Slovenes, the Croatians, as well as the remnant of the Huns. Charlemagne then incorporated this territory with the diocese of Salzburg. Hence, Bavarian missionaries soon pressed after the colonists and carried Christianization as well as Germanization among the Slavic tribes newly settled there. The first bishop regularly settled among the Slovenes was Deodoricus, who was ordained by Archbishop Arno in 799. His diocese extended to the River Drave[22], which formed a boundary between the see of Salzburg and that of Aquilea.

In the thirties of the ninth century there arose in Pannonia a Slavic Croatian state organized by Margrave Pribina, under the overlordship of King Ludwig the German. Pribina's great zeal for Christianization of his subjects was based upon considerations of policy which proved successful, for in 847 Ludwig rewarded his apostolic labors by granting him a hereditary title to the lower Pannonian territory. Pribina's chaplain, Dominic, became quite famous for his missionary fervor. When in 850 the archbishop of Salzburg, Liutpram, consecrated to the Virgin Mary the first Christian church in Pribina's dominions, which was built at Moseburg on the Balaton Lake, more than one-half

22. *MGH.*, Conversio Bagoariorum, sec. 8.

of the number of the notables present on the occasion bore German names. This is an eloquent testimony not only to the heavy German immigration into these regions but also to the success of the Germanizing policy of the Bavarian missionaries. Within fifteen years Pribina's territory boasted more than thirty-two churches and many monasteries.

The greatest impetus to Christianization of the Slavic population of Pribina's dominions came from the work of the two "apostles of the Slavs," the Greek brothers Cyril and Methodius. In 863 they had been sent by Emperor Michael III and Patriarch Photius of Constantinople to Moravia, (a territory roughly corresponding to modern Czechoslovakia) at the request of its duke, Rastislav. This ruler grew apprehensive of the pronounced nationalistic spirit of the missionary work carried on by the German missionaries sent into his territories by the bishop of Passau, for he well knew the dangerous political consequences of such work. The two Greek brothers, who knew the Macedonian dialect in use among the Slavs of their native Thessalonica, preached the gospel in a language easily understood by the Moravians and the Slovenes. In such a way, the process of Christianization, no longer synonymous with a policy of Germanization, for the first time afforded the possibility of setting up a native Slavic Christian church.

The founding of a Slavic church in Moravia by the two "apostles of the Slavs" (863), occasioned a brief interference with the process of Germanization of Pannonia. When in 869 Methodius was returning from Rome after having received from Pope Hadrian II episcopal consecration, he paid a visit to the court of the Pannonian ruler, Kocel (861-76), the son and successor of Pribina. This astute ruler quickly saw the advantages of a native Slavic church for his dominions, for such an organization would tend to free him from the German overlordship. He therefore requested Pope Hadrian to permit Methodius to remain in Pannonia permanently and to set up an independent Slavic church there. But instead of complying with this demand, Hadrian, as reported in the most important source, the Pannonian *Life of Methodius*,[23] decided upon a much more ambitious and bolder project of restoring the defunct ancient metro-

---

23. Teodorov-Balan, A.: *Kiril i Metodi*, Sofia, 1920, vol. I, Zhitie Metodiovo, VIII.

politan see of Sirmium (present Mitrovitsa), traditionally the see of St. Andronicus, consecrating Methodius as its archbishop, and thus combining both Pannonia and Moravia into a new archepiscopal see. The pope was thus able to secure direct control over the new diocese which hitherto had formed a part of the Salzburg archbishopric.

Methodius was most likely actuated by motives not of personal ambition, but of zeal for the expansion and firm establishment of his Slavic work. The historic see of Sirmium would confer upon the Slavic diocese an existential justification which a new foundation would find difficult to acquire. But such a flagrant injustice to the rights of the archbishop of Salzburg could not be passed over without a protest. The latter dignitary might have possibly acquiesced in the erection of a Moravian bishopric under his own immediate jurisdiction. But the reestablishment of the independent archbishopric of Sirmium with Methodius at its head, by which act the Pannonian and Moravian ecclesiastical jurisdiction, along with a great deal of valuable property, were lost to the Salzburg see, made conflict inevitable. Methodius was taken prisoner by the archbishop and most shamefully mistreated. To be sure, after some years in consequence of papal intervention he was released and restored to his office. But after his death (885) the Germanizing party in his archdiocese everywhere proved victorious, so that ultimately Christianity in the Slovene and the Pannonian-Croatian territories became an all-powerful Germanizing cultural force. In 894 the occupation of Pannonia and Slovakia by the Magyars, an Ural-Altaic nation probably of Finnish origin (although another theory sees in them Turco-Tartars) once more and radically changed the cultural character of these regions.

In the case of the Dalmatian Croatians, the process of Christianization was much more complicated. Its beginnings are ascribed to Emperor Heraclius (610-41) who called for the purpose missionaries from Rome. Emperor Constantine VII Porphyrogenitus, who preserved this information, writes: "Emperor Heraclius sent for and brought from Rome priests, and made some of them archbishops, bishops, presbyters, and deacons, and baptized the Croatians"[24]. It is not surprising that the emperor should have called upon

---

24. Constantine Porphyrogenitus, *op. cit.*, chp. 31.

Rome to furnish the missionaries, since the mission field lay within the territory under Roman ecclesiastical jurisdiction. But it is impossible to believe that the evangelizing labors among the Croatians were begun with a complete hierarchy from archbishops down to deacons, for the work in its earliest stages could not have required the presence of the princes of the church. When one remembers the difficulties encountered two and a half centuries later by the Bulgarian khan Boris in his efforts to secure an archbishop for his much more mature church, one grows quite sceptical about the accuracy of Constantine's assertion. At any rate, this mission, whatever its size or personnel, could not have been very successful in its work, for nothing more is heard of it or of the results obtained.

Most of the territory held by the Croatians along the Dalmatian coast had formerly been ecclesiastically subject to the archbishop of Salona. But when this city was ruined during the invasions of the barbarians (c. 614), a new city, Spalatum arose in its place. By the end of the eighth century this newer city became the heir of Salona even in respect of the ecclesiastical rights of the ancient metropolitan see. But it was not until 925, at the synod held there under the authority of papal nuncios, that Spalatum was raised to the rank of a metropolitanate.

In 678 the Dalmatian Croatians acknowledged the supremacy of Emperor Constantine IV Pogonatus (668-85) and thus came under the political influence of the Byzantine Empire. Nevertheless, ecclesiastically the territory was still subject to Rome, and the see of Spalatum, whose first bishop was John of Ravenna (c. 780), did much to spread Latin Christianity among the new settlers of the country. But when in 732 Emperor Leo III transferred Illyricum to the jurisdiction of the Constantinopolitan patriarchate, Spalatum became an Orthodox see and an effort was made to gain the whole country for the Eastern rite. In 792 Charlemagne conquered so much of the territory occupied by the Croatians in his *Drang nach Osten* that he became a neighbor of the Bulgarians, and in accordance with his set policy promptly undertook Christianization of his newly-won lands by Latin missionaries. Thus the Croatians along the Save and the Drave rivers were drawn within the orbit of Western civilization—an event of momentous importance for their culture and history.

The chief missionary among the Dalmatian Croatians was St. Ursius, and the first among their princes to be converted to Christianity was Visheslav (c. 800). The Latin influence soon became paramount, especially when during the reign of Vladislav (821-35) a Croatian Latin bishopric was established at Nin (the Roman Nona), and this diocese which comprised all of Croatia from Rascia to the mouth of the river Cetina was thus lost to the Eastern see of Spalatum. The rest of Dalmatia, with Spalatum, remained Byzantine. The reason for establishing a separate bishopric for the Croatians is to be sought in the desire of the papal curia to regain at least a part of the territory of Illyricum lost in 732 by the decree of Leo III. In order to guard against the eventuality that Spalatum might reassert its authority over the diocese of Nin, the latter was subordinated directly to the pope. During the next reign, that of Prince Mislav (835-45), the bishop of Spalatum actually made an attempt to win the Nin bishopric to his own jurisdiction, but without success. This goal was reached in 925, after Spalatum had again passed to the papal jurisdiction and was made an archbishopric; the Nin diocese then lost its independent existence and its territory was divided among other Dalmatian sees. With the passing of the Nin bishopric, the Slavic liturgy was abolished and prohibited, and gave place to the Latin rite. Thereafter, the archbishop of Spalatum bore the title of *archiepiscopus totius Dalmatiae et Croatiae.*

During the reign of Mislav and his successors, the country was somewhat disturbed by heretical teachers. For a time it became the field of labors of that unhappy Calvinist born before his time, the unwilling monk Gottschalk of Orbais (c. 805-868) whose championship of the doctrine of absolute double predestination brought upon him the condemnation of the church. The popes found it necessary to take vigorous steps to prevent the spread of the heresy.

Mislav was succeeded by the pious Prince Trpimir (c. 845-65) who constructed at his magnificent residence at Klis, near Spalatum, a church and probably the first Benedictine monastery in Dalmatia, and settled these foundations with monks whose task it was to stablize the people in their new faith. This policy of close alliance with the West was followed by his successor, the brave and warlike Domagoy (c. 864-70), known to his Venetian neighbors on account of his ruthless prowess as the *Sclavorum pessimus dux*. During his reign, the energetic and warlike Byzantine emperor, Basil I the Macedonian (867-86) determined, at the request of an embassy from Dubrovnik, to relieve that mighty commercial center from the Arab corsairs who were besieging it and were playing havoc with Mediterranean shipping and commerce. Aided by the Roman Emperor Ludwig II (825-75), who was accompanied by Domagoy as well as his other Slavic subject princes, Basil succeeded in his design. By 871 the important south-Italian city of Bari was again in Ludwig's hands, having been for the previous thirty years a Saracen stronghold. But soon after Bari passed over to the Byzantine emperor, and with it gradually the whole of southern Italy. Basil also tried to win the allegiance of the Croatian prince who acknowledged Ludwig as his overlord. In this project, however, he failed, and the venture resulted in the estrangement between the two emperors. Basil was able, however, to secure an ascendency over the Serbians. Domagoy also succeeded to steer clear of the entangling alliances with the Byzantine church and to remain in communion with the Roman see. This is attested by a letter of Pope John VIII (872 or 873) in which the latter complained of the treachery of Patriarch Ignatius of Constantinople in alienating the Bulgarian church from papal jurisdiction[25].

But Croatia possessed a strong pro-Byzantine party, probably led by the dispossessed sons of the former Prince Trpimir, which was not afraid even to assassinate their ruling prince in order to bring about a change of the dominant pro-Western policy. When their treasonable conspiracy was revealed, Domagoy had all the revolters put to death.

In spite of his thwarting of the incipient rebellion, Domagoy's pro-Western policy proved his undoing. One of the sons of Trpimir, Prince Zdeslav (878-79), secured the help of Emperor Basil I in his project to overthrow Domagoy, and having succeeded, seized the throne himself. Thereupon he acknowledged, according to the report of

25. Jaffé, P., *Regesta pontificum Romanorum*, Lipsiae, 1885, I, no. 2964.

Constantine Porphyrogenitus, Emperor Basil as his suzeraign and asked at the same time for Byzantine missionaries
to Christianize those of his people who had not as yet been
baptized.   These missionaries are said to have baptized even
the fierce pagans and famous pirates, the inhabitants of the
Narenta valley, who hitherto had withstood all attempts at
conversion; the Byzantines also extended their labors to the
Serbs of the hinterland.   The Nin bishopric, which hitherto
had exercised jurisdiction over the entire territory of
Croatia, now became subject to the patriarchate of Constantinople.

These events greatly alarmed Pope John VIII who
feared that Croatia might be definitely lost to the papal
jurisdiction as Bulgaria had been.   It may have been at the
instigation of the papal legate who in 879 visited Zdeslav's
court on his way to Boris of Bulgaria with a letter from Pope
John pleading with the khan to return to the papal
obedience[26], or as the result of the machinations of the
bishop-elect of Nin, Theodosius, that one of the zhupans,
or provincial governors, Branimir, revolted against the
prince.   The revolt, during which Zdeslav was assassinated,
was successful, and Branimir seized the throne for himself.
He thereupon became the real founder of the independent
Croatian state.

Branimir's reign (879-892) witnessed the final adoption, on the part of Croatia, of the policy of Western political and ecclesiastical orientation.   As soon as he ascended
the throne, Branimir sent the papal legate, John, back to
Pope John VIII with letters of complete submission to the
papal see in behalf of himself and of his people.   The pope,
responding in two letters dated June 7, 879, most gladly
welcomed the Croatian prince and his people into the bosom
of the Catholic church[27].   The Croatian bishopric of Nin
was restored to papal obedience and the bishop-elect,
Theodosius, was confirmed in his office.   John VIII likewise
sought to secure the obedience of the Byzantine prelates of
the Dalmatian coast, but in this effort he did not succeed.

Beginnings of the Christianization of the Serbians, who
for the greatest part occupied the inner lands of the "old

26. MGH., Epistolarum tom. VII, Karolini aevi tom. V, Berlin, 1928, epp. 182-
184.
27. Jaffé, P., Regesta, I, nos. 3259 and 3260.

Serbia" and were thus less directly exposed to foreign influences than their Croatian cousins, are likewise ascribed to Emperor Heraclius. Constantine Porphyrogenitus affirms that "having brought representatives ($\pi\varrho\varepsilon\sigma\beta\acute{\upsilon}\tau\alpha\varsigma$) from Rome, the emperor baptized them (the Serbians) and taught them to do pious works well"[28]. How effective or lasting this work proved we have no means of knowing. The more frequent contact of the Serbian inhabitants of the maritime territories with the Byzantino-Latin culture undoubtedly resulted in the spread of Graeco-Roman Christianity among them. Moreover, interest of the Greek church in carrying on active propaganda among the Slavs is evident from the fact that the patriarchate of Constantinople was wont to appoint inspectors ($\pi\varepsilon\varrho\iota\upsilon\delta\varepsilon\upsilon\tau\acute{\eta}\varsigma$) to oversee the missionary work in the European themes as the imperial provinces were then called. Thus although no general conversion of the Serbs occurred till the middle of the ninth century, the number of Slavs who had accepted Christianity prior to that date must have been considerable. This may be inferred from the fact that one of the patriarchs of Constantinople, Nicetas I, (766-780) was a Slav. He had been one of the secular priests attached to the Church of the Holy Apostles in Constantinople; tradition affirms that he had never learned to speak Greek correctly.

Another, this time more definite and successful attempt to convert the Serbians, occurred during the reign of Emperor Basil I the Macedonian (867-86). During the preceding reigns, from the time of Emperor Michael II the Stammerer (820-29) to that of Michael III the Drunkard (842-867), the Byzantine Empire suffered a decline in power and prestige. Taking advantage of this weakness, the Serbians asserted their independence of the Empire whose overlordship they had acknowledged since the days of Leo III the Isaurian. They organized themselves under the leadership of five principal zhupans or provincial rulers; those of Dioclea, Trebinye, Hum, Bosnia, and Rascia. The three first-named zhupas or provinces were maritime, while the two last-named comprised inner lands. It is also possible that this political revolt was accompanied by a relapse into paganism, since the Christianity of these people—as much of it as there was—sat rather lightly upon them and was

---

28. Constantine Porphyrogenitus, *op. cit.*, ch. 32.

largely regarded as a concomitant of the Byzantine rule.

Emperor Basil's interest in their conversion was aroused in the following manner: the Serbs living along the Dalmatian coast, and especially those of the Narenta valley, took to the highly lucrative business of piracy, and became a considerable menace to Mediterranian commerce and trade. Their depredations finally provoked the emperor to a determined effort to suppress the raids. In this punitive undertaking he was eminently successful and not only swept the Serbian pirates off the seas but pursued them into their settlements which he then promptly laid waste. Having thus chastized them and having brought them to a tractable state of mind, Basil sent them a number of priests and compelled these fierce pirates to accept Christian baptism. It would certainly be too much to expect that the somewhat innocuous rite of baptism would immediately change the fierce pirates into gentle doves.

The zhupan of the Serbian territory of Rascia, Mutimir (c. 850-91), seeing the exemplary and thoroughgoing chastisement administered by Basil to the inhabitants of the Narenta valley, became somewhat apprehensive for the safety of his own rule. It appears that the work of Christianization of his people was being quietly carried on by some unauthorized missionaries. At least Pope John VIII in a letter written in 873[29] complained to the zhupan about it, and advised him and his people to submit to the spiritual direction of the newly-created archbishop of Sirmium, Methodius. But when Emperor Basil became aggressive in the matter of the Narenta piracy, in order to forestall any hostile move on his part, Mutimir, possibly in behalf of the other Serbian zhupans as well, sent an embassy to Constantinople professing his submission to the emperor and requesting him to send missionaries into the Serbian territories to baptize his people. Basil gladly complied with the request; and it was at this time that the official, if not actual, conversion of Serbians to Christianity took place.

It must be understood that this "Christianization" accepted on the part of zhupans as a strictly political measure and on the people's part as an act of obedience, left much to be desired. Not only were there many who refused to receive even the outward sign of Christianization—baptism—

---

29. Jaffé, *op. cit.*, I, no. 2973 (2259).

but those who did receive it did not manifest any noticeable change in their môde of life. Christianity remained for centuries a foreign cult. The church services, conducted in Greek, were naturally incomprehensible to the people, who therefore continued secretly or openly to worship their ancient deities. This was especially true of the worship of the family god—the deified ancestral spirit. In consequence, there resulted a curious co-mingling of Christianity with paganism which has remained the religion of a part of the populace ever since. It was not until toward the end of the ninth century, when the disciples of Methodius, especially Clement of Ohrid and Nahum, began their missionary work in Western Macedonia in the vernacular, that Christianity took deeper root among the Serbian and the Macedonian Slavs. These missionaries brought with them Slavic translations of the Scriptures and of the liturgical books. The work carried on by these pious and worthy men and their disciples was far more effective and successful than that of their Greek colleagues had been.

As for the Slavic tribes living in the region between the Danube river and the Haemus mountains and from the river Isker to the Black Sea, little is known about the process of Christianization among them prior to the invasion of the territory by the Bulgars. But there is no doubt that the process had been quietly going on: the Slavs of the region came into commercial contact with the Greeks both at the Black Sea ports and on the great overland commercial routes; great numbers of them served in the army; moreover, many of them became slaves. In all these several ways they came in contact with the Byzantine culture and with Christianity. But these influences affected only individual groups and communities, not whole tribes. Since the eight Slavic tribes occupying this region developed no sort of confederation or union, the method of converting the ruler of the nation and through him the subjects was excluded.

This peaceful and piecemeal process of Christianization was rudely interrupted by the invasion of the Bulgarians. The original home of these nomads extended over the regions of the central Volga to the river Kama, and they were probably of Finnish (Ugrian) or else of Tartar origin mixed with Turkish stock. Some tribes of these people had moved south to the shores of the Sea of Azov, but in the seventh century, after the death of their Christian khan Kubrat (or Kurt), his five sons separated. Four brothers left the ancestral steppes to seek other settlements; one remained behind as the heir of Kubrat's dominions. One of the four brothers, Asperuch, settled with his followers on the Lower Danube, somewhere in modern Bessarabia.[30] Even prior to this event, the name of the Bulgars appears in Byzantine history. Emperor Zeno (474-491) asked their aid against the Goths, and since his day they were employed several times by the Empire. Asperuch's hordes, however, soon were attracted by the fertile lands south of the Danube, and sometime between 650-679[31] they crossed the river and occupied a part of the imperial territory. Emperor Constantine IV Pogonatus (661-685) undertook an expedition against them with the purpose of expelling them. But some infirmity of his described by Theophanes as "sore feet" —possibly gout—prevented him from taking energetic measures. At any rate, his army fell back before the invaders who penetrated as far south as the present-day Varna. They settled in the country which they had occupied, and the emperor was forced to negotiate with them for terms of peace (679). Thus Asperuch became the founder of modern Bulgaria.

As for the Slavic population settled in the territory, they not only offered no resistance to the invaders, but appear to have entered into a voluntary political union with the Bulgars, by the terms of which the Slavs were obliged to render their Bulgarian overlords military aid and possibly pay a yearly tribute. The Slavic population which comprised eight tribes, appears to have promptly acquiesced in this arrangement, either because they were in revolt against the Romans, or possibly because they still remembered the terrible yoke of their former masters, the Avars, against whom the Bulgars would now protect them. The two racial groups, however, did not amalgamate. In accordance with the treaty, as Theophanes says[32], the Slavic tribes, under their own tribal leaders, were moved from their settlements and planted on the fringe of the territory occupied

30. Theophanes, *Chronographia*, ed. C. de Boor, Leipzig, 1883, vol. I, p. 357-59.
31. Niederle, L., *op. cit.*, vol. 2, p. 405, places the event in 679.
32. Theophanes, *op. cit.*, I, p. 359.

by the Bulgars, to guard it against the Avars. At the center of this strategic and well-protected territory lay Pliska, northeast of Shumla, where the sublime khan, as the ruler of the Bulgars was called, built his palace and held court. This form of governmental organization of the Bulgars and Slavs is further confirmed by Frankish sources of the ninth century which speak of it as *Bulgarorum societas*. Thus the Slavic tribes were for the first time definitely held together by the military overlordship of the Bulgars. The sway of the new masters of the north-eastern Balkans extended south to the Haemus (Balkan) Mountains, and on the north to an undefined boundary somewhere in Wallachia and Transylvania, where it adjoined the Avar empire. On the west it was probably bounded by the Isker River. This extensive territory was ruled by the sublime khan, who was no more than a chief of the khans of various Bulgarian clans, although he was scion of the famous dynasty of Dulo, who held the office of sublime khan in a hereditary fashion. It was because of their iron military discipline, a characteristic in which the Slavic tribes were ever deficient, that the Bulgars were able to impose their overlordship upon the far more numerous Slavs. The state organization of the Bulgars proved sufficiently strong to withstand the successive attacks of the Empire even after the death of Asperuch, which occurred in 701.

The mightiest of Asperuch's successors was the grim warrior Krum (797-814), under whose rule the Bulgarian territory was greatly extended. He conquered the Avars, and later (in 811) when his growing strength alarmed Emperor Nicephorus (802-811) to the extent that he led his armies against the barbarian khan, Krum caused him a terrible defeat, in which the Greek army, finding itself caught in a trap engineered by the Bulgarian khan who had closed the Balkan passes behind it, was annihilated. Nicephorus himself fell in the battle, and Krum had the emperor's skull fashioned into a drinking goblet.[33] In 813 Krum defeated Emperor Michael I Rangabe near Hadrianople, and besieged Constantinople. This task proved, however, too great for him, and he retired, having first utterly devastated Thrace.

After Krum's death (814), caused by the bursting of a

33. Theophanes, *op. cit.*, v. I, p. 761-5.

blood-vessel as he was preparing for another siege of Constantinople, the throne was to have passed to his young son, Omortag; but it was usurped for a brief period by three nobles. During this interregnum there appears to have occurred cruel persecution of Christians who had been taken prisoners by Krum at Hadrianople in 813. Among these, a late Slavonic source mentions even the archbishop of Hadrianople, Manuel, whose arms Ditzeng, one of the ephemeral rulers, ordered cut off. Tsok, another of the infamous trio, went so far as to demand that all Christian captives, lay and clerical, renounce their faith; those who refused were massacred. Whether or not the persecution extended to native Christians, the sources do not say.

There is no doubt that the numerous Christian captives who had been brought into Krum's dominions carried on a lively campaign of proselytism, especially among the Slavic population. When Omortag finally established himself on the throne (late in 815), he regarded the Christian propaganda as sufficiently dangerous to adopt a policy of persecution. The cause of his decision appears to have been not so much religious fanaticism as state policy. The dissemination of Christianity was regarded as a means employed by the Byzantine emperor to subvert the allegiance of the Bulgar subjects, since the former represented the Christian prince *par excellence*. It was now that the mutilated Archbishop Manuel lost his life[34] along with some other Christians.

The story of the Christian Greek captive, Cinamon, must be viewed in the same light. Cinamon was among the captives whom Krum had taken at Hadrianople. The khan had presented him as a slave to Omortag. On account of his physical beauty, Cinamon soon became a favorite at Omortag's court; but later, for refusing to abjure his faith— a passage eloquently magnified by the narrator, the Bulgarian Archbishop Theophylact[35]—he was imprisoned. After Omortag's death (831), his oldest son, Enravotas, befriended Cinamon, and secured his freedom. In turn, Cinamon converted the Bulgarian prince and baptized him. But this brought upon Enravotas, who held some important position

---

34. Theophanes continuatus, *Chronographia*, p. 217. In *Corpus Scriptorum Historiae Byzantinorum*, Bonn, 1838.
35. Theophylactus, *Historia martyrii xv martyrum*, in Migne, GP, CXXVI, p. 192ff.

in the army,[36] suspicion of Hellenophilism. The baptism of
the prince was undoubtedly a political *faux pas*: it was dis-
tinctly awkward to have a Christian suspected of Hellenophilism occupy a high army command and to encourage,
by his example, an undesirable political tendency. Viewing it as a potential betrayal of Bulgarian interests, khan
Presiam or Malamir, as he was known in Slavic, strove to
dissuade his brother from persisting in his new faith. But
failing in this task, he sentenced Enravotas to death (849).
The Christian prince was decapitated.[37] Theophylact, writing much later, interprets the episode as a case of Christian
martyrdom; but there appears to have been no general persecution, as this is the only case cited.

But with the death of Malamir and the accession of his
successor Boris, Bulgaria entered a new era. The reign of
Boris (852-889), one of the most outstanding during the
history of Bulgaria, is specially significant on account of
Boris' conversion to Christianity, the consequent adoption
of that religion as the national creed, and the fundamental
change in the political character of the Bulgarian government which resulted therefrom. Back of these changes,
political factors were preeminent. It is this political back-
ground which must be understood in order that the reasons
for Boris' conversion may become clear.

Among the first acts of Boris after he ascended the
throne of his fathers was the conclusion of a treaty with the
powerful Moravian prince, Rastislav, whereby the two rulers
allied themselves to oppose the expansionist policy of
Emperor Ludwig the German. In pursuance of Ludwig's
policy, the bishop of Passau had sent into Rastislav's country missionaries, who ostensibly had played the rôle of
messengers of the Prince of Peace, but in reality had been
political agents of Ludwig, who bore but little resemblance
to the former Prince. But the great defeat which the two
allies, Rastislav and Boris, suffered at the hands of the
bellicose German, caused Boris to withdraw from the coali-
tion. Indeed, in course of time he even became an ally of
Ludwig against the latter's rebellious son, Karloman, who

---

36. This conjecture is based upon Runciman's interpretation of Theophylactus'
remark that the prince was nicknamed Voicus, which he takes to mean, from its similarity to the Bulgarian word for soldier, some high position in the army. Runciman,
S., *A History of the First Bulgarian Empire*, London, 1930, p. 89.
37. Theophylactus, *op. cit.*, p. 197.

with Rastislav's aid took up arms against his father (862).
The Bulgarians then actually fought on Ludwig's side
against their erst-while allies, the Moravians. There has
ever been but little consistency in the Balkan politics.

In view of these close political relations between Boris
and the formidable Ludwig it is not surprising to learn that
the latter made attempts to induce Boris to accept Christianity. Whether or not it was a part of the treaty concluded between the two rulers at the time of Karloman's revolt
(862), Ludwig at any rate informed Pope Nicholas of Boris'
intention of receiving baptism, at which news the pope was
effusively gratified.[38] The same report was recorded by
Archbishop Hincmar of Rheims.[39] Thus although there is
no certainty about the exact nature of the negotiations, it
is evident that the subject of Boris' acceptance of Christianity was broached. As for the Moravian prince Rastislav,
he had even before this (although in the same year, 862),
requested for his people missionaries from Constantinople
capable of speaking the Slavic language. He appealed to
the distant Byzantine capital not only to ward off the political danger consequent upon the missionary work conducted by the bishop of Passau, but also because wishing to control the church within his dominions, he knew that such a
pope as Nicholas I would never permit the establishment of
a practically autonomous Slavic church. Patriarch Photius
of Constantinople was far more likely to acquiesce in
Rastislav's policy: having been pronounced deposed from
his see by Nicholas, he became, by reason of his struggle
with the pope a champion of the theory of the essential
equality of the patriarchates. Thus he was much more likely to be amenable to Rastislav's ecclesiastical policy, since
he needed all the outside support he could gain, and furthermore because the policy of the Moravian prince was essentially anti-papal.

Thus the two Slavic rulers, Rastislav and Boris, began
elaborating schemes of acceptance of Christianity at about
the same time. But the political dangers involved therein
led them to adopt mutually opposed means. Boris, fearing
the political pressure from the age-long enemy of Bulgaria,
the Byzantine Empire, and hence not desiring to subject his

---

38. Nicolai Papae I *Epistolae*, in Migne, PL, CXIX, col. 875, xii.
39. *MGH.*, *Scriptorum* tom. I, Hincmari Remensis Annales, p. 465.

people to the jurisdiction of the ecumenical patriarch, whose subservience to the emperor was notorious, turned to his German ally for help in the matter; while Rastislav, for the same political reason—although in his case the source of danger was the Frankish Empire—turned to Constantinople.

Emperor Michael III the Drunkard (842-867) and his uncle, Caesar Bardas, who was the real ruler of the Empire, gladly complied with Rastislav's request. In cooperation with Patriarch Photius, they selected the renowned teacher of philosophy at the court school of the palace of Magnaura, Constantine, and his brother, Methodius, Greeks from Thessalonica who were well acquainted with the language of the Macedonian Slavs, as best fitted missionaries for the Moravian field. Therefore, in 863 the two brothers, having prepared Slavic translations of the most necessary parts of the Scriptures, for which purpose Cyril had adapted and partly invented the so-called Glagolitic alphabet, set out for Moravia.

But Boris' project of subjecting his territories to the ecclesiastical jurisdiction of the West could not be viewed with indifference on the part of Michael and Bardas or of Photius. The latter's quarrel with Pope Nicholas had gone so far that in April, 863, the pope called upon Photius to resign his office on pain of excommunication. Hence, the patriarch was greatly alarmed about the possibility of Bulgaria falling under papal jurisdiction, thus strengthening the power of the hated papacy. Emperor Michael and Caesar Bardas had no difficulty in recognizing the danger in the far-reaching Bulgaro-German alliance contemplated by Boris and decided to act quickly.

In regard to Boris' actual conversion, several legends gained currency. One of them resembles the story of the Greek slave Cinamon and prince Enravotas, and for that reason is not inherently impossible. A Greek monk, Theodore Kupharas, a slave at the khan's court, exerted himself to convert his master. Later he was redeemed from captivity, having been exchanged for the khan's captive sister who had embraced Christianity in Constantinople. She then put pressure upon her brother in an attempt to induce him to accept her faith. Finally, as Theophanes continuatus tells the story, a very severe famine compelled Boris to seek succor of the Christian God, and when his prayer was favorably answered, he became a Christian.[40]   According to another story, a monk, Methodius by name, painted a scene of the Last Judgment in which he, like an early Dante or a pre-incarnated Jonathan Edwards, depicted the sinners in the hands of an angry God with such startling and fearinspiring realism that the khan was overcome with terror and forthwith received baptism to escape the tortures of such fiery furnace of hell.

Although it is not inherently improbable that one or several of such influences may have been operative upon Boris, the actual historical conversion came about in an entirely different manner.   When in 864 the Bulgarian armies were out of the country, helping Ludwig to put down the rebellion of his son, Karloman, Emperor Michael decided to strike.   He invaded the country by land and blockaded it from the sea.   Boris, in whose land a famine was just then raging, was unable to withstand the overwhelming imperial forces.   Without risking a battle, he offered his submission. The demands made by the Greeks included an acceptance of Christianity and an acknowledgment of the imperial sovereignty, although Bulgaria was permitted to retain autonomy.   Seeing no alternative, Boris accepted the terms. To sweeten the bitter pill, the emperor granted Boris a slight extension of his territory.   A number of nobles were then sent to Constantinople to arrange the details of the peace treaty, and were there baptized.   Patriarch Photius, who was greatly interested in the extension of his jurisdiction over Bulgaria, organized a mission to the newly won eparchy.   The Greek clergy, with a bishop at their head, were then dispatched to Bulgaria with the returning emissaries.   They reached their destination some time in 865. Thereupon, Boris himself received baptism at the hands of the Greek hierarchs delegated by Photius, having on this occasion as sponsor (by proxy) Emperor Michael himself whose name he assumed in the rite.[41]   Otherwise, no details respecting the ceremony are known.   Theophylact of Ohrid affirms that along with Boris many other nobles and outstanding Bulgarians were baptized.

40.   Theophanes continuatus, *op. cit.*, pp. 162-3.
41.   According to Zlatarsky, this took place between Sept. 1 and 19, 865, and probably on Sept. 14.   (Zlatarsky, V. N.: *Istoriya na B'lgarskata d'rzhava prez srednite vekove*, Sofia, 1927, v. I, part 2, p. 30).

Although the particular ecclesiastical jurisdiction to which Bulgaria was subjected had been decided by force, and hence Boris had had no choice in the matter, it must not be concluded that the acceptance of Christianity itself was wholly foisted upon him. As his subsequent career proves, he personally favored Christianity—a creed which his sister as well as his uncle Enravotas had confessed. Moreover, politically, he could not but see the great advantage which would accrue to his people by such an act. In the first place, a considerable part of the Slavic population was already Christian, and as such it naturally sought contact with other Christian lands; Boris likewise was conscious of the grave danger of possible political subjugation of his country by his powerful Christian neighbors—the East Frankish realm on the west and the Byzantine Empire on the southeast —unless he took away every pretext for such action by accepting Christianity. Moreover, as a Christian he legalized, in the eyes of the Christian neighbors, his position as a ruler, for all power was regarded as coming from God and as a Christian Boris could claim his right to the throne far better than as a pagan. Moreover, Boris had the sagacity to discern in the conversion forced upon him by Michael a means toward the realization of his own political projects. He was then ruling a divided people: the governing Bulgarian class with which he shared his power formed an increasingly diminishing minority in the midst of the Slavic masses. Boris conceived the plan of centralizing the political power in his own hands by subverting the existing balance of power and favoring the Slavic element. Adoption of Christianity (many Slavs already being Christian) as the official state religion, making Slavic the language of the state as well as of the church, were to be the means to the end of changing his status from a Bulgarian khan to an absolute prince ruling a united nation. Of course, such plan required time for maturing, and undoubtedly only dim outlines of it were originally in Boris' mind; nevertheless, the above considerations were among the motives actuating him to accept Christianity.

* * * *

And now viewing the period prior and during the process of Christianization of the various Slavic peoples as a whole, it would be of great interest if it were possible to establish just what the effects of that process were. What changes has the life of the Slavs undergone as the result of their conversion? In what specific instances can the uplifting, humanizing, cultural, or ameliorating influences which the new religion exercised upon the pagan Slavs be definitely traced?

It is to be regretted that for lack of source material bearing upon them, these pertinent queries can not be answered with any degree of fulness. Among the Elbe and the Baltic Slavs, and even among the Russians, the situation is far better known than among the Balkan nations. It would not of course be safe to assume a complete analogy between the Southern Slavs and the rest; hence, we must be content with the meagre data which the sources yield respecting the former, despite the fact that they do not suffice to answer the questions raised.

In the first place, it must be borne in mind that Slavic paganism was not a religion of morality, but was predominantly magical in character. It was a matter of satisfying one's wishes or needs either by cajoling or propitiating the supernatural powers to grant the desired ends. Christianity came to the Slavs in a form which in character differed but little from the religion held by them. It was all too often presented to them as a superior magic by which the needs of its votaries could be satisfied more unfailingly than was the case with paganism.

Under such circumstances the "conversion" of the Slavs was often characterized by crass superficiality. Believing in the magical efficacy of baptism, Christian missionaries were often satisfied with not much more than a mere administration of this rite, thereafter insisting upon a more or less regular attendance upon the other sacraments. The people accepted the new faith, retaining their own ancient beliefs alongside with it. This "double faith" persisted for many centuries. The Bulgarian monk Spiridon, writing in the eighteenth century, complained that many of his compatriots still worshipped Perun.[42] The penitential books of the fifteenth century forbade the worship of the sun and the moon. No wonder that John the Exarch, who lived in the age of the Bulgarian Tsar Simeon (893-927), had much to say regarding the survival of paganism in his day!

_____

42. Niederle, L., *op. cit.*, II, part I, ed. 2, p. 99.

Along with this open adherence to the gods of the ancient Slavs, their worship was perpetuated under the guise of the worship of Christian saints. As already mentioned, Perun became St. Elijah and continued to wield the thunderbolts of the sky; Volos was converted into St. Blasius; an interesting survival of the faith in the goddess who fixed the fate of each newborn child—*rozhanitsa*—is to be seen in the perpetuation of her worship, even including the offerings of flour and cheese to her, by identifying her day with the holiday of the Virgin Mary. These same offerings were then presumably brought "in honor of the Theotokos."

Ancestor worship has survived in the Slavic Balkans in the forms of the Bulgarian *zadushnitsa*—a species of the Roman Catholic "all souls' day"—and the Serbian *slava*. On these days, the people still bring food and drink to the graves of their dead, a patent survival of the rites performed in ancient times in connection with the worship of the household *děd*.

Similarly, various sacrifices and pagan rites were by no means uncommon among the Balkan Slavs throughout the centuries in connection with sowing, reaping, cattle breeding, digging of foundations, weddings, funerals, and other significant occasions in their lives. Animal sacrifices were offered on the days dedicated to St. George and St. Elijah, a clear witness to the perpetuation of the ancient practices.

Probably an unconscious survival of the worship of idols is to be seen in many Christmas customs, such as the throwing of a log, called *badnyak,* on the fireplace. In Serbo-Croatian, Christmas day is still called *badnyi dan.*

Naturally, the sway of the magicians, the *volkhvi,* long survived among the common people who devoutly believed in the power of their charms and magic. Pope Nicholas I in 866, in his *Responsa,* forbade the Bulgarians *auguria et incantationes exercere.* In the tenth century, Presbyter Cosmas still vigorously denounced the pagan *volkhvi* in his *Sermon.*

The Christian church addressed itself rigorously to the task of establishing at least an outward conformity with its ritual requirements. Since it looked upon the sacraments as saving ordinances, attendance upon these seemed of utmost importance. In this regard the church found the canons respecting Christian marriage most difficult of enforcement. The *Code* of the Serbian Tsar Stephen Dushan (middle of the fourteenth century) enacts many regulations which plainly indicate that the Serbians even then did not fully conform to the Christian usages in this regard.

Turning now to the political and cultural results of the Christianization of the Balkan Slavs, it becomes clear that the struggle for hegemony between the patriarchates of Rome and Constantinople resulted in a permanent political, cultural, and ecclesiastical division of the peoples of the Balkans. Latin influence became paramount among the Slovenes and the Croatians, while the Bosniacs, the Serbians, the Macedonian Slavs, and the Bulgarians fell under the sway of the Byzantine culture. Moreover, it is abundantly clear that the process was motivated predominantly by political considerations. The cleavage among the Slavic peoples, closely related to each other in language and in ethnic origin, had the most far reaching influences tragically affecting their entire history. The Serbs and the Croatians, in spite of their racial unity, were separated into two national groups which historically revolved in different orbits. The culture of the Slovenes and the Croatians became thoroughly Western, while the cultural traditions of the Serbs and the Bulgarians link them closely to the Byzantine civilization. The estrangement of a thousand years produced in the two groups widely different outlooks. Their religious affiliations, one strongly Roman Catholic, the other Eastern Orthodox, further accentuated their cultural differences. No wonder that Yugoslavia of today finds it difficult to weld its racially homogeneous but culturally antagonistic peoples into a harmonious national unit! Such then was the result of the age-long struggle between the two patriarchates: their animosities and rivalries were perpetuated in the history of the Balkan nations to this day.

It is not within the scope of this study to follow the fortunes of those Slavic peoples which accepted the claims of papal supremacy. Having surveyed the causes which produced the cultural cleavage, our attention shall henceforth be occupied exclusively with the history of Balkan Slavic Orthodox Christianity.

BULGARIAN CHRISTIANITY AFTER THE CONVERSION OF BORIS

The wholesale acceptance of the new creed ordered by Boris soon provoked a spirited revolt on the part of the nobles. Opposed to the policy which threatened to deprive them of their privileged position, they stirred up the people of ten provinces, and the mob besieged the khan's palace at Pliska. The revolt which broke out early in 866 placed Boris in desperate straits. In fact Archbishop Hincmar of Rheims in his *Annales* could see no means to extricate Boris from his predicament save miraculous divine aid.[1] Fortunately, the khan was able to overcome the rebels, whereupon he inflicted a summary vengeance upon them: fifty-two of the revolted nobles with their wives and children were cruelly put to death, and others were punished in a milder fashion. Henceforth, the opposition was wiped out, and Boris had a free hand.

From the political point of view, the revolt is easily explicable. Acceptance of Christianity meant a victory of the Slavic over the Bulgarian element in Boris' realm. The former, always numerically greatly in majority, now became politically dominant by supporting Boris' new policy of Christianization, and hence of centralization of government in the hands of a divinely anointed ruler. The Bulgarian element, with its traditional concepts of division of authority among the heads of clans, well understood that the change of religion was a step toward the overthrow of their own power.

As a far-seeing statesman who knew that ecclesiastical dependence upon the Constantinopolitan patriarchate meant an indirect subjection to the emperor, all too often supreme in Byzantine ecclesiastical affairs, Boris determined to secure for his church complete autocephaly. In order to establish a truly national church, he demanded from Photius either a patriarch, or a metropolitan, or at least an autocephalous archbishop. Although Photius sent the illustri-

---

1. *MGH.*, *Scriptorum* tom. I, Annales Bertiniani, p. 473-74.

ous neophyte an extremely long and erudite epistle (865) in which he explained to him the mysteries of the faith as well as the duties of a well-behaved prince, Boris' chief request was studiously ignored.[2] It was obvious that the patriarch and the emperor desired to make the Bulgarian church a part of the Constantinopolitan patriarchate, as indeed the terms of peace of 864 had specifically stipulated.

Dissatisfied with the attitude of Constantinople, Boris decided to profit by the dissensions between Patriarch Photius and Pope Nicholas. Under the circumstances, Boris had a good chance to drive a hard bargain with the pope. Therefore, a year after his conversion, he sent an embassy to Pope Nicholas, headed by his cousin, bolyar Peter. The embassy arrived in Rome in August, 866, and brought the pope many gifts, as well as a list of one hundred and six questions dealing with matters of faith and morals. Above all, the Bulgars requested the pope, whose supreme authority they readily acknowledged, to grant Bulgaria a patriarch and to send Latin clergy along with him. At the same time Boris sent another embassy to Regensburg to his friend, Ludwig the German, asking him for suitable teachers of Christianity.[3]

The pope, who saw in Boris' request an opportunity to offset the loss of territories of which Emperor Leo III had deprived the Roman See, joyfully expressed his satisfaction with the action of the sagacious Boris. He detained the embassy until he had time to prepare replies to the questions. By the middle of November, 866, the delegation was ready to return. Nicholas sent with them two able legates, bishops Formosus of Porto and Paul of Populonia, who carried papal gifts and sacred vessels as well as books and the *Responses*[4] in which in one hundred and six paragraphs the questions of Boris were answered with remarkable restraint and insight. In respect to the chief request of Boris—the establishment of an independent patriarchate— the pope replied that it could not be granted immediately, but that he would be guided by the report of his legates as to the strength of Christianity in Bulgaria. In the meantime, he promised Boris one bishop whose rank would be

2. Photios, *Epistolae*, in Migne, *PG.*, CII, col. 628-696.
3. *MGH., Scriptorum* tom. I, Annales Fuldenses, p. 379.
4. Responsa Nicolae papae I ad consulta Bulgarorum, Migne, *PL*, CXIX, col. 978-1016. (Dated Nov. 13, 866).

raised to that of an archbishop as soon as the dioceses would grow sufficiently large to require the services of more than one bishop. Thereupon, the first archbishop would be ordained by the pope, but the succeeding archbishops could receive their ordination at home, provided they would secure papal pallium before assuming their office.

The papal legates were received by Boris with great honor and he promptly submitted to their direction; Greek clergy were obliged to leave the country, their places being taken by Latin priests. These latter showed no great consideration for the work of their eastern colleagues: they proceeded to reconfirm the Bulgarian Christians on the ground that the sacrament of confirmation administered in accordance with the Greek rite was not valid. They also reordained the priests who had remained in the country. Besides, they opposed fasting on Saturdays, ordered fasting on the first Sunday in Lent, introduced the *Filioque* clause into the Creed, and denounced married clergy.[5] Thus if Photius had condemned the Latin usages as heretical, the Roman clergy were not at all reticent about expressing their abhorrence of the Greek local customs. Needless to say that activity of this sort was highly confusing to the newly-converted Bulgarians. Moreover, the Latin language with which the poor Bulgarians were quite unfamiliar replaced the equally unintelligible Greek in church service.[6]

Soon after the arrival of the Latin mission, Bishop Hermanrich of Passau with a retinue of priests and deacons arrived in Bulgaria, having been sent there by Ludwig the German. They brought some service books, vestments, and other ritual paraphernalia as a gift from their royal master. But since the papal legates were already in possession of the field, the German mission left the gifts and returned home.

The *Responses* of Pope Nicholas to the anxious questions submitted to him by the Bulgarian khan-neophyte were milder and less exacting than the instructions previously sent him by Photius. The pope eased the rigor of the fasts imposed by the Greeks, although it is puzzling why he forbade the royal convert any food before nine o'clock in

---

5. *MGH., Scriptorum* tom. I, Annales Fuldenses, p. 380.
6. Boris' praises were sung loudly by the Latins that he became a popular hero in the West. *MGH., Scriptores*, I. Regionis Chronicon, p. 580.

the morning; he set Boris' mind at rest in regard to the legitimacy of wearing or not wearing trousers, although he upheld the Greek command of removal of the turban in churches. He informed the khan that the Bulgarian custom of eating apart from his family was bad manners although not a sin. He ordered a strict observance of the right of sanctuary asylum in cases of transgressors of the law, and roundly condemned polygamy. But above all, he stressed the utter hideousness of apostacy, and exhorted the Bulgarian khan to punish it mercilessly.

Although greatly pleased with the zealous missionary work of the Roman legates, Boris naturally hoped that they would report favorably regarding his request upon their return to Rome, so that he could expect the appointment of the promised archbishop soon. Hence, toward the end of 867 he sent a delegation to Rome with the request that Bishop Formosus, whose tact and vigor greatly pleased him, be appointed archbishop of the Bulgarian church. That Formosus was actually a man of unusual ability and ambition may be judged from the fact that he later (891) became pope; Liudprand tells a gruesome story of the treatment accorded his exhumed corpse by his spiteful successor, Pope Sergius.[7] But Nicholas would not be commanded: he categorically refused Boris' request on the ground that Formosus could not be spared from his own see. It may be said in passing that Pope Nicholas consistently adhered to the policy of enforcing the canon forbidding removal of bishops from one see to another. But it is possible that Formosus, whose hatred of the Greeks originally recommended him for the Bulgarian mission, came to be distrusted at the papal curia. The pope may have feared that the ambitious bishop, if placed at the head of the Bulgarian church, might aspire to make himself wholly independent of the Roman see. In fact, Boris was said to have pledged himself to further Formosus' candidacy at all odds, which may have seemed suspicious to the pope. Hence, deciding upon a general reassignment of posts, Nicholas sent to Bulgaria a small number of priests, placing at their head bishops Dominic of Treviso and Grimoald of Polimarti. Formosus and Dominic were ordered to go on to Constantinople, while Paul and Grimoald were to administer the Bulgarian church

7. Liudprand, *Works*, tr. by F. A. Wright, New York, 1930, Tit-for-Tat, p. 52-53.

till a permanent archbishop should be appointed. These instructions were actually carried out after Nicholas' death (Nov. 13, 867) during the pontificate of his successor, Pope Hadrian II (867-72).

Nicholas adopted this high-handed policy toward Bulgaria because he no longer needed to fear the machinations of Photius. For after the assassination of Emperor Michael III by Basil the Macedonian (867-886), who had risen from the humble post of stable-master to that of co-emperor and had, after his bloody deed, been proclaimed the sole emperor, Photius was deposed. The new emperor was prompted to take this measure by his dislike of Photius, abhorring "the knavery of this sage," as well as by his desire to win the good-will of the West. Thereupon the ex-patriarch Ignatius was restored to the patriarchal throne. Basil then wrote a conciliatory letter to Nicholas, requesting him to send his legates to a council called to compose the late differences between the two patriarchates. Consequently, the pope did not feel the necessity of an indulgent policy toward Bulgaria; hence his autocratic action.

Bishop Formosus being a *persona non grata* with Pope Hadrian, the latter adopted his predecessor's policy regarding Bulgaria as his own. In lieu of Formosus, Boris was offered the choice of a candidate from among the Latin clergy dispatched to Bulgaria. Although dissatisfied with being thwarted in his original choice, Boris, after almost two years' indecision, acquiesced and selected (in the summer of 869) for the dignity deacon Marinus. The latter had been sent to Constantinople by Nicholas, but was refused entry. Thereupon, he took refuge at the court of Boris. Being without a stated charge, he seemed to qualify admirably for the exalted post offered him by the Bulgarian khan. Hence, Boris again dispatched, in 869, his cousin Peter to Rome, requesting the appointment of deacon Marinus as archbishop, unless a Roman cardinal of proper qualifications could be found instead. But even then Boris' wishes were rudely ignored: Hadrian appointed Marinus a delegate to the forthcoming Council at Constantinople, and instead of substituting a Roman cardinal for him, sent a subdeacon, Sylvester by name, to replace him.[8] Boris was deeply of-

---

8. Anastasius Bibliothecarius, *Vita Adriani*, pp. 1393-6; Jaffé, P: *Regesta*, I p. 372.

fended and sent Sylvester ignominiously back to Rome, at
the same time requesting, apparently in no gentle manner
(*importunissime,* Anastasius the Librarian calls it), the appointment of his original nominee, Bishop Formosus.[9] Once
more the pope refused to comply with the wishes of the
imperious Bulgarian khan, and Boris in disgust dropped the
parley.   According to Anastasius, the disagreement over
the appointment of the archbishop was the sole reason why
Bulgaria ultimately turned away from Rome and submitted
to Constantinople.   Essentially an opportunist in his ecclesiastical policy, Boris was determined to play Rome
against Constantinople and vice versa, in accordance with
the chance of the best bargain to be secured from either.
From the political point of view, there is no doubt that Boris
would have preferred to see his church in communion with
the West, which threatened less danger of subjugation. But
the pope's intransigence blocked the way.   Hence when
Constantinople, greatly chagrined by Boris' negotiations
with Rome, showed itself amenable to his aspirations, he
once more, and this time of his own will, turned to it.

The new emperor, Basil I, put forth much effort to
induce Boris to return to the Constantinopolitan ecclesiastical jurisdiction.   Indignant at the fractious attitude of
Rome, Boris decided to try his luck with the new emperor
and the restored Ecumenical Patriarch Ignatius.   The
Council of 869 which called itself the Eighth Ecumenical,
had been assembled in an attempt to restore amicable relations between the see of Constantinople and Rome, which
had been severed on account of the Photian schism.   Basil
prevailed upon Boris to submit the question of the proper
jurisdiction over the Bulgarian church to this Council.   After having consulted an assembly about the advisability of
the measure, Boris accepted the invitation and sent a delegation to the Council which arrived in Constantinople three
days after it had been formally closed on February 28, 870.
Thereupon the emperor reassembled the Council, and submitted to it the question of the Bulgarian jurisdiction.   The
answer could of course be easily foreseen: since the Eastern-
ers had the majority, a decision adverse to Rome was a fore-
gone conclusion.   A few days after the arrival of the Bulgarian delegation and in spite of the vehement protest of

---

9.   Jaffé, *op. cit.,* I. No. 2925, p. 372.

the papal legates, the Council decreed that the Bulgarian church fell properly within the jurisdiction of the ecumenical patriarchate. Thereupon, it instructed Patriarch Ignatius to ordain an archbishop for Bulgaria, to whom were to be granted extensive powers of autonomy. The Bulgarian archbishop, though subject to the patriarch, held a rank next to his own.

The newly restored Patriarch Ignatius immediately, on March 4, ordained to the office Bishop Joseph, a Bulgar by birth, apparently Boris' nominee, and dispatched him with ten bishops and a large retinue of Greek clergy to his new field. Upon his arrival, Bishop Grimoald and the Latin clergy left peaceably and abandoned the field to their Greek rivals. Once more was the Greek liturgy introduced into the church of Bulgaria, and as could be expected, Greek culture and commerce soon followed in the wake of the missionary work. Churches were erected in Greek style by Greek architects and artisans. The Greek language became fashionable among the ruling classes, and the nobles soon saw the wisdom of sending their sons to Constantinople for education. Boris himself gave impetus to this custom by sending his younger son, Simeon, to the famous court school of the Magnaura palace, that he might there prepare himself for leadership of the Bulgarian church, a career for which he had been destined by his father. Thus the action of the Council of 869-70 had a far reaching effect: it definitely determined the character of the Bulgarian Christianity, and with it the cultural and partly even the political history of Bulgaria. The struggle waged between Constantinople and Rome for the last six years was permanently decided in favor of the former.

Upon learning of the state of affairs, the pope naturally strove to regain his lost jurisdiction. In 871 Pope Hadrian wrote to the emperor as well as to the old Patriarch Ignatius, remonstrating especially with the latter whose gratitude to Rome for her valiant championship of his cause against Photius should have prevented such "treachery." But his exertions bore no fruit. Hadrian's successor, Pope John VIII (872-82), promised the Roman clergy at the time of his election to be true to the masterful policy of Nicholas I. He at first wrote to Boris, threatening him, the patriarch, and the Greek clergy with excommunication, "that

they may thus join the Devil"[10] unless Bulgaria be restored
to papal obedience. When this vehement exhortation proved
ineffective, the Pope wrote a somewhat less violent letter
to Boris in 875, forbidding his subjects as well as himself to
receive the sacraments at the hands of Greek priests on pain
of being declared schismatics.[11] At the same time, John
wrote to Emperor Basil, citing Patriarch Ignatius to Rome
for a trial.[12] Again, the thunders passed unheeded except
that Boris sent an embassy to Rome to present his compli-
ments to the pope.   Three years later (878) John sent two
legates, bishops Eugene and Paul to Constantinople, instructing them to deliver *en route* four letters at the court of
Pliska: one, addressed to the Greek hierarchy and clergy of
"the Illyrian provinces" ordering them categorically to
leave Bulgaria within thirty days, on the ground that
Illyricum belonged to Rome.[13] The second, a very conciliatory epistle, was addressed to Boris, exhorting the khan to
abandon Constantinople.[14] The remaining two were addressed to the cousin of the khan, Peter, and to another Bulgarian noble, probably Boris' brother; the pope fervently
besought them to use their influence with the khan to induce his return to Roman obedience.[15] The legates then
proceeded to Constantinople to deliver a letter to Ignatius,
ordering him on pain of deprivation of his office to recall his
clergy from Bulgaria within thirty days,[16] and another one
to Basil, requiring him to aid in execution of the order. But
Ignatius had died before the letter reached him (Oct. 23,
877), and Photius, who had thereupon resumed the patriarchal throne, paid no attention to it.

All these attempts failed ignominiously, although Pope
John wrote still other letters in 879.[17] And yet John was
to have another chance to regain Bulgaria.   Photius, in
order to secure the full support of Emperor Basil, thought
it politic to seek Pope John's approval of his assumption of
the patriarchal office. The Pope saw in it his opportunity
to secure by bargaining what he had failed to get by threats

---

10. Johannes VIII Papa, *Fragmenta*, Ep. 7, p. 277.
11. *Ibid.*, Ep. 37, p. 294-5.
12. *Ibid.*, Ep. 40, p. 296.
13. *Ibid.*, pp. 62-67.
14. *Ibid.*, pp. 58-60.
15. *Ibid.*, pp. 61-62-66.
16. Jaffé, P., *Regesta*, I, No. 3133, p. 397.
17. Jaffé, P., *op. cit.*, I, No. 3246, p. 408; No. 3261 p. 410; No. 3265.

and blandishments. He was willing to acknowledge Photius providing that Bulgaria be returned to his jurisdiction.

The Council of 879 which was to bring about a satisfactory arrangement between the two parties met in Constantinople, and in the absence of the emperor, rendered completely apathetic to all public concerns by the death of his son, Constantine, was dominated by Photius. By none too scrupulous means the latter succeeded in hoodwinking the papal legates into an approval of measures which they would have never dreamed of approving had they understood them properly. When it came to the crucial question of the return of the Bulgarian church to the papal jurisdiction, the matter was adroitly referred to the emperor for decision. To the utter astonishment of the legates, he decided in favor of Rome. Hardly able to believe their good fortune, and of course willing then to concede to Photius the coveted papal approval, the legates hastened home with the good news. John was overjoyed. He wrote a number of lyrically jubilant letters to Boris during 880 and 882,[18] to most of which no reply was returned, although Boris had sent a noble, Funticus by name, to Rome to deliver to John the laconic assurance that all was well. At last Bishop Marinus, who had learned the real state of affairs while on an embassy in Constantinople, enlightened the puzzled John. The truth of the matter was that the Council of 879 had merrily given away a bride who had no desire to marry the offered bridegroom—and Photius knew it. The Bulgarian church no longer had any desire to cut her connection with Constantinople, and there was no way of compelling her. The infuriated pope deposed the two legates who had permitted themselves to be so grossly duped, but that did not bring Bulgaria back. It was never to come back. The renewed excommunication of Photius availed nothing in this matter, either. The pride of Nicholas and Hadrian which had led them to refuse Boris bishops Formosus or Marinus was punished by the loss of papal hegemony in the Balkan peninsula.

Although Boris gained one of the objectives of his ecclesiastical policy, viz., the autocephaly of the Bulgarian church, yet his was a church whose leaders were foreign to the great mass of his people, and as such it could never be-

---

18. *MGH., Epistolarum* tom. VII, Iohannis VIII Epistolae, 298, 308.

come a thoroughly national institution. Such a church must speak the language of the people. But the idea of providing a Slavic liturgy and Slavic priesthood for Slavic people was no longer novel. The two Thessalonian brothers, Cyril and Methodius, who had been working in the Greater Moravia since 863, had translated the greater part of the Scriptures and the liturgical books into Slavic and had introduced that language into the church service and had trained a devoted band of Slavic disciples. Archbishop Methodius made a visit to Constantinople in 881-82; whether or not at the time he visited Boris' court on his return from Constantinople—as Zlatarsky suggests[19]—does not matter. Boris had good means of learning of the work of Methodius irrespective of any personal contact with the great Moravian archbishop. This work naturally suggested to him the idea of introducing into his own country the Slavic liturgy and the Slavic priesthood, and thus thoroughly nationalizing the church of his realm.

When Archbishop Methodius died at Velehrad in Moravia on April 6, 885, his grandiose plan of establishing an extensive Slavic archdiocese on the fringe of Greek and Latin patriarchates collapsed completely. Papal opposition to the Slavic liturgy, combined with a fierce hatred of Methodius' designs on the part of the German party in Moravia led by the Latinizing bishop of Nitra, Wiching, who had even resorted to downright forgery, compassed the downfall of the Slavic liturgy in central Europe. But this defeat in turn led to the most important event as far as the formation of the character of the Bulgarian Christianity was concerned, namely, to the expulsion of the disciples of Methodius from Moravia by order of Prince Svatopluk, and their eager reception on the part of Boris.

The leader of the Slavonic party in Moravia, Gorazd, whom Methodius had designated as his successor, as well as other prominent men like Clement, Nahum, Angelarus, Laurentius, and Sabbas, together with their disciples, had been imprisoned and some time later were sentenced to perpetual exile. They were accompanied by soldiers to the Danube, and there left to their own devices. The less prominent members of the group were sold into slavery to Venice as heretics. Crossing the Danube, the exiled band

---

19. Zlatarsky, *op. cit.*, I², p. 219.

found a most cordial reception by the Bulgarian governor of Belgrade, Tarkan Boris. This man obviously knew of Khan Boris' wish to secure Slavic priests, for he quickly dispatched them to the khan's court at Pliska. They were received with great honor by Boris, for they fitted in excellently with his program of nationalizing the Bulgarian church. Later other Slavic priests, who had been sold to Venice as slaves, were redeemed by a representative of Emperor Basil sent to that city on some business. They were quickly dispatched to Constantinople where they were gladly received by Basil, who provided some with benefices and later sent them into Bulgaria.[20] The Bulgarian church to this day reveres the memory of the "holy seven," members of these saintly bands of Slavic missionaries. In their newly found home, they continued the work begun by Cyril and Methodius in Moravia, and thus became the organizers of the Slavic Bulgarian church and creators of a great deal of Slavic literature. It is due to them that the young Bulgarian church exerted a profound and creative influence upon all the rest of the Slavic Orthodox national churches when they came to be organized, for it furnished them with priests capable of conducting the services in Slavic and provided them with ready-made liturgical and devotional books. Thus Church Slavonic became the liturgical language of all Slavic Orthodox churches.

Among the protagonists of the Slavic culture the greatest fame was achieved by Clement who later came to be known as of Ohrid. Boris chose him as the chief instrument of his ecclesiastical policy. The problem which Boris faced was not a negligible one: he wished to introduce Slavic liturgy into his church and ultimately to displace the Greek hierarchy and clergy by native priesthood. How could this be done in the face of opposition which such a program would necessarily arouse on the part of the actual Greek holders of ecclesiastical power in Bulgaria? Even supposing that Emperor Basil and Patriarch Photius were for the present favorable toward the Slavic missionary work, would not their attitude change as soon as the supremacy of the Greek clergy would be seriously endangered? Moreover,

20. This story is found in the recently discovered Life of Naum; cf. Ivanov, J.; *B'lgarski starini iz Makedoniya*, Sofia, 1908, p. 51-58. I have not been able to verify it.

even though the Slavic population received Christianity gladly, the remaining Bulgarian element, especially the nobles, were not showing much enthusiasm for it. Would they be likely to receive it more readily at the hands of Slavic missionaries? Certainly not. Unless they were over-awed by the culture and prestige of the Byzantine Empire, there was not much hope that Christianity would make speedy headway among them.

Boris solved his problem as befitted the statesman he was: he retained the Greek clergy at the court, but on the other hand he founded a center of Slavic culture at the monastery of St. Panteleimon near Preslav by settling some of the Slavic monks there, while the remaining Slavic missionaries, under the leadership of Clement, he sent to evangelize the outlying Macedonian provinces predominantly settled by Slavs (886). It is possible that Clement's field of labor was near his own birthplace, for he appears to have been a Byzantine Slav. The districts selected for Clement's missionary work were located in the southwest region of Macedonia and were known as Kutmichevitsa and Devol. To ensure full cooperation of the civil authorities of the region, Boris recalled the Bulgarian governor of the place and sent an official—probably a Slav—Dometa by name, to administer it in cooperation with Clement. In fact the latter seems to have acted as the superior of the former. Clement was granted several places of residence: three in the district of Devol, where under his leadership a Slavic school for the training of priests and other clerics was established, and houses at Ohrid and Glavenitsa. At the Devol training school, Clement hoped to train in time a sufficient number of Slavic clergy to enable Boris to displace the entire Greek hierarchy and clergy. During the seven years of Clement's headship of the Slavic school in Devol it is said that 3,500 pupils received their education there, and were then ordained as readers, singers, deacons, and priests and sent to their posts to carry on Slavic work. They were sent in large groups into twelve regions of the province, but extended their work even among the neighboring Serbian population. It was in this manner that the ideas and work of the great Slavic apostles of Moravia found abundant fruition in Bulgaria as well as in Serbia.

Besides his preaching and teaching activity, Clement

produced many translations from Greek. Later he was appointed bishop of the dual see of Debritsa and Belitsa, northwest of Prilep, his place at the head of the Devol school being taken by Nahum who had hitherto been presiding over the monastery of St. Panteleimon.[21] Clement thus became the first Slavic bishop of Bulgaria.

Many of the disciples of Methodius who, having been redeemed from slavery by Emperor Basil, were dispatched to Bulgaria at the time when Boris' youngest son, Simeon, was returning home from his studies at the Constantinopolitan palace school of Magnaura, were settled at the newly founded monastery of St. Panteleimon at the mouth of the river Ticha, near Preslav. Simeon himself became a monk there and the community developed into a veritable center of Slavic learning and of literary culture. Boris, who fondly cherished the scheme of unification of his nation through the establishment of a national Slavic church, following the example of many devoutly Christian rulers, decided to lay down his rule and give the remaining years of his life to the furtherance of his ecclesiastical project. In 889 he resigned his throne, after thirty-seven years of reign, and assuming the monastic habit, joined his beloved community of St. Panteleimon. He gave himself there to the task of furthering the production of Slavic literature and to organizing of like activity on the part of others. His voluntary abdication of power bears witness to the depth of his devotion to the religion he had adopted.

His oldest son, Vladimir (889-93), who ascended the throne after Boris' abdication, did not prove to be a worthy ruler. He associated himself with the reactionary party of nobles who wished to overthrow the policies of Boris and to restore the hegemony of the Bulgarian pagan element. This party consisted of a group of Bulgarian nobles who wished to subvert the centralizing tendency of Boris' policy and to regain their ancient prerogatives. Vladimir began a persecution of the church, especially of the clergy, and had Archbishop Joseph either imprisoned or possibly even put to death. Moreover, he was a weak character, spending his time in hunting and revelry. As for his political orientation, the new ruler was inclined to favor the advances of the

---

21. Nahum founded a monastery near Ohrid on the lake Prespa, where he died in 910.

German King Arnulf (887-99) who tried to win him for an alliance. Such a course would have necessarily led to a break with the Byzantine state and to an overthrow of the existing ecclesiastical arrangements.

Seeing his entire life-work in danger, Boris, supported by his son Simeon and a party of nobles still faithful to him, left the monastery and drew the sword against Vladimir. He succeeded in dethroning him; thereupon he had the unworthy son blinded and imprisoned (893). Thus the second forcible attempt to subvert Boris' Christianizing and pro-Slavic policy was frustrated.

The same autumn Boris called together a council to Preslav comprising "the whole tsardom" (*convocato omni regno*), which selected at his bidding as the tsar in place of Vladimir his third son, the monk Simeon, who was then about thirty years of age. This assembly also effected the reforms for which Boris had striven throughout his reign: it approved the Slavic as the official language of the state and the church, and substituted the newly translated liturgical and Biblical books for the Greek. Boris regarded it as highly important for the unification of the nation that one language should be spoken by all his subjects, Slav and Bulgar alike. It is probable that the vacancy in the archipiscopal see offered a good opportunity to effect a fundamental change of such magnitude. Moreover, the capital was now transferred from Pliska, where the pagan associations were too deeply rooted, to the great center of Slavic missionary and literary work, Preslav. The residence of the archbishop was likewise transferred there. Thereupon, seeing the dream of his lifetime well on the way to realization, Boris returned to his monastery where he died in 907.

Simeon's reign (893-927) represents the fruition of the ideas and policies of his father, and opened the greatest epoch in Bulgarian history. The efforts of Boris to make his country an independent national and ecclesiastical unit and to secure for it the riches of the Byzantine culture in the language of his own people were gloriously realized by Simeon. His reign was surnamed "the golden age of Bulgaria," and "the golden epoch of the Bulgarian literature." He himself is known to history as Simeon the Great—a title which he bears with relatively better justification than many other rulers similarly honored.

Educated at the palace school of Magnaura, Simeon became imbued with the best which Byzantine culture could afford. Greeks themselves, in their admiration for Simeon's learning, flattered him by regarding him as "half a Greek."[22]

Politically, Simeon made his country the dominant force in the Balkans, wresting the hegemony from the then decadent Byzantine Empire. A war soon broke out between Bulgaria and the Empire provoked by a dispute over extortionate duties levied on Bulgarian traders by the Greek holders of the trade monopoly. Simeon defeated the imperial forces and concluded with Emperor Leo VI an advantageous peace treaty. But when after Leo's death (912) the treaty was disregarded by the regent, the drunken and dissolute Alexander, Simeon once more took up arms against the Empire, and brought his armies to the very walls of Constantinople (913), just a century after his grim ancestor, the terrible Khan Krum, had similarly put the fear of God into the hearts of the haughty inhabitants of the capital. But Alexander had opportunely died in the meantime (June 6, 913) and the regency passed into the hands of the fearless old Patriarch Nicholas Mysticus. This remarkable man, who had defied Emperor Leo the Wise in the matter of his fourth marriage and had suffered exile in consequence of it, had exerted himself to the utmost to avert Simeon's siege, and in his capacity of ecumenical patriarch had written his "beloved son" a long series of pathetically pleading letters in which he tried to induce him to keep peace with the Empire.[23] But Simeon was no longer to be dissuaded from his purpose. In the face of the overwhelming power of the Bulgarian army, Patriarch Nicholas could do nothing but conclude a treaty of peace with Simeon. By its terms, the boy-emperor, Constantine VII Porphyrogenitus, was to marry one of Simeon's daughters, thus giving Simeon the influential position of a father-in-law of the Byzantine emperor. This was to be a stepping stone to the assumption of the imperial purple. But the patriarch's regency was

22. Liudprand, op. cit., Antapodosis, Book III, ch. 29.
23. Nicholas Mysticus, Epistolae, V-X, Migne, PG., vol. CXI, col. 45-83.

overthrown in October of the same year by the machinations of the partisans of the shrewd and ambitious Zoë, Constantine's mother, who repudiated the promise of marriage on behalf of her son. Simeon promptly responded with a new war, in which the imperial leader, Nicephorus Phocas, suffered such a decisive defeat (917) in the battle of Anchialus that the imperial forces were utterly annihilated. The bones of the slain could be seen on the battle-field in large heaps half a century later. This ended the contest between the mighty Bulgarian ruler and the Empire: henceforth Bulgaria was unquestionably the mightiest power in the Balkans.

Simeon once more demanded the fulfilment of the marriage treaty between Constantine and his daughter. Zoë refused. The intrigues among various rivals for the throne became so rife that had Simeon attacked Constantinople during 918, he might have seized the throne for himself. But he became entangled in a war with the Serbians and missed his opportunity. For by a new revolution in Constantinople, Drungarius (Admiral) Romanus Lecapenus seized sole regency (in March, 919) and married his daughter Helena to the young emperor. By the time the year was out, Romanus forestalled the plans of Simeon by assuming the imperial title himself. Balked of his ambition to dominate the imperial politics, Simeon decided to make himself an emperor in his own name. According to Zlatarsky,[24] he had assumed the title of "the tsar and autocrat of all Bulgarians" as early as 915, but did not have himself crowned as such till 918. The reason for the delay is to be found in the fact that Simeon, in accordance with the generally accepted notions of the time, regarded it legally absolutely necessary for an emperor to be crowned by a patriarch. Of course, Nicholas Mysticus, patriarch of Constantinople, would never lend himself to such treasonable action. The only other method left was to raise the rank of the archbishop of Bulgaria to that of patriarch. This would inevitably produce an estrangement, and probably even a schism, between the Bulgarian archdiocese and the patriarchate of Constantinople—a calamity which the revered Bishop Clement of Ohrid most earnestly sought to avert.

24. Zlatarsky, *op. cit.*, I², p. 381.

While Clement lived, Simeon, out of consideration for the venerable bishop, contented himself with a mere assumption of the imperial title. But after Clement's death (July 27, 916), and especially after the signal slaughter by the Bulgarians of the whole imperial army at Anchialus (917), Simeon hesitated no longer.[25] Having called all Bulgarian bishops together in a council, he induced them first to proclaim the Bulgarian church autocephalous and then to elect a patriarch, or more likely to raise the rank of the existing archbishop to that of patriarch. The first holder of that dignity, according to the *Synodical of Tsar Boril* (1211)[26] was Leontius. Thereupon, the new patriarch solemnly crowned Simeon with the imperial crown as "the tsar and autocrat of all Bulgarians." Of course, the ecumenical patriarch refused to acknowledge Leontius as patriarch and Simeon as emperor. The latter retaliated by denouncing the usurpation of Emperor Romanus and by carrying devastating expeditions into the imperial territory. Nevertheless, desiring some outside recognition of his new title, Simeon resumed the policy of Boris of bargaining with the Holy See. Whether he offered Pope John X submission of his church to the papal jurisdiction, is not known. At any rate, in 926, a papal legate, Madalbert, brought the papal recognition to the court at Preslav.[27]

Simeon was not only a great warrior: during his reign and under his own fostering care the Slavic culture and literature reached a high degree of development. The group of scholars he had gathered about him at the court were busily engaged in translating what was then regarded as the best in Greek literature, also producing some original works. For this purpose they adapted the Greek uncial letters to the requirements of the Slavic language and wrote their works in the script which received the name of Cyrillic, although as a matter of fact neither Cyril nor Methodius ever had anything to do with its adoption. The involved

25. Runciman, *op. cit.*, p. 173, places the elevation of Simeon as emperor and the papal recognition of the title in the year 925. But his ingenious theories (foot note, p. 174) are not convincing. On the whole, Zlatarsky has presented a more tenable theory.

26. Popruzhenko, M. G.: *Sinodik Tsarya Borila*, Sofia, 1928.

27. Runciman (p. 173, foot note 3) supports this statement by quoting Pope Innocent's letter, Migne, *PL*, CCXIV, col. 1112-13. The letter in question is really Kaloyan's to the Pope, and although it mentions Peter and Samuel, does not mention Simeon by name but merely says "*et alii qui eos in imperio praecesserunt*".

script developed by Cyril and known as Glagolitic, continued in use by Methodius' disciples settled in Macedonia and Western Bulgaria. Thus there developed two distinct literary schools in Bulgaria, the Cyrillic and the Glagolitic. The latter also spread to the Dalmatian coast and among the Croatians in general.

The court school, supported and directed by Simeon, besides preparing a translation of the Bible and of the liturgical books into the ancient Bulgarian language, produced translations of works of theological, homiletical, legal, hagiographical, and historical character. Simeon himself, probably before he ascended the throne, had made a translation of selections from the works of John Chrysostom, *Zlatostruy,* which became very popular among the Bulgarians as well as among other Slavs. Bishop Constantine, a teacher at the monastery of St. Panteleimon, and possibly the second Slavic bishop in Bulgaria, wrote a collection of homilies on the gospel-lessons for the year, entitled *Didactic Gospels,* culled largely from Chrysostom, Cyril of Alexandria, and Isidore of Palusia. He placed an "alphabetical prayer" at the beginning, which is the first attempt at Slavic prosody. Besides, he made a translation of some passages from the work of Athanasius. John the Exarch, who appears to have been the vicar of the archbishop, was one of the most active and fertile of the writers of Simeon's time. He headed the court school. Among his productions the first rank is accorded to his *Shestodnev* (Hexameron), a detailed exposition of the six days of creation after the works of Basil the Great and others. The work is overrun with citations from the Fathers and the classical philosophers. Besides, he translated a part of Πήγη γνώσεως[28] of John of Damascus under the title *Heaven and its Dialectic,* as well as his *Treatise of the Orthodox Faith.* A monk Gregory translated the *Chronicle* of John Malalas.

As for the Glagolitic school which was headed by Clement, since it was farther removed from direct Greek influence, it tended to be characterized by greater originality. Clement himself, who made the school at Devol a center for dissemination of culture and of religious zeal, produced some translations. Monk Khrabr, who belonged

---

28. Migne, *PG.,* vol. 94, col. 521-675.

to this school, left a treatise *On the Letters*[29] in which he de-
fended the legitimacy of the Slavic script against the assaults of the Greek theologians who denied its propriety,
holding to the current theory that only Hebrew, Greek, and
Latin letters could be used in the service of the church.
Further adumbrations of the same struggle are clearly discernible in the Pannonian legend of the *Vita Methodii*, a
work of Bulgarian origin, which ascribes to Cyril in his in-
vention of the Slavic alphabet a divine inspiration, in an
effort to prove the legitimacy of Slavic books for liturgical
purposes.

In spite of the benefits which Simeon's cultural policy
brought to Bulgaria, his program had its indubitable faults.
Fundamentally, the Greek culture which Simeon wished to
make available in the Slavic language, was too technical and
not free from decadent tendencies. For one thing, its character was predominantly theological; the religious works
stressed so uniformly the esoteric virtues of monasticism as to
suggest that no other kind of life could be truly Christian.
Hence, such literature could appeal to a comparatively small
group in Bulgaria—the theologically-trained monastic
community. In other words, it served the purposes of religious recluses, but had no great cultural influence upon
the masses. The common people, even if they could read,
would not find the type of literature extant well adapted to
their needs. The culture fostered by Simeon was therefore in its very nature exclusive while popular education
was neglected.

In this manner the essentially Byzantine cultural influences became domesticated in Bulgaria, from which
they were extended, in their Slavic form, to the other Slavic
nations when they in turn adopted Christianity. The most
important example of such spread of Byzantine culture is
the case of Russia when Vladimir, in his desire to introduce
the Greek civilization into his country, accepted Christianity for himself (987) and labored to make his country Christian. Bulgarian Slavic literature then proved to be a pre-
cious ready-made means by which the Christianization and
Byzantinization of Russia were enormously facilitated.
The same potent influence of the Slavic culture emanating

---

29. Reprinted in Vondrák, V., *Církevněslovanská chrestomatie*, Brno, 1925,
p. 135ff.

from Bulgaria was exercised in the neighboring Serbian territories, where in the end it displaced the hitherto dominant Greek influence.

The successful realization of Boris' and Simeon's policy of centralization of the governmental power in their own hands resulted in a permanent differentiation of the social classes in Bulgaria. The Bulgarian nobility, now utterly dependent upon the favor of the tsar, little by little became imbued with the Byzantine notions of imperial power which came into Bulgaria along with Christianity. Following the lead of Simeon, whose splendid palace at Preslav became a legendary wonder, they adopted the forms of thought prevailing at the court of Constantinople and aped the ceremonial and legal arrangements in vogue in the Empire. Thus arose a privileged class of nobles and a class of commoners. The nation was divided socially, and within a short time economically as well.

Simeon greatly widened the gulf which existed since the latter days of Boris between the ruling nobility and the masses of the common people by his reliance upon the nobles and the church for the realization of his grandiose schemes. During his long wars with the Empire, Simeon's dependence upon the higher classes became very marked: they were rewarded for their military and diplomatic services by extensive grants of land, while the heavy costs of the numerous military expeditions were met by greatly increased taxation of the masses. Thus the rich grew richer and the poor grew poorer. Many free peasants became landless proletarians or serfs. The nobility took on more and more the airs and forms of the imperial aristocracy, and increased their prerogatives at the expense of the common people. The hierarchy followed suit; they aspired to imitate the pomp of the Byzantine patriarchal court and vied with the nobles for power in the state.

BULGARIAN PATRIARCHATE OF
THE FIRST EMPIRE

The eventful reign of Simeon, terminated by his death on May 27, 927, at the very moment when he was preparing to deliver the Byzantine Empire a *coup de grâce,* was followed by a rapid decline of the power of Bulgaria which finally ended with the loss of her independence. Simeon's successor, his second son Peter (927-69), still a child, was not a person forceful enough to conserve the gains of his father. Moreover, a multiplicity of causes contributed to the downward trend of Bulgarian fortunes. Peter's father before his death had designated his brother-in-law, George Sursubul, as the young tsar's regent and chief counsellor. Sursubul promptly concluded a treaty of peace with the Greeks (927) which was accepted with alacrity by Romanus Lecapenus because of the utter exhaustion of his resources. By the terms of this treaty, Emperor Romanus acknowledged Peter's imperial title, confirmed him in the possession of most of Simeon's conquests, and promised to pay him a yearly tribute. With the acknowledgment of Peter's imperial title came the recognition, on the part of the ecumenical patriarch, of the patriarchal rank of the head of the Bulgarian church. The first patriarch thus acknowledged was Demetrius,[1] the successor of Leontius. But the terms of recognition stipulated that the Bulgarian patriarch must not take his title from the Bulgarian capital, Preslav, but from some bishopric the foundation of which went back to the earliest times of Balkan Christianity. Hence, it was finally agreed that the Bulgarian patriarch should be the metropolitan of Silistria, the ancient Durostorum. His title then ran: "the metropolitan of Silistria (Drster) and patriarch of all Bulgaria." It seems that this stipulation had for its object the removal of the patriarch from the di-

---

1. There is a queer confusion in Runciman regarding this admittedly mooted question. He states (*op. cit.*, p. 182) that Damian of Dristra was the first acknowledged patriarch of Bulgaria, and not Demetrius. In support of this assertion he quotes Zlatarsky. But this latter author (*op. cit.*, I², p. 529, footnote 3) asserts just the opposite, namely that Damian was the last patriarch of the period, who ascended the throne in 972, not 927.

rect influence of the tsar, and thus possibly a more immediate influence over this dignitary on the part of the ecumenical patriarch. Finally, these various treaty provisions were capped by the marriage of Tsar Peter with Princess Maria, daughter of the third emperor Christophorus and the granddaughter of Emperor Romanus Lecapenus. The young princess was renamed Irene, in commemoration of the peace thus concluded. The marriage was a great concession on the part of the Empire which hitherto refused to ally itself by marriage with any "barbarian" nation. Thus viewed superficially, Sursubul seemed to have gained all that Simeon in vain had fought for throughout his life.

But the gains were only apparent, not real. Peter was not suited to his arduous task for which he had a positive distaste. He was of a fervently pious disposition, inclined by temperament to the monastic vocation. He surrounded himself by monastic advisers who had an overweening influence upon the conduct of state affairs. No wonder that this period is known as "the monastic reign." Moreover, Peter quickly fell under the guiding influence of his Greek wife, the shrewd and masterful Maria-Irene. She became the center of a Hellenophil court coterie through which the will of the Byzantine emperor was carried out. The tsaritsa brought with her many Greeks in her retinue and gradually made the court thoroughly Byzantine.

The disaffection of "Simeon's nobles" with the abandonment of the traditional national policy soon flared up in a revolt, headed by the tsar's youngest brother, John. It had for its object the deposition of Peter and the elevation to the throne of John. But the revolt was discovered in time and John was forced to become a monk, imprisoned, and later exiled to Constantinople. But some time later, Emperor Romanus permitted him to leave his monastic prison and to marry an Armenian lady.

Nevertheless, the spirit of disaffection did not abate, and in 930 a more serious political outbreak occurred when the elder brother of Peter, Michael, having left the monastery into which he had been forced, organized a revolt for the purpose of seizing the supreme power. It was again destined to fail, for at the very beginning of the uprising Michael had died and the movement thereupon had collapsed. But the Serbs took advantage of the internecine wars, and led by Prince Cheslav, with the Byzantine help they threw off the Bulgarian overlordship and set up an independent political organization (931). With this event, the fall of the Bulgarian empire was initiated.

Moreover, during the decade following, Bulgaria was repeatedly invaded by various nomadic hordes, as the Turcoman Magyars who at the beginning of the tenth century had settled in the fertile plains of Hungary and the related fierce Patzinaks whose seats were in the southern steppes of Russia. The nobles, detecting the weakness of the government, proceeded to avail themselves of the opportunity to extend their privileges at the tsar's expense. The common people attributed the misfortunes which overtook Bulgaria to the pro-Byzantine policy of the court, and were bitter against the government on account of their increasingly difficult economic situation. The free peasants, who had suffered much misery during Simeon's wars, regarded with discontent the luxuries of the court, while they themselves groaned under the burden of endless exactions. On the other hand, the landless peasantry who tilled the soil of the nobles became thoroughly dissatisfied with their hard lot, for they were gradually sinking to the status of serfs.

Under such unfavorable circumstances, the government of Peter sought support in the church. But the church proved a broken reed, because of the loss of prestige on the part of the hierarchy and the clergy. The tenth century was a time of general decline of monastic life and ideals both in the Byzantine Empire and in Bulgaria, which ever since the establishment of the patriarchate had zealously imitated the pomp and vices of her Constantinopolitan model. It was probably because of the munificent and lavish support given the Bulgarian monasticism and the church in general by the tsar and the nobles that their condition, morally and spiritually, greatly degenerated. Peter is directly credited with the founding of some twenty-two monasteries, among which the magnificent establishment of Rila, "the mother of the Bulgarian monasteries," might be especially singled out. Many other monastic establishments were founded by the court nobles. On account of the magnificence of these monasteries, Bulgaria came to be known as "the second Holy Mountain." Peter's beneficence extended even to Mount Athos, where the monasteries of

5

Zographou and Xeropotamou received such generous support from him that they came to be regarded as Bulgarian foundations. Thus the church and the monasteries became large land owners, and as such adopted the oppressive measures toward the peasantry exercised by the nobles. Hence the higher clergy, both the hierarchy and the monastic superiors, gave themselves to luxury and ease, woefully neglecting their duties and earning for themselves the hate and detestation of the common people, whose miserable lot, whether under the nobles or under their ecclesiastical masters, grew increasingly more wretched.

The conditions of the monasteries and among the clergy were denounced in the strongest terms by a contemporary, presbyter Cosmas, in spite of the fact that he was a doughty defender of the church and an opponent of heretical movements. He was a younger contemporary of those "who saw and knew" John the Exarch, although no further biographical details concerning him are preserved. His only surviving work, *Sermon against the Heretics,*[2] affords an excellent description of the contemporary religious conditions.

In spite of his desire to uphold the cause of the church against its opponents, Cosmas was constrained to admit that the monastic vows were honored oftener in the breach than in their observance: many monks re-entered "the world" and married. Others assumed the habit, but retained their connection with the world. They often turned into wandering vagabonds, begging for their daily bread, and causing grave scandal by their licentious living. In some instances, the monasteries came to be used as prisons for men of rank, or even of royal lineage. Many monks transgressed the rule of chastity. In fact, the more pious and truly religious among the monks left their monasteries and retired into wilderness where they lived the life of hermits. The most outstanding of these was Ivan (946) who was later surnamed Rilsky, because he lived in the wilderness of the Rila mountains. In time, he became the patron saint of Bulgaria.

As for the hierarchy and the clergy, Cosmas complains that they were equally censurable on account of their abandoned, profligate, lazy living, although he still regards them

---

2. Popruzhenko, M. G., *Sv. Kozmy presvitera Slovo na eretiki*, St. Petersburg, 1907.

as better than the heretics: "Even if the Orthodox priests live in laziness, as you (i. e., Bogomils) accuse them, they do not blaspheme the Godhead. . . ." They were indifferent toward their duties, so that Cosmas lays upon them the responsibility for the anti-ecclesiastical movements. "Whence come the commotions, the evil dogs, the heretical teachings? Are they not caused by the laziness and the coarseness of the pastors? Whence are the rebels and such (i. e., heretical preachers) as spread sin and lies? Are they not caused by episcopal laxness?" As for the lower clergy, Cosmas repeats the accusations of the Bogomils against them without directly denying them: "for the priests do just the opposite (i. e., to evangelical virtues) in all respects. They get drunk, they rob, and there is none to forbid them these evil practices." Cosmas further quotes the Bogomils saying: "They (i. e. the priests) sin secretly and clearly live according to the flesh and not according to the spirit as we do". To all this Cosmas seems to have nothing else to reply but: "Do you not see, O heretic, that it is commanded that we keep priests in honor even though they be wicked?"[3] The worldly-minded, venal hierarchy, imitating Byzantine practices, disdained any contact with the lower clergy and the people, and became bureaucratic and unapproachable. Some of the pro-Byzantine clerical party went so far as to reject the Slavic liturgy as unsuited for liturgical purposes, and to extol the Greek as the only one acceptable to God.

Under such sorry circumstances it is no wonder that revolutionary movements directed both against the church and the state soon made their appearance. Thus early in the reign of Peter a particularly important anti-ecclesiastical movement arose. The earliest notice of it is found in a letter written by the profligate and utterly worldly Constantinopolitan patriarch, Theophylact (933-956), to Tsar Peter. The patriarch was the fourth son of Emperor Romanus Lecapenus, and hence an uncle of Peter's wife, Maria-Irene. The letter was found recently in the Ambrosian Library in Milan.[4] It appears that Peter had been greatly exercised over the appearance of the movement, and had written twice to the patriarch for instructions as to

3. Popruzhenko, *op. cit., p.* 16-17.
4. It is reprinted, in Bulgarian translation, in Zlatarsky, *op. cit.*, I², Appendix 11, pp. 840-45.

how to deal with it. Theophylact, who was a great deal
better acquainted with the breed of horses and the merits
of different wines than with matters of theology, did not
spend much time investigating the new teaching.   The
sportsman-patriarch, possibly jumping at hasty conclusions,
assured the pious tsar that he knew the teaching of the
group well, and pronounced it "an ancient and newly appeared Manichaeism mixed with Paulicianism".[5] The patriarch seems to have been good at guessing.   Some two
centuries previously, Emperor Constantine V Copronymus,
one of the most energetic of the Iconoclastic emperors, after
having defeated the Bulgarians in Thrace, took the opportunity to weaken the strength of the iconodule party by
transplanting to the depopulated regions strong colonies
of Syrian and Armenian Paulicians, who in their pronounced
dualism were closely related to the Manichees.   Besides
the Paulicians, some Monophysites were likewise trans-
ported.[6] The emperor wished to oppose these strongly
iconoclastic dualists, the Paulicians, to the Orthodox icono-
dules, but they were also to serve as guardians of the
border against the wild hordes of the Bulgars. From Thrace
the zeal of the Paulicians carried their teaching westward
into Macedonia, where, as George Hamartolos testifies,
they founded congregations as early as the first half of the
ninth century.[7] The patriarch's explanation of the new
movement therefore possesses a good deal of verisimilitude.
Although he nowhere mentioned the leaders of the new
movement, and above all did not refer to it as Bogomilism—
a name the movement received later—Theophylact was not
at a loss how to classify the phenomenon.   To him it was
the well known ancient heresy of Manichaeism and Paulicianism emerging anew in Bulgaria.   Theophylact gave
Peter specific instructions how to deal with the priests who
had fallen into these errors. It is thus evident that a considerable number of Orthodox priests had become identified
with the movement, although at the time the patriarch was
writing the letter no one among them seems to have become
the recognized leader of it. From Theophylact's insistence
that it was "a newly appeared heresy" it would seem that

5.   Zlatarsky, op. cit., I², p. 841.
6.   Theophanes, op. cit., p. 422.
7.   Georgios Hamartolos, ed. Muralt, p. 607.

neither he nor Peter were concerned with the ancient Bulgarian Paulician groups as such, but that the movement which caused Peter so much uneasiness was distinct from, although closely allied to them.

While we have no historical data regarding the practical steps taken by Tsar Peter to suppress the movement, it seems logical to suppose that he followed the patriarch's advice he had so earnestly sought and persecuted the adherents of the "heresy." If that supposition be correct, it must have been during this period of persecution that one person gained such preeminence as leader or reorganizer of the movement that it was ever after known by his name. That man was the Orthodox Bulgarian priest Bogomil.

Our sources of information about this remarkable man, unfortunately, are extremely scanty. That doughty opponent of the Bogomil movement, presbyter Cosmas, contributes practically all that is known concerning him, and that is almost nil. He tells us that "in the time of the Orthodox Tsar Peter there lived in the Bulgarian land a priest, Bogomil by name, who in reality was *Bogu ne mil,*[8] who first began to teach heresy in the Bulgarian land".[9] According to the editor of Cosmas' *Sermon against the Heretics,* the Russian scholar Popruzhenko, Cosmas wrote between 977 and 1014. Since Patriarch Theophylact, who died in 956, knew nothing of Bogomil, while to Cosmas he was the heresiarch *par excellence,* it follows that Bogomil must have secured leadership of the movement some time between the date of Theophylact's letter (which is not known) and the date of the death of Tsar Peter, in whose reign Cosmas affirms Bogomil made his appearance. Hence, roughly speaking, the date falls between 956 (or some years earlier) and 969. Moreover, Bogomil must have died sometime before the date of Cosmas' writing (earliest 977), for this writer speaks of him in the past tense. Unsatisfactory as this approximation is, it affords some idea of the period during which Bogomil lived. The *Synodical of Tsar Boris* (1211)[10] gives a list of Bogomil's "apostles"—apparently leaders of the movement in various territories—but several of them are known to have lived over a century later than Bogomil.

8. This is a pun on the name of Bogomil (Theophilos), the beloved of God; *Bogu ne mil* means *not beloved of God.*
9. Popruzhenko, *op. cit.,* p. 2.
10. Popruzhenko, M. G., *Sinodik tsarya Borila,* Sofia, 1928.

Thus it would not be safe to affirm that the list comprises the names of his immediate associates or successors.

What was "the ancient and newly-appeared" heresy which had caused the good Tsar Peter so much concern and had stirred Cosmas to such a pitch of denunciatory zeal? It must be realized, first of all, that no sources of their teaching coming from the members of the group are extant. All that is known about their doctrinal positions comes from their professed opponents. Cosmas, for instance, was their pronounced antagonist. If the thesis of Blagoev were to be accepted[11] that Cosmas simply copied Petrus Sicilus' *History of the Manichees*[12] and other Greek authors well known in Bulgaria, there could be no talk of teachings of the Bogomils. But it must be remembered that Bogomilism was genetically related to the Manichean-Paulician tenets, and therefore the similarity of its teaching to the former need not necessarily be taken as a clear proof that a description of it has been bodily copied from the former. Besides, one can not feel certain that the tenets ascribed to Bogomils by Cosmas were in every instance and in every particular correctly and unbiasedly stated. It must, however, be conceded that Cosmas knew the Bogomils personally and lived close enough to the beginnings of the movement to be able, if willing to be fair, correctly to portray its original, undeveloped, and unmodified state. But whether or not he did so or to what extent he may be trusted, is at present impossible to say.

In his *Sermon*, Cosmas plainly affirms that the Bogomils were dualists, who like the Gnostics of old held that the material world had been created not by the good God, the Father of Jesus the Christ, but by the devil.[13] Although Cosmas did not go into details in elaborating this teaching, it is obvious that it formed the foundation of the entire system. As dualists, they logically taught renunciation of the world, and insisted upon strictly ascetic ethical practices. Cosmas describes them as meek in deportment, gentle, modest and quiet, given assiduously to fasting and other practices of self-mortification. "For the heretics outwardly appear like sheep—meek, humble and quiet, visibly pallid

---

11.   Blagoev, N. P., *Besedata na presviter Kozma protiv Bogomilite*, Sofia, 1923.
12.   Migne, *PG*, CIV, col. 1240ff.
13.   Popruzhenko, *op. cit.*, p. 28, 37.

from their hypocritical fasting."[14]   They ate no meat and drank no wine.   Theoretically, marriage was forbidden them, for it implied continuation and extension of the kingdom of evil.   They lived in all respects an austere, strictly ascetic moral life.

Since the Old Testament speaks of the creator of the world as God, they rejected it and adhered only to the New.[15] In their interpretations of the Scriptures, they came surprisingly near to modern conclusions, employing fundamentally rationalistic methods in their exegesis.   Cosmas reports that "since they call the devil the creator, they deny that Christ performed miracles.   On hearing the gospel writer who mightily affirms the miracles of the Lord, they subvert the words to their own ruin, saying: 'Christ neither gave sight to the blind, nor healed the lame, nor raised a dead man; these are only parables and images employed to indicate healing of sins!'   They likewise do not believe the gospel writer who wrote that the multitude in the desert were fed with five loaves of bread; they say, 'It was not with loaves of bread, but with the four gospels and the Acts of the Apostles'."[16]   Too bad that the Bogomils had to mar such a perfectly good bit of biblical criticism by silly allegorizing!

Furthermore, the Bogomils rejected the historic Christian church in all its branches as false, and with it rejected its orders, rites, and doctrines.   They ridiculed the reverence paid to the cross on the ground that since it represented the tree on which Jesus had been crucified, it should by all means be held in horror and detestation as an instrument of murder.[17]   They called icons idols, and rejected the worship of saints as well as of the Virgin Mary.   Cosmas affirms that the Bogomils "went so far astray about her that their words and insolence can not be set down in these books".[18] Furthermore, they fulminated against the liturgy and the vestments.   As for prayers, they acknowledged as rightful only the Lord's Prayer, which they recited four times a day and as many times a night.   They categorically rejected all

14.   *Ibid.*, p. 3.
15.   *Ibid.*, p. 25, 31.
16.   *Ibid.*, p. 37.
17.   *Ibid.*, p. 6.
18.   *Ibid.*, p. 22.

holy days and all sacraments. They confessed and gave
absolution one to another.[19] Cosmas is especially indignant that this latter custom was in vogue among both sexes.

As for the protest of the Bogomils against social
and political oppression and injustice, Cosmas is disappoint-
ingly and exasperatingly brief in describing it. He merely
remarks that "they teach their own people not to obey their
masters; they blaspheme the wealthy, hate their father
(according to another reading, the tsar), ridicule the elders,
condemn the nobles, regard as vile in the sight of God those
who serve the tsar, and forbid all slaves to obey their masters".[20] In spite of its regrettable brevity, it is possible to
discern in this diatribe the rôle which the Bogomils, who
came from among the common people and were led by
ordinary parochial priests, played in an attempt to bring
relief and liberation to the enslaved masses. They represented the latter's protest against the tendency toward serfdom, and in behalf of economic justice and recovery of land
ownership on the part of the common people. They undoubtedly represented likewise the patriotic Bulgarian party
opposed to the bolyars (nobles) because of their selfish and
cruel policy of grinding the common peasantry into dust.

Naturally, a strictly ascetic régime, imposing upon its
adherents non-marriage and the consequent childlessness,
would have quickly led to the group's extinction. Under
the stress of circumstances and need of self-preservation,
the Bogomils developed, just as the Manichees had done
before them, a double standard which effectually insured
the continuance of the movement. The adherents were ultimately divided into two groups: the full-fledged members,
"the perfect," who were bound by a solemn pledge to observe all the rigors of the ascetic régime, and "hearers,"
who constituted a kind of life-long novitiate. Of course
the former, who comprised the élite of the society, were
comparatively few in number, and were supported by the
far more numerous class of the "hearers." The "perfect"
zealously gave themselves to missionary work, traveling
from place to place and preaching their gospel of world-
rejection and other-worldliness, and fulminating their fiery
denunciations of the evils of this world. The "hearers"

19. *Ibid.*, p. 45.
20. *Ibid.*, p. 40.

could marry and were permitted to engage in any honorable occupation.

Such then was the sorry plight of the Bulgarian society—political and spiritual—in the days of the immediate successor of the great Simeon! No wonder that the incompetent rule of Peter terminated in a grave disaster. Soon after the death of the debauched Emperor Romanus II (959-63) who was probably poisoned by his notoriously vicious wife Theophano, the Byzantine imperial power was seized by the ablest general of the time, Nicephorus Phocas, who as guardian of the imperial children, Basil II and Constantine VIII, ruled as emperor, having married Romanus' widow, Theophano, in spite of her reputation and the fact that she was thirty years his junior. Nicephorus II soon found a pretext for a quarrel with the Bulgarian Tsar Peter in the latter's demand for imperial tribute even after Tsaritsa Maria-Irene's death (965); after publicly insulting the Bulgarian embassy, he went to war with Peter (967). Since Nicephorus himself was not able to prosecute the war, he adopted the time-honored expedient of calling to his aid some barbarian chieftain who was glad to avail himself of the sanction to invade and plunder the unfortunate country at enmity with the emperor. In this instance, instead of calling upon the Magyars, the Patzinaks, or the Cumans, he turned to the Grand-Prince of Kiev. This principality, set up by the "Rus" whom the Byzantines knew under the name of Varangians and about whose identity a fierce battle is still raging, had for some time been well known to the Empire. Under their Prince Igor a commercial treaty had been concluded with the Empire from which it appears that some of the Rus were already Christian. Igor's wife, Olga, became openly Christian, and was personally known in Constantinople which she had visited. But her son Svyatoslav (945-72) was a fierce warrior of the true Viking type—a soul naturally pagan. The business of war was his meat and drink. It was with this grim and lusty cut-throat that Nicephorus Phocas made arrangements for invasion of Peter's dominions in spite of the fact that the terrified Peter had sued for peace and had sent his two sons to Constantinople as hostages. The fierce Russian warrior gladly consented to receive the bribe offered him for the task so congenial to him and in the summer of 968 came to

the mouth of the Danube. He gained an easy victory over
the Bulgarian army and occupied a large part of the country. But the Russian bear had no intention of relinquish-
ing his prey: he openly boasted of his determination to
retain his conquest permanently. It is said that he was so
delighted with the country he had conquered that he contemplated abandoning Kiev and setting up his capital in
Bulgaria.

Such a plan could not prove acceptable to Nicephorus
Phocas, who had no desire to permit a dangerous neighbor
like Svyatoslav near Constantinople. He therefore readily
consented to Peter's plea for peace and promised him aid to
drive out the Russians.

But before Svyatoslav could be expelled or any other
benefits of the newly concluded peace be reaped, Peter died
(Jan. 30, 969). Before his death, he assumed the monastic
habit, and the Bulgarian church soon added him to the number of her saints. Peter's death ushered in a period of interregnum which effectually added to the existing confusion.
Peter's sons, Boris and Romanus, were away in Constantinople, and this gave the disaffected elements in Bulgaria an
opportunity to seize the throne. The uprising which now
occurred was led by four brothers, David, Moses, Aaron,
and Samuel, and was carried on a larger scale than the
previous revolts. These four men, known in history as
"Comitopouloi", or young counts, were the sons of Shishman, a zhupan or governor of the Western part of Bulgaria.

In such imminent danger, Boris and Romanus, sent
back by Nicephorus, returned to Bulgaria with Greek military aid to claim the throne of their father. The elder of
them, Boris II, became tsar (969-72), but was too weak to
cope with the difficulties facing him. Since Svyatoslav's
Kievan territory had been attacked in his absence by his
southern neighbors, the Patzinaks, and he had been forced
to withdraw his forces from Bulgaria in defense of his own
lands, Boris was enabled to reoccupy for a few months the
territories thus evacuated. But to cope with the revolts of
the "Comitopouloi" he was too weak. Hence, the Bulgarian empire was torn into two halves, of which only the
Eastern remained under the rule of Boris; David and his

brothers succeeded in seizing the reins of government in Western Bulgaria.

But the Russian grand-prince had no intention of surrendering his conquests easily. During the autumn of 969, Svyatoslav reappeared at the mouth of the Danube. Boris II was in a terrible quandary: unable to withstand the superior forces of the invader, he appealed to Constantinople for help. In the meantime, the Russians quickly reconquered Preslavets and occupied a great deal of the territory between the Danube and the Balkan mountains. Finally, they took even the capital, Preslav, where they captured both Boris and his brother Romanus with their families.

In the meantime, Constantinople was greatly alarmed at the rapid conquests of Svyatoslav, especially when the latter crossed the Balkan range and took Philippopolis where he barbarously impaled 20,000 of its inhabitants. Moreover, there occurred palace revolutions at Constantinople. Empress Theophano had her husband, Nicephorus II Phocas, murdered by her lover and quondam friend of Nicephorus, the renowned Armenian general John Tzimisces, and in turn she was exiled by the faithless John. The latter then usurped the throne of Nicephorus (Dec., 969). The first task of the new emperor was to induce Svyatoslav, by an offer of a payment, to withdraw, or in case of rejection of the offer, to fight with him. The latter turning out to be the choice, Tzimisces, in a terrible battle near the modern Lüle-Burgas, succeeded in defeating the fierce Russian grand-prince. Constantinople was saved.

After a delay of over a year, Tzimisces decided (971) to drive the Russians from the whole of the Bulgarian territory. Proclaiming everywhere that he came as liberator of Bulgaria, he penetrated the passes of the Balkan range and laid siege to Preslav, which he took on Good Friday, 972. Boris and Romanus fatuously rejoiced to have regained their freedom. Thereupon, the Bulgarians everywhere willingly submitted to Tzimisces, who was thus enabled to lay siege to Silistria (Drster) where Svyatoslav took up his last defensive stand. After three months of the most ferocious fighting, hunger compelled the Russian forces to sue for peace. It was granted on terms compelling the Russian grand-prince to give up all his conquests and to retire from Bulgaria. Svyatoslav accepted and started for Kiev, but on his return he lost his life in a skirmish with the Patzinaks (973).

But the victorious Tzimisces did not for a moment desire to play the rôle of Boris' magnanimous defender. Having taken the Bulgarian tsar and his brother prisoners, he triumphantly carried them in his train to Constantinople along with the tsarist crown. There Tsar Boris II was constrained to divest himself publicly in St. Sophia of the imperial purple and to take off his head the jewelled crown, and then at the palace to abdicate his throne. Thereupon, he received the rank of a magister. His brother was emasculated. This done, Tzimisces proclaimed Boris' territory a province of the Byzantine Empire. The Bulgarian patriarchate of Preslav, to which place it had been moved some time previously from Silistria, was abolished, and Patriarch Damian who had fled to Western Bulgaria was declared deposed, the Bulgarian church being subjected to the ecumenical patriarchate as a mere metropolitanate (972). Silistria was once more made a metropolitan see subject to Constantinople.

The territory which had so recently suffered the terrible devastation caused by the Russian, the Patzinak, and the imperial armies, was denuded of population. In order to repopulate the conquered territory, as well as with the intention of weakening the native Bulgarian population and of providing a strong military cordon to protect the Empire from possible future invasions, Tzimisces transplanted the remnants of the Paulicians into the Philippopolis region. The Armenian newcomers came from the strongly Paulician territories of Melitene and Theodosiopolis (Erzerum) in eastern Asia Minor. The plan of transplanting them was suggested by Patriarch Thomas of Antioch, who thus got rid of dangerous religious malcontents, but unwittingly strengthened the anti-ecclesiastical groups, such as the native Bogomils, in Bulgaria.

In the meantime, Western Bulgaria, under the rule of the four brothers, David, Moses, Aaron and Samuel, proclaimed itself an independent political entity. Its rulers refused to acknowledge the abolition of the imperial rank assented to by the weak Boris, and claimed the imperial title (whether in common or on the part of only one of the brothers, is not known) as their own. At the same time, they resolved to regain the lost eastern half of Bulgaria from the Empire. The four rulers likewise refused to acknowledge the legality of the abolition of the Bulgarian patriarchate: they gladly received Patriarch Damian who had fled to them (972) for refuge, and set up for him a new see at their capital, Sredets (in Greek Triaditza), the ancient Sardica and modern Sofia.

At first the four brothers were not fortunate in their struggle to regain eastern Bulgaria. In fact, they were not able even to retain all of their own territory. The imperial armies continued to drive them westward, so that they and the patriarch were forced to change their residence successively to Vodena, Moglen, and Prespa, until finally they set it up at Ohrid. By that time they held no more than the extreme western Macedonia and Albania. At last, however, the sudden death of John Tzimisces (January, 976) changed the whole situation. Young Emperor Basil II, who now took the government into his own hands, was preoccupied with the dangerous revolt of Bardas Sclerus. Given a breathing spell, the four Bulgarian rulers were able to drive the Greek armies from western Bulgaria and from the Danube region; the Greeks retained only northern Thrace. But the two elder brothers of the four rulers lost their lives fighting, and the third, Aaron, was put to death, having been accused by Samuel of treason. Thus in the summer of 976 Samuel found himself the sole ruler of the Western Bulgarian Empire.

Samuel (976-1014) was an able and energetic administrator and excellent warrior. By waging war with the Empire almost incessantly, he was able to recover in general the territory of Simeon's realm with the exception of the region south of the Balkan Mountains. The center of his realm therefore shifted westward, and he finally made Ohrid, the holy city of Clement and Nahum, the capital of his empire and the see of the Bulgarian patriarchate.

Unfortunately for the independence of Bulgaria, Emperor Basil II, having overcome the revolt of Bardas Sclerus with the help of the Russian Grand-prince Vladimir, for which service he had to give the latter his sister, Anna, in marriage and to help Vladimir Christianize his dominions, was able to turn his attention to the territories of Samuel. In 996 the imperial army so signally defeated the Bulgarian forces that Samuel's military strength was permanently shattered. Thereupon, in several campaigns, stretching in time over almost twenty years, Basil subjugated a great part of Bulgaria to himself. The final terrible defeat of Samuel's army occurred in 1014 at the battle of Belasitse.

Samuel himself died the same year. His successors, Radomir and John Vladislav, were not able to withstand the victorious Basil, and by the year 1018 the latter completed the conquest of the whole country. As an independent empire, Bulgaria ceased to exist. With the deposition of her last autocephalous patriarch, David, the Bulgarian church as a national institution also came to an end. Basil regarded his brilliant victories over the Bulgarians as his chief claim to glory and on their account assumed the title of Βουλγαροκτόνος—the Bulgar-killer.

SERBIAN CHRISTIANITY BEFORE THE TIME OF ST. SAVA

As has already been narrated, the official conversion of the Serbians is to be placed in the reign of Mutimir, the zhupan of Rascia, in the second half of the ninth century. Emperor Basil I sent him a large number of priests, and it is probable even a bishop. The episcopal see, which is first mentioned in 1018, may have been established as early as Mutimir's time at his seat, Rascia, and was placed under the jurisdiction of the metropolitan of Dyrrhachium (Durazzo). Later it was transferred to the jurisdiction of the Bulgarian see of Ohrid. It must not, however, be forgotten that there existed in the country several episcopal sees of the Latin rite. In the Orthodox eparchy of Rascia the liturgy was of course sung in Greek and the character of the church in general was Greek. During Mutimir's reign, Byzantine influence remained predominant. But after Emperor Basil's death (886), and prior to the reign of Nicephorus II Phocas, the Empire lost much of its prestige and the rising state of Bulgaria replaced it as the chief power in the Balkans. The Serbians, little by little, fell under the domination of Bulgaria, especially during the reign of the Bulgarian Emperor Simeon (893-927) when the native Serbian zhupans were replaced by Bulgarians. With the hegemony of this chief protagonist of Slavic culture, Bulgaria, the use of Slavic liturgy gradually displaced the Greek, and the ecclesiastical jurisdiction passed over to the Bulgarian church.

The disastrous defeat of Bulgaria by Emperor Basil II the Bulgar-killer, who in 1018 put an end to the independence of Bulgaria, changed the whole aspect of the situation. With the loss of the Bulgarian lands proper, the Serbian dependencies of Dioclea, Trebinye, Hum, Bosnia, and Serbia or Rascia likewise passed under the imperial sway. In addition to these, even the province of Sirmium with Belgrade as its capital was incorporated within the Byzantine Empire. The Serbian bishopric of Rascia remained under

73

the jurisdiction of the former Bulgarian patriarchate of
Ohrid, but this see became thoroughly Hellenized. The
bishop of Rascia had under his control an immense eparchy,
manned with a surprisingly limited personnel. The three
Latin sees within the Serbian territories were subject to the
jurisdiction of Dubrovnik, which in 1022 was raised by Pope
Benedict VIII to the rank of an archbishopric. They comprised the Serbian episcopal sees of Hum (i. e. Ston), of
Serbia (the see unknown), and of Trebinye.

The radical change in the political situation of the Balkans produced a corresponding change in the foreign policy
of the Serbian zhupans. The Serbian lands were then organized into two centers: the maritime, comprising Dioclea-
Zeta, Trebinye, and Hum, and the inner lands of Bosnia and
Rascia. The uncomfortable and menacing proximity of the
Byzantine Empire which now surrounded the Serbian lands
on three sides threatened the latter with a disaster similar
to that which had overtaken Bulgaria. In view of that fact,
Serbian foreign policy became anti-Byzantine.

An important expansion of the territorial and political
status of the Serbian zhupans occurred during the reign of
the statesmanlike Zhupan Michael (c. 1050-81), the son of
Zhupan Voyislav. He began his career as ruler of the
Dalmatian territory of Dioclea-Zeta (essentially the pre-
war Montenegro), but soon expanded it considerably. He
acknowledged the overlordship of the Byzantine Empire,
and being in favor at Constantinople, received from Emper-
or Constantine IX Monomachus (1042-55) the title of
protospatharius (c. 1052) as well as an imperial princess in
marriage. During the next twenty years he kept peace with
the Empire. But during the period of disorders consequent
upon the disastrous defeat of the imperial forces by the
Seljuq Turks at the battle of Manzikert (1071), the Bulgars
rose up in revolt against Emperor Michael VII Parapinaces
(1071-78), and chose Michael's son, Constantine Bodin, as
their tsar. Acceptance of this dignity on Bodin's part necessarily involved Serbia in hostilities with the Empire, during
which the Serbian zhupan succeeded in enlarging his territories.

Zhupan Michael even succeeded in securing the royal
title from the papacy. Pope Gregory VII (1073-85) who
was anxious to procure aid in the Balkans for his aggressive

policy against the patriarchate of Constantinople, deemed it advantageous to bind to himself the Croatian and the Serbian rulers. In 1076 the pope conferred the royal dignity upon Demetrius Zvonimir of Croatia, who thus signalized his independence of the Byzantine overlordship, and in 1077 the like dignity was granted to Michael of Serbia on the condition that Pope Gregory be acknowledged as Serbia's overlord. That action, of course, likewise implied a declaration of independence from the Empire. In spite of the dependence upon the papacy which the transaction involved and which was not taken very seriously, this was an important victory for the Serbian ruler who thus secured a legal sanction for the increase of his rank. As for Pope Gregory, he pursued a policy of recovering as much of the lost diocese of Illyricum as he could, thus extending his jurisdiction.

After King Michael's death (c. 1082), the royal title passed to his son, Constantine Bodin, who had been co-regent with his father for some time before the latter's death. Bodin still further extended the inherited territory by imposing his rule upon the zhupas of Bosnia and Rascia. He likewise rendered an important service to the Serbian church by consolidating the ecclesiastical jurisdiction in the hands of the archbishop of Antivari.

It has been thought formerly, on the basis of a spurious document attributed to Pope Alexander II,[1] that the archbishopric of Antivari was founded in 1067. It used to be commonly affirmed that King Michael had cleverly made use of an opportunity offered him by the dissatisfaction among the Dalmatian Slavs with the decisions of the Synod of Spalato of 1060. This gathering not only promulgated the strict decrees of the Vatican Council of 1059 comprising the demands of the Cluniac reform, but also reaffirmed the prohibition of the Slavic liturgy which had originally been issued by the Synod of Spalato in 925. But although there is no doubt that much dissatisfaction existed among the Slavic population, zealously and fervently attached to the use of the Church-Slavonic liturgy, with the prohibition of it, yet this did not lead directly to the establishment of an independent archbishopric for the Serbian lands. That

1. Thalloczy et al., *Acta Albaniae*, I, No. 63, p. 17; Jaffé, P., *Regesta*, I, No. 4628.

result was obtained during the reign of Constantine Bodin. In 1088 he and the bishop of Antivari, Peter, sent a petition to Pope Clement III Wibert appealing to him to "renew" what they claimed—probably also on the basis of forged documents—to have once been the archbishopric of Dioclea, by raising the bishopric of Antivari (which claimed to be the heir of Dioclea) to the rank of archbishopric. The pope complied readily with the request and sent Bishop Peter the archepiscopal pallium. The "renewed" see was granted jurisdiction over nine bishoprics, which, it was claimed, had been formerly comprised by the mythical archepiscopal see of Dioclea. All these Slavic sees were a part of the dominions of Bodin. In this manner the Serbian bishoprics, formerly subject to several jurisdictions, were now unified and consolidated. The supremacy of Antivari was acknowledged even in modern times, when in 1902 Pope Leo XIII conferred upon its archbishop the title of "Primate of Serbia."

During the latter part of the reign of King Constantine Bodin, and especially after his death (c. 1101), Zeta lost the hegemony it had wielded. Bodin's death ushered in a period of indescribable anarchy which lasted during the long and wearisome struggles for succession. Various rivals for the throne succeeded each other with great swiftness, each leaving the confusion worse confounded.

During this time the leadership among the Serbian zhupas passed over to Rascia. This zhupa was ruled by the able Zhupan Vlkan, a quondam appointee and subordinate of Constantine Bodin, who now felt strong enough to assert his independence. Bosnia also fell away from the group which had been united under Bodin's sway, and in 1120 voluntarily submitted to the overlordship of Hungary. Because of the disharmony existing among these important nuclei of Serbian power, as well as on account of the raids conducted by the Serbs into the imperial territory, Emperor John II Comnenus (c. 1122) invaded Rascia and later Zeta, and reasserted Byzantine authority over the zhupans of these territories. The situation was especially galling during the reign of Emperor Manuel I Comnenus (1143-80) whose bellicose chivalry made him a Byzantine counterpart of the English Coeur-de-Lion. Wishing to reestablish the ancient boundaries of Byzantium, Manuel forced the Ser-

bian zhupans to seek an alliance with the Magyar king in
order to preserve their autonomy. The grand zhupan of
Rascia went even further and espoused the idea of full national independence by unification of the various zhupas
into one strong unit. Grand-Zhupan Desa (c. 1161-65)
realized that as long as the feudal decentralization of the
Serbian lands obtained, and as long as the Serbian zhupans
regarded themselves as independent of any central authority, acknowledging only nominally the supremacy of the
grand-zhupans, Serbia would remain a prey to the Empire
or some other strongly organized state. He therefore initiated the policy of centralizing the power in the hands of
the grand-zhupan by subjugating the zhupa of Zeta to
himself. But Desa's policy of uniting the Serbian territories under the aegis of Rascia seemed dangerous to Emperor
Manuel, who thereupon deposed Desa and divided his territory among the sons of an old Serbian ruling family, the
Zavidas, appointing the eldest, Tihomir, to succeed Desa as
grand-zhupan.

But the youngest of the Zavida brothers, Stephen
Nemanya, espousing the policy of Desa, completed the task
undertaken by the deposed grand-zhupan. When by singular favor of Emperor Manuel this able man was appointed
grand-zhupan (1168), Stephen Nemanya immediately turned against his benefactor and taking advantage of the
emperor's war with Hungary, reconquered certain Serbian
lands surrendered to Manuel at his accession. The latter
sent an army against Stephen under the leadership of
Stephen's eldest brother, Tihomir, but Stephen defeated it and thus became the master of the situation (1168). Two years later he conducted a successful
invasion of Zeta and the territory of Narenta on the
Dalmatian coast and subjected these countries to his own
rule, although the process of consolidation was not fully
completed till 1183. By making the title of grand-zhupan
mean something in terms of centralized actual power, and
thus making it comparable to that of a king, Stephen
Nemanya became the founder of a consolidated and independent Serbian state. Unfortunately, his domains failed
to comprise all Serbian territories, for Bosnia and Hum remained outside Stephen's rule and organized themselves
separately. The tragic disorders which broke out in the

Empire before and after the revolt of 1185 against the hated rule of the last emperor of the house of Comnenus, Andronicus I, continuing under the Angeli rulers till the plots and counterplots for regaining the throne for the deposed Emperor Isaac II led to the sacking of Constantinople in 1204, greatly facilitated the consolidation of the Slavic power in the Balkans. The anarchic conditions in the Empire enabled Stephen Nemanya to assert his country's independence, and afforded an opportunity to Theodore (who later assumed the name Peter) and John Asen to set up the Second Bulgarian Empire of Trnovo in 1186. Stephen Nemanya of Serbia and Tsar Peter of Bulgaria then made a common cause against the Empire.

Thus under the Grand-Zhupan Stephen Nemanya (1168-95) a large part of Serbian lands was consolidated and the power of the grand-zhupan centralized. To the nucleus of Rascia were added the zhupa of Zeta (1183) and the territories conquered from the former Bulgarian possessions. But the grand-zhupan was statesman enough to realize that along with political independence he must secure for his land ecclesiastical unity. Christianity instead of amalgamating his people into a single cultural group, had played a divisive rôle in his dominions. The eastern territories, principally Rascia, lay within the orbit of the influence of the Constantinopolitan patriarchate, while the Western regions, especially the Adriatic littoral, were predominantly Catholic. Besides, Bogomilism had penetrated the Serbian lands from Macedonia and presented by no means an easy problem for an ecclesiastical statesman. Furthermore, because of the constant rivalry between the Eastern and the Latin patriarchates for hegemony in the Balkans, the spread of Christianity in Serbia had been greatly retarded. There were still many pagans among the conservative-minded masses, as well as those who adhered to a curious mixture of paganism and Christianity, desiring to be equally safe no matter which religion should prove right in the life beyond. Stephen was conscious of the grave danger inherent in such ecclesiastical disunity, knowing that the pretense of spreading the true faith was always the favorite excuse of every political adventurer actuated by purely secular ambition to subjugate his neighbor's country to himself. To guard his dominion against the possibility of such danger,

Nemanya realized that he must consolidate the ecclesiastical organization of his land.

The grand-zhupan therefore decided upon a radical ecclesiastical policy of unification: in the first place, he proclaimed as the state church that rite which claimed the adherence of the majority of the population of Rascia—namely, Eastern Orthodoxy—to which he himself had become fervently attached. This was an important decision as far as the future of his country was concerned. One is moved to speculate how different the history of Serbia might have been had Stephen remained a steadfast adherent of the Latin rite in which he had been baptized![2] Nevertheless, Stephen was no religious bigot: since his maritime provinces were under the jurisdiction of the Latin church, he devoted himself most energetically to the task of preserving friendly relations with the Roman curia and with the two Catholic archbishops in his dominions, those of Dubrovnik and of Antivari, and sent presents to Rome. As for the third religious group which he found entrenched in Rascia, the Bogomils, which was heartily hated by the other two dominant groups as heretical, Stephen decided to deal harshly with it, for its existence contravened his policy of unification. Having called a "great council" to consider what policy to adopt regarding the Bogomils, he had "the godless heretics" anathematized and condemned in spite of considerable opposition to the measure on the part of some of Bogomil nobles. When these leaders resisted the grand-zhupan's forcible measures with weapons in their hands, Nemanya decided to conduct a crusade against them. The Bogomils were defeated and the great majority of them were expelled or fled to the neighboring independent states of Bosnia and Hum. The biographers of Stephen Nemanya, his son King Stephen the First-Crowned and his more famous younger son, St. Sava, heap extravagant praise upon him for these harsh measures which not only made Orthodoxy supreme in Serbia but also cleared the land of heresy.[3]

The organizer of the autocephalous Serbian national church was the youngest son of the grand-zhupan, Rastko

2. Šafařík, P. J., *Památky dřevního písemnictví Jihoslovanův*, ed. 2, Praha, 1873; Život sv. Symeona, od krále Štěpána, p. 2.
3. *Ibid.*, Život sv. Symeona, od krále Štěpána, a Život sv. Symeona, od sv. Sávy.

(possibly a diminutive form of Rastislav, as the Russian church-historian Golubinsky suggests),[4] who came to be generally known under his monastic name of Sava. He was born in 1174, and was educated at his father's court. When about eighteen years of age, his parents wished to see him married, but he was won for the monastic ideal by a visiting Russian monk from Mount Athos who had come in company of others to the court in quest of alms. Rastko, rightly fearing his parents' strenuous opposition to his design, secretly ran away from home with the monk, having taken leave of his parents on the pretext of going on a hunting expedition. He entered the Russian monastery of St. Panteleimon on Mount Athos, and after his father's emissaries had tracked him to this retreat, threatening to take him back in chains unless he return voluntarily, he outwitted them by a ruse and assumed the monastic habit.[5] After a short time he left St. Panteleimon, having accepted an invitation to join the monastery of Vatopedi where he assumed "the great rite", i. e., the full monastic vows, and with it the name of the famous Serbian saint, Sava (Sabbas). His former princely rank was, however, by no means forgotten—a circumstance which was not to his disadvantage.

When his father, Stephen, abdicated his throne in 1195,[6] to devote the rest of his life to works of piety, he also assumed the monastic cowl from the hand of Callinicos, the bishop of Rascia, and changed his name to Simeon. Stephen's wife, Anna, became nun Anastasia. After having spent two years at his own foundation, the monastery Studenitsa, monk Simeon, bringing richly wrought gold and silver presents with him, joined his son Sava at Vatopedi. Many Serbian nobles accompanied the royal monk, and joined the monastic community with him. The two monks, father and son, then tramped all over the Holy Mountain, acquainting themselves with the best that this great center of Orthodox culture had to offer, incidentally distributing princely gifts among the monasteries. They undertook the

4. Golubinsky, E. E., *Kratki ocherk istorii pravoslavnykh tserkvei bolgarskoi, serbskoi, i rumynskoi*, Moskva, 1871, p. 450.
5. Domentiyan, *Zhitie svyatykh serbskykh prosvêtitelei, Symeona i Savvy.* Ed. by Cyril Zhivković, Paris, 1858, p. 8; also Yanich-Hankey, *Lives of the Serbian Saints*, London, 1921, p. 13.
6. Burković, T. J., *Khilandar u goda Nemanića*, Beograd, 1925, p. 8.

journey with the purpose of founding a Serbian monastery
which might become a religious and cultural center of the
Serbian church life and to perform the function fulfilled
by the Greek monasteries in the Byzantine ecclesiastical
economy.   They finally fixed upon the site of the ruined
ancient monastery of Khilandari which then belonged to
Vatopedi. Emperor Alexius III Comnenus, Simeon's cousin
by marriage, on the suggestion of the Vatopedi brotherhood
granted by an imperial diploma the abandoned monastery
to the Serbian princely monks, who thereupon set about
restoring it.   When their building labors were completed,
they forthwith settled the new and magnificent foundation
with Serbian monks, and it was thereafter officially acknowledged by the Synod of Mount Athos as well as by the
emperor as a Serbian monastery.[7]   Khilandar, which was
finished in 1199, became within a short time the chief center
of Serbian monastic culture and of literary activity. Sava,
who had previously received holy orders of deaconate and
priesthood at the hands of Nicholas, bishop of Mt. Athos,
was elevated to the rank of archimandrite of the new monastery by the archbishop of Thessalonica and the bishop of
Mt. Athos. He organized a school at the monastery which became the training ground for practically all the future leaders of the Serbian church.

   After Simeon's death, which occurred in 1200,[8] a civil
war broke out between his two elder sons over the question
of succession to the rule of Rascia. The eldest son of
Nemanya, Vlkan, had been appointed in 1195 the ruler of
the minor principalities of Zeta, Trebinye, Hvostno, and
Toplitsa, which had been for that purpose detached from
Rascia. But when Nemanya had abdicated his throne in
that same year, Vlkan, despite of his primogeniture, was
passed over in the matter of succession to the throne of
Rascia in favor of his younger brother, Stephen (1195-
1228), because the latter was strongly supported by Emper-
or Isaac II Angelus, whose niece, Eudocia, he had married.
In order to secure the coveted throne by force, Vlkan entered into a close alliance with Pope Innocent III and with
the Hungarian King Henry (or Emerich, 1196-1204), both
of whom were exceedingly glad of the opportunity to se-

7.   Miklosich, *Monumenta Serbica*, Vindobonae, 1858, item 14.
8.   Domentiyan, *op. cit.*, p. 38.

cure a measure of control over the Serbian territory. A strong man like Pope Innocent could not be presumed to allow himself to forget that Illyricum had once belonged to the papal jurisdiction. Moreover, the only power which could help him to realize his ambition of regaining the lost diocese was Hungary. He was therefore quite ready to join forces with Henry who, for his part, wished to extend his political influence over Serbia. Vlkan's appeal was therefore eagerly responded to. Thus with the Magyar military aid, Vlkan drove Stephen out of the country and assumed the rule over Rascia. In return for the aid rendered him by the pope and the Hungarian king, Vlkan was obliged, in 1199, to acknowledge the papal primacy,[9] to proclaim Roman Catholicism the religion of the state, to permit the Roman legates, chaplain John and sub-deacon Simeon, to set up a Latin ecclesiastical organization in his territories,[10] and to acknowledge Henry as his overlord. Since that time, the kings of Hungary added to their already long and pompous titles that of kings of Serbia. But a few years later, while Hungary was busily engaged in a war with the Bulgarians, Stephen organized a counter-attack upon Vlkan (1203) and succeeded in driving him out of the country. Thereupon, he resumed the throne.

The conquest of Constantinople by the Crusaders in 1204 completely changed the situation not only in the Empire, but in the Balkan peninsula as well. The son of Emperor Isaac II Angelus, Alexius, had been able, by promises of financial and military aid to the leaders of the Fourth Crusade, as well as of reunion of the churches, to deflect them from their original purpose of attacking Alexandria to what was regarded as a temporary expedition to Constantinople for the purpose of restoring the throne to Isaac. They were successful in this undertaking (1203), but when Isaac regained his throne and associated his son Alexius with himself, the two rulers found their resources insufficient to redeem their pledges to the Crusaders. Moreover, an opposition party inspired by a feeling that the two emperors betrayed the interests of Byzantium to the Latins, stirred up a popular revolution which swept both rulers off

9. Theiner, A., *Vetera monumenta Slavorum meridionalium*, Romae, 1863, I, No. 10, p. 6.
10. Thalloczy et al., *Acta Albaniae*, I, No. 115.

the throne. This was then seized by the anti-Latin leader of the revolters, Alexius V Ducas (1204), who repudiated the promises altogether. Thereupon, the Crusaders decided to take Constantinople by storm. In this undertaking they were successful, whereupon they sacked and looted the capital in such furious and barbarous manner that the treasures gathered there by the husbandry of centuries were lost to it forever. Villehardouin, the historian of the Crusade, bears testimony that "never since the world was created, was so much taken in a city." The looting over, the conquerors, having abandoned their original intention to go on an expedition to the Holy Land, settled down as new masters of the Empire. They created out of it the Latin Empire of Romania which comprised the bulk of the former Byzantine Empire, although it was parceled out among warring and mutually opposed factions of the various leaders. The remainder left in Greek hands fell into three parts: the Empire of Nicaea ruled by Theodore I Lascaris, son-in-law of Emperor Alexius III, with the seat of the emperor as well as the patriarch at Nicaea; the Empire of Trebizond, ruled by Alexius, grandson of Emperor Andronicus I; and the despotate (later Empire) of Epirus, under the bastard Michael Angelus, first cousin of Emperor Isaac II. The latter territory comprised the arch-episcopal diocese of Ohrid, to whose jurisdiction the Serbian bishopric of Rascia had long been subordinated.

Under such greatly changed circumstances Stephen Nemanyich decided to alter the traditional political orientation: he divorced his wife, Eudocia, daughter of Emperor Alexius III, turning her out of doors all but naked as gossip persisted to affirm, and in 1217 married the Roman Catholic Anna, grand-daughter of the powerful doge of Venice, Enrico Dandolo, who held the lion's share of the newly created Latin Empire. With the help of his new friends, and while the jealous Hungarian king Andrew II was away on a crusading expedition, he secured in the same year from Pope Honorius III (1216-1227) the royal crown. A papal legate having been sent to Serbia with the crown, performed the ceremony of coronation of Stephen and his Venetian wife Anna in behalf of his master. Thus Stephen became the first crowned king of Rascia or Serbia, although Zeta had

formerly been ruled by kings.[11] Of course, in exchange
Stephen, who came to be known to history as "Prvovyen-
chany", i. e. the First-Crowned, was obliged to acknowledge
on his own behalf as well as on that of his country the
claims of papacy to supremacy, and to give solemn pledges
of obedience to the pope. It may be remarked in passing
that throughout the history of Bulgaria and Serbia the
rulers manifested no hesitation in giving such solemn
pledges whenever there was anything to be gained from the
papacy, but thereafter displayed an equally remarkable
propensity to forget them.

The papal legate, having crowned the royal pair,
promptly set about organizing the Latin church in Serbia.
But the Serbian clergy, which ever since Sava's return to
Serbia from Mount Athos in 1208 had been under his influence and leadership, remained loyal to Orthodoxy and
vehemently opposed the Latin cult. They refused to
acknowledge the Latin hierarchy or to adopt the Latin rite.
The common people were likewise seriously disaffected toward the new ecclesiastical policy of their king. Thus
Stephen, having gained his political objectives of securing
the royal crown, soon discovered abundant reasons for
abandoning his pro-Roman orientation.

Eleven years before (1208), at the request of his
brother, Sava returned from Khilandar, three years after
the Holy Mountain had been conquered by the Latins who
had introduced the Latin rite there. He brought home the
body of his father, the monk Simeon, and interred it in the
monastery of Studenitsa. At this monastery Sava settled
and became its archimandrite. He took part in the diplomatic affairs of the country, faithfully supporting his
brother Stephen. Moreover, according to the *Life,* "like an
apostle he travelled through all his fatherland, teaching the
people the divine dogmas of the Orthodox faith, building
churches, setting forth the method of singing and praising
the Lord in the churches, as it was done at the Holy Mountain of Athos".[12] Sava brought with him from Khilandar

---

11. Archdeacon Thomas of Spalato, *Historia Salonitanorum,* cap. 25; in Farlati,
Illyricum Sacrum, v. 5. But the *Regesta* of Honorius do not make any mention of
this important occurrence, nor does Theiner's monumental work, *Vetera monumenta
Slavorum meridionalium,* contain any papal document referring to it. Jireček, *op. cit.*
I, p. 297 accepts the account as authentic.
12. Yanich-Hankey, *op. cit.,* p. 21.

many of his former pupils who had been trained in the Slavic cult; they were now employed as his helpers in the wide-spread missionary labors he was carrying on. Some biographers of Sava give him a great deal of credit for combating heretics: Domentiyan says that Sava, "ranging throughout his Fatherland, everywhere corrected disorders and evil customs, assailing and converting the unrepentant heretics and expelling from the kingdom those who refused to be converted and were causing confusion".[13] His brother, the Grand-Zhupan Stephen, at first loyally supported Sava's zealous apostolic labors in behalf of Orthodoxy, and together the two brothers founded the famous monastery of Zhicha, which later became the first see of the Serbian archbishopric. But when Stephen so greatly jeopardized the national faith as to subject his country to the jurisdiction of the pope, Sava most resolutely expressed his disapproval of the course, and rather than to submit, left the country and returned to Mount Athos (1217).

Undoubtedly the danger in which the Serbian Orthodox eparchy found itself by Stephen's acceptance of the royal crown at the hands of the papal legate was great. In order to make Serbia safe for Othodoxy, Sava determined to secure its ecclesiastical independence. He therefore undertook a journey to Nicaea and presented his appeal on behalf of the Serbian church to the patriarch, stressing the necessity of autocephaly as the only effective means of preventing the subversion of the bishopric of Rascia to the Latin jurisdiction. To be sure, in accordance with the *Life,* he had gone to Nicaea primarily on account of some "needs of the monastery".[14] Moreover, Sava is said to have suggested "one of the brethren" accompanying him for the office; but this may safely be understood as Domentiyan's attempt to shield Sava from the charge of an unmonastic conduct in seeking archepiscopal honor for himself. At any rate, both Patriarch Manuel and Emperor Theodore Lascaris readily acknowledged the gravity of the situation and in 1219 Patriarch Manuel I (1215-1222),[15] with the approval

13. Domentiyan, *op. cit.,* p. 61.

14. Yanich-Hankey, *op. cit.,* p. 22; also Domentiyan, *op. cit.,* p. 54, where the destination of Sava is given as Constantinople, clearly under the impression that this city was still held by Emperor Theodore Lascaris.

15. Domentiyan, *op. cit.,* p. 55 credits Patriarch Germanos II with having granted the autocephaly to the Serbian church. But this hierarch held office from 1222 to 1240; cf. Cobham, C. D.: *The Patriarchs of Constantinople,* Cambridge, 1911, p. 91 and 93.

of the Holy Synod, granted the Serbian church autocephaly, raising it at the same time to the rank of an archbishopric. Sava was thereupon consecrated the first "archbishop of all the Serbian lands", the emperor with his court being present at the ceremony. By the terms of the *Tomos* issued at the time, the Serbian hierarchy was granted the right to consecrate its own archbishop, without requiring him to undertake the arduous journey to the patriarchal court.[16]

Having successfully accomplished the purpose of his journey, Archbishop Sava returned to Serbia via Mount Athos and Thessalonica. He made a visit to Khilandar where he selected among his disciples such as he thought worthy of leadership in the newly created autocephalous see. He likewise made a pause in his journey at Thessalonica in order to prepare the necessary books for his church. Domentiyan informs us that Sava, as guest of the metropolitan of Thessalonica, "completed all that was needed for his great church,[17] and having informed his brother, King Stephen, of his coming, proceeded on his journey". Whether or not this comprised needed books, and whether the nomocanon was included or what the books were, is not known.

Upon arriving in Serbia where in the meantime a considerable reaction against the Latin ecclesiastical domination had taken place, Sava was received at the border by King Stephen and his retinue with great honor. He settled at the unfinished monastery of Zhicha.

A few days later, according to Domentiyan,[18] Sava called Stephen and his court to the monastery and there not only announced to the assembly his own assumption of the duties of his office as archbishop of Serbia, but also, as is said, by virtue of that office conferred upon his brother the royal rank, consecrating and crowning him as the First-Crowned King of Serbia. In view of the fact that any mention of the previous crowning of Stephen by the papal legate had been studiously avoided by Domentiyan, it seems plain that the loyalist and Orthodox monastic author simply ascribed to Sava the function which really had been performed by the papal legate.

16. Domentiyan *op. cit.*, p. 56.
17. *Ibid.*, p. 57.
18. *Ibid.*, p. 59.

There appears to have been no difficulty about securing acknowledgment of Sava on the part of his brother, King Stephen, as the rightful head of the Serbian church. Having secured the royal crown for himself, there was no reason why Stephen should oppose the raising of the rank of the Serbian church to that of an archbishopric. The papal legate retreated and withdrew his clergy from the dioceses so recently occupied by them, for the sources proceed to inform us that the new archbishop immediately set about the work of organizing his archdiocese. First of all, he divided the country into ten eparchies[19] of which eight were new foundations, for the eparchies of Rascia and of Prizren were already in existence. Thereupon he ordained for them bishops, archpriests, priests, and deacons, having selected candidates for these offices from among his monastic pupils brought from Khilandar.

Naturally enough, the former superior of the Serbian church, the archbishop of Ohrid, the learned Demetrius Khomatianus, (1220) vigorously protested against this high-handed and uncanonical diminution of his diocese occasioned by the cutting off the Serbian eparchies. He refused to acknowledge the act of the ecumenical patriarch on the ground that the archbishopric of Ohrid was autocephalous, and that the patriarch had no jurisdiction over it; hence, he had no canonical right to dispose of its component parts without Khomatianus' own consent. There is no doubt that canonically Archbishop Demetrius was quite right; the eparchies of Rascia and Prizren belonged to the jurisdiction of Ohrid, and the ecumenical patriarch had no right to disturb or to change the existing status. Sava was wrong in appealing to Patriarch Manuel over Demetrius' head. But he knew that it would have been in vain to make his appeal to the archbishop of Ohrid whose see lay within the despotate of Epirus and who was therefore under political restraint to oppose the expansionist policy of Serbia. Sava therefore, as well as his brother, King Stephen, calmly disregarded the protests and the threats of excommunication hurled against them by Archbishop Demetrius. Similar protests addressed to the ecu-

19. There is some doubt as to their number, given variously as ranging from eight to twelve. The uncertainty is occasioned by the fact that the sources do not clearly specify whether or not the existing eparchies were included in the count.

menical patriarch Germanos II likewise proved of no avail.

Before the newly consecrated Serbian hierarchy and clergy dispersed to their respective fields of labor, Sava instructed them in their duties: he read them the Symbol of Faith, exhorted them to show zeal in protecting the true doctrine as well as uprooting the plentiful remains of the old pagan and heretical beliefs and practices.

His own activity comprised, among much other labor, the establishment of monastic schools at Zhicha and Studenitsa, which in time became important cultural centers. He is said to have been tireless in traveling all over the country, supervising and inspiring the clergy and the bishops by his own zeal and example, and expelling from the country those who proved obdurate in their opposition.[20] Whether other outstanding personalities were associated with him in these apostolic labors, the extant sources do not inform us.

The church organized by Sava was thoroughly national, a character which it has retained ever since. In this feature, the Byzantine parentage of the Serbian church clearly manifests itself. The Byzantine church had always been Erastian in character — subservient to the state. Erastianism, both at its best and its worst shows itself in the character of the Orthodox national churches. Many of them proved themselves leaders of vigorous national culture; during the period of the Turkish supremacy, the churches of Serbia, Bulgaria, and Greece became the chief conservers of the spirit of nationality. In course of time, the terms Orthodox and Serbian, or Bulgarian, or Greek, became almost synonymous. On the other hand, Erastianism had often been, ever since the reign of Emperor Justinian, synonymous with an abject subserviency to the dictates of the caesaropapal state to the extent of surrendering the things that were God's to Caesar. In respect to Serbia, it may be said with a great measure of accuracy that the Serbian kingdom was politically created by Stephen Nemanya, while its spiritual and cultural life owes its character to the formative labors of St. Sava. That is at least the rôle ascribed to these men by Serbians.

After the death of Stephen the First-Crowned (1228), Sava crowned the latter's son, Radoslav, as king. Radoslav

---

20. Domentiyan, *op. cit.*, p. 61.

married a daughter of Theodore of Epirus; this ruler, who since 1223 bore the title of emperor, was then the dominant spirit of Balkan politics. Thanks to his wife's influence, Radoslav became so strongly Hellenistic in policy that he is said even to have submitted the Serbian church once more to the jurisdiction of Ohrid, which was the archepiscopal see of Theodore's dominions. In protest, Archbishop Sava thereupon left the country and went on his first pilgrimage to the Holy Land.[21] But when in 1230 Emperor Theodore in his overweening pride thought the time opportune to attack Bulgaria, he suffered a crushing defeat at the hands of the Bulgarian Tsar Asen II in the battle of Klokotnitse; thereupon, his hegemony was definitely lost. The weak Radoslav was unable to retain his throne and was deprived of it by his younger brother, Vladislav (1233-1243). Archbishop Sava, who had in the meantime returned from Palestine, resigned his office, transferred it to his disciple Arsenius (1233-63), then hegumen of the monastery of Studenitsa, and departed on his second pilgrimage to the Holy Land. In order to avoid crossing the country, he chose the Adriatic route.

On this pilgrimage Sava visited Jerusalem and the holy places, Alexandria, Libya and the Thebaid, Sinai, and Antioch, from which he returned once more to Jerusalem. On his return homeward, he possibly made a stop at Nicaea. The probability rests on the fact that in the next year (1235) the ecumenical patriarch granted his approval of the reestablishment of the patriarchate of Bulgaria—a measure with which St Sava may have had something to do. Sava then proceeded to Bulgaria via Constantinople. He fell sick at the capital of Bulgaria, Trnovo, where he died at the court of his relative, Tsar John Asen II, on January 25, (n. s.) 1236. His body was brought to Serbia two years later and was interred at the Mileshevo monastery. In 1595, the Turks took his remains to Vrachar and burned them there.

The reason for Sava's success in an undertaking in which his Greek and Latin precursors had so largely failed lay in the fact that he realized the danger of trying to uproot the old national customs too radically. He decided to

21. Domentiyan, op. cit., p. 64.

compromise; he "Christianized" as many of the immemorial folkways and mores of his people as he could, and adapted the rest to the genius of the Christian cult. He was neither the first nor the last among the great missionaries of the church to resort to this method of furthering the Christian cause. Christianity, like a mighty river, has been swelled by tributary streams and brooks deriving from many and widely scattered regions. The appearance of a new Orthodox state in the Balkans at a time when Orthodoxy of the Byzantine Empire suffered a serious defeat at the hands of the Latins was a fact of great importance. The Balkan Slavs then joined hands with the Greeks in the defense of their common Byzantine culture. Thus the work of St. Sava assumes an importance beyond the limits of Serbian national history.

THE BULGARIAN CHURCH OF THE SECOND EMPIRE

The fall of Tsar Samuel's empire resulted in the reconquest, on the part of the Byzantines, of the entire Balkan peninsula, for the Serbian zhupans were forced to submit to the conqueror along with the Bulgarians.

Emperor Basil II, who had promised to respect the Bulgarian ecclesiastical organization, kept his word. He appointed a Bulgarian, John, hegumen of Dibra, in place of the unworthy Patriarch David, the last of the autocephalous patriarchs of the first Bulgarian Empire. Whether Basil deposed the patriarch for his own private reasons or on account of popular demand, is not known. The new head of the Bulgarian church did not succeed to the patriarchal title, however, having been demoted to the lesser title of archbishop. Nevertheless, by three imperial chrysobulls,[1] Archbishop John was granted all the privileges and rights possessed formerly by the patriarchs. He was fully independent of the ecumenical patriarchate, and possessed the unrestricted autonomy enjoyed by the Bulgarian church prior to the conquest. He was nominated by the Bulgarian Holy Synod, the choice being merely approved by the emperor. Ohrid was retained as the archepiscopal see. Ultimately, although not immediately, the archbishop of Ohrid ruled over thirty-one eparchies, which extended over the entire territory of Peter's and Samuel's empire. Some episcopal dioceses belonging to the metropolitans of Durazzo, Thessalonica and other jurisdictions were transferred to the jurisdiction of Ohrid. But later the metropolitanate of Silistria (the ancient Durostorum) as well as many other dioceses were severed from Ohrid and placed directly under the jurisdiction of Constantinople, or were otherwise disposed of. By this measure the Ohrid archbishopric was reduced to one-half its former size. The emperor explicitly acknowledged the Ohrid archbishopric to be a direct con-

---

1. Thalloczy, *Acta Albaniae*, I, nos. 58 and 59.

tinuation of the historic Bulgarian patriarchate, i. e., autocephalous, an acknowledgment which was later denied by
the ruling Greek hierarchy which affirmed it to be a continuation of the metropolitanate of Justiniana Prima, and thus
a Greek imperial foundation.

Basil's recognition of the Bulgarian national character of the Ohrid archbishopric availed it but little. Successors of Archbishop John, who died in 1037, were all
Greeks, as were the occupants of the majority of the episcopal sees. The Greek language became the official and
liturgical language of the archdiocese. With the helleni-
zation of Ohrid came a partial loss of its autocephalous
character: beginning with the successor of John, Archbishop
Leo, the occupants of the see were appointed directly by
Constantinople without the previous nomination of the candidate by the Ohrid Holy Synod. Usually a member of the
Constantinopolitan clergy was chosen to fill the post. Such
was the case with archbishops Leo, the famous theological
writer Theophylact, and Michael. The bishops were also
quite generally chosen from among the Greeks, and by
preference from the Constantinopolitan clergy. Thus the
privileges granted the Ohrid archbishopric by Basil were
soon disregarded, for it must be remembered that the throne
of St. Chrysostom in Constantinople was then occupied by
the domineering and insatiably ambitious Patriarch Michael
Cerularius (1043-59) who was guided by a policy of centralizing all power in his own hands. In consequence, the Bulgarian church lost its national character, to the great detriment of its cultural and even religious influence.

The general situation of the Bulgarian population grew
steadily worse. Although the rule of the native nobles had
been oppressive, the government of the Greek officials
proved far worse. They treated the subject population as
their legitimate prey, and the tax collectors behaved no better than robbers. In course of time, most of the population
fell to the level of serfs bound to the soil (πάροικοι), and
the system of latifundia increased enormously. As far as
the holding of land or treatment of serfs were concerned,
there was no difference between the lay and the ecclesiastical masters. The only group which to a certain extent escaped the doom of serfdom was that of the nomadic shepherds known as Wallachians. But since in accordance with

the Byzantine as well as Western European legal notions all land not actually in possession of a private owner belonged to the ruler, even the shepherds finally came to be held in a form of serfdom. Thereupon, many of them emigrated northward beyond the Danube where they strengthened the Roumanian element of Wallachia.

When during the reign of Emperor Michael IV the Paphlagonian (1034-41) the Byzantine officials decided to levy the various taxes in money instead of in produce, for money was needed for the absurd benefactions of the emperor, the wars of the chief minister John the Orphanotrophos, and the insatiable greed of the whole tribe of Michael's family, although the insufferable burden of taxation was laid upon the masses of the whole Empire, the Bulgarians as subjected people felt it the most, and their pent-up dissatisfaction broke out into an open revolt. The Serbians joined them in their effort to throw off the Byzantine yoke. Unfortunately for the Bulgarians, the imperial armies defeated the revolters (1041). Thereupon, the oppression became worse than before. Greek officials displaced all Bulgarian administrators still left in possession of their office, and thus the political autonomy of Bulgaria definitely came to an end. The general misery was increased by the invasion of the land by a vast horde of Patzinaks, who are said to have numbered 80,000 men, and who devastated the northeastern territories most terribly (1048). In 1064 the unfortunate country suffered another invasion by the barbarian Ghuzz or Uzes who, numbering 600,000, penetrated as far as the neighborhood of Thessalonica and even threatened Constantinople itself. The weakness of the Empire was such that it could not efficiently protect the inhabitants from these barbarian raids. Finally, when Emperor Constantine X Ducas (1059-67), wishing to break the dangerous power of the nobility and of the army leaders, drastically reduced the army, the measure had for its consequence in the next reign the defeat of the Byzantine armies by the Seljuq Turks at Manzikert in 1071. Thereupon, the Turks overran all Asia Minor.

This disaster and the consequent weakening of the Empire had for its sequel a new uprising on the part of the Bulgarians. In 1073 the leaders offered the tsarist crown to Bodin, a son of the Serbian King Michael, in consideration of Serbian military aid. The offer was accepted and Bodin was actually crowned tsar at Prizren. But the conspirators were defeated, and Bodin was taken prisoner. Thus the second attempt at regaining national independence failed.

In spite of the disheartening failure, the Bulgarian discontent continued. To the political and economic grievances was added religious dissatisfaction. The bigoted persecuting policy of the Byzantine rulers, Michael VII Ducas (1071-78) and Nicephorus III Botaniates (1078-81), the brunt of which was borne by the Manichees-Paulicians and the Bogomils of Bulgaria, finally drove these dissenters into an open rebellion. A Greek Paulician of Philippopolis, Lecus by name, incited the populace of the neighborhoods of Sredets (modern Sofia) and Nish to revolt; he was joined by malcontents led by a Bogomil of Mesembria, Dobromir. The two leaders secured the aid of the wild Patzinaks and Cumans, and their bands caused frightful havoc wherever they went. The bishops of Sredets and of Vidin lost their lives in this uprising. But the brilliant Byzantine general, Alexius Comnenus, the future emperor, defeated the motley hordes of the insurgents. The two leaders were taken prisoners, but for some reason were released in 1080.

At this time and later, the Ohrid archbishopric lost some of its privileges, such as the exemption from taxation and other rights granted it by Emperor Basil II. These privileges were not restored until the time of Emperor Manuel I Comnenus (1143-80).

The Bogomils, free from the incubus of the hellenizing hierarchy of the Orthodox church, developed into a strong nationalistic anti-Greek and anti-imperial party. Their rejection of the dogmas and claims of the Orthodox church now assumed the character of a Bulgarian nationalistic revolt against the Greek tyranny in state and church. Their success in gaining numerous adherents during this period may be partly understood on the basis of their strong nationalistic spirit, and partly because they formed the best-organized anti-Byzantine element in the country. During the Norman invasion of the Balkan peninsula (1081-85) under Robert Guiscard and his son Bohemond, the former of whom aimed at no less than the imperial diadem of

Byzantium, a detachment of the imperial army composed of Manichees-Paulicians and Bogomils, fighting the invaders, withdrew from the fight. This so greatly infuriated Emperor Alexius Comnenus (1081-1118) that he ordered a severe punishment of the officers of the regiment. The order led to a mutiny under the leadership of a high officer, Traulos by name. He had been chosen by Alexius as one of his intimate servants, and although born a Manichee, had received baptism, and had married one of Empress Irene's maid-servants. According to Emperor Alexius' learned daughter, Anna Comnena, the author of the *Alexiad*,[2] he had an additional reason for the mutiny inasmuch as his four sisters had been driven out of Philippopolis by reason of their Manichaean faith. At any rate, Traulos, in spite of his baptism which seemed to have produced no miraculous change in him, felt enough sympathy with his former Manichee-Paulician coreligionists to organize them into an army and to occupy with this force the fortified castle of Byelatov. From this base he then conducted raids into the neighborhood (1086). The Bulgarian nobles, always ready to take up arms against the hated Byzantine régime, rose up in revolt in the vicinity of Silistria (on the Danube), allied themselves with the ever ready and willing Patzinaks and Cumans, and with a force amounting to 80,000 invaded Thrace. For two years the emperor was not able to expel the formidable invaders who even threatened Constantinople, and his two generals who had been sent against them, Pacurianus and Branas, were not only defeated but lost their lives as well. It was not until 1091 that Alexius, for a high payment, was able to secure the services of another horde of Cumans, and with their help defeated the Patzinaks and their Bulgarian allies in the battle on the river Leburnium.

When in 1114 the Cumans again invaded the imperial territory, Alexius made his headquarters at Philippopolis, and beguiled the tedium between campaigns by the favorite pastime of the Byzantine Empire—theological disputation. According to Anna Comnena, "all the inhabitants of Philippopolis were Manichaeans except a few; they tyrannized over the Christians there and plundered their goods,

---

2. Anna Comnena, *The Alexiad*, transl. by Elisabeth A. C. Dawes, London, 1928, p. 143.

caring little or naught for the envoys sent by the Emperor.
They increased in numbers until all the inhabitants around
Philippopolis were heretics. Then another brackish stream
of Armenians joined them and yet another from the most
polluted sources of James. And thus, metaphorically speaking, it was a meeting place of all evils; for the rest disagreed
indeed with the Manichaeans in doctrine, but agreed with
them in disaffection".[3] Alexius seized the opportunity of
dealing summarily with the dissenting and politically dangerous population. Attended by his son-in-law, Nicephorus
Bryennius, the husband of Anna Comnena, as well as by
the famous theologian, Eustratius, metropolitan of Nicaea,
he held passionate disputations with the Manichaean-
Paulician population of Philippopolis. Their three outstanding leaders were in attendance at these disputations daily,
but to Alexius' chagrin held their ground against the imperial "defender of the faith" all too well. But they found that
disputing with an imperial adversary had its peculiar draw-
backs: Alexius could not win in argument, but he could shut
them up in prison. The unfortunate victors in debate were
finally sent to Constantinople, and two of them were imprisoned and "allowed to die in company with their sins
alone," as Anna euphemistically puts it.[4] The third leader
must have found the persuasion of the imperial prison more
potent and convincing than Alexius' arguments had been.
Anna claimed that Alexius won over to Christianity the
majority of the population of the Manichaean citadel, although to be sure not by purely spiritual means: he granted the more important personages who consented to receive baptism "great gifts" and lucrative military posts. As
for the smaller fry, he built a new city for them, Alexiopolis,
or as it was more commonly known, Neocastrum, near Philippopolis, transferred the "converted" population there,
granted them much land, and secured them in their possessions by a special imperial edict to all subsequent times.
Those who stubbornly resisted even these alluring arguments in favor of Orthodoxy and remained steadfast in
their faith, Alexius imprisoned, confiscated their property
and gave it to Greeks, or drove them out of Philippopolis.
    It seems likely that it was during this period of perse-

---

3. Anna Comnena, *The Alexiad*, book XIV, p. 385-86.
4. *Ibid.*, p. 389.

cution that the Manichee-Paulician group, driven out of
Philippopolis, amalgamated to a certain extent with the native Bogomils to form a separate group known as the
Dragovitian Church. At any rate, this organization came
to assume the most definitely and radically dualistic form
of doctrine of all the various branches of the Bogomil movement. It was far more radical than the Bulgarian Church,
as the group which had remained true to the teachings of
Bogomil came to be called. This characteristic of the
Dragovitian group suggests some unusually strong Manichee-Paulician influence.

In spite of the temporary persecution of the dualistic
group at Philippopolis, Bogomilism was gradually gaining
ground and found many adherents among the Bulgarians
on account of its nationalistic opposition to the hellenizing
policy of the Greeks. Bogomilism found favor not only with
the common people, but even among the nobles. Its propaganda was successfully carried on in spite or Alexius'
persecuting policy. Among the most outstanding apostles
of Bogomilism of this period, the first place must be accorded to the physician Basil. He was a Bulgar born in Macedonia. Having become a monk in some monastery of the
Ohrid diocese, he learned Greek there and became proficient
in the rudiments of the healing art, so that he was later
spoken of as a physician. Later he left the monastery for
some unknown reason and returned to lay life, but soon
passed over to the Bogomil community as one of the "perfect." In course of time he became the most prominent
leader of the movement, being an energetic organizer and
a fiery missionary of the gospel of renunciation of the world.
Personally, he became noted for his strict asceticism and
his austere moral life. Anna Comnena describes him as
dressed "in monk's habit, with a withered countenance,
clean-shaven, and tall of stature".[5] He gathered about him
twelve disciples whom he called his apostles.

After having scored a remarkable success among the
people of Macedonia, Basil decided to invade the capital
itself, for Bogomilism had been introduced into Constantinople long before the reign of Alexius. He organized and
directed wide missionary labors there. His teachings found
ready reception, especially among the adherents of the

5. Anna Comnena, *op. cit.*, p. 412.

Platonic, anti-ecclesiastical teachings of John Italus, whose doctrines had been condemned in 1082; moreover, not only lay common people and nobles became Basil's followers, but even the clergy.

But Basil's energetic apostolic labors were rudely interrupted when in 1118 Emperor Alexius learned of the spread of the heretical movement in his capital and ordered his officials to ferret out and arrest the leaders of the Bogomils. Basil and his twelve apostles were seized, having been betrayed by a member of the Bogomil community who under torture had revealed their hiding place. Basil was taken before the emperor, who together with his brother, Isaac Comnenus, examined him as to his teaching. Anna unblushingly and even exultingly relates that Alexius secured Basil's confession by a direct lie: he feigned an interest in Basil's doctrines as if wishing to accept them, and by denouncing the Orthodox clergy as unfaithful. When Basil fell into the trap and freely expounded his doctrines to the emperor, Alexius suddenly threw aside the curtain separating the room from the adjoining one, and revealed the presence of a scribe who had taken down the confession in full.[6] Thereupon, Alexius called together a council consisting of many high civil and ecclesiastical officials, under the presidency of Patriarch John IX (1111-1134),[7] which sentenced Basil to die at the stake.

Immediately after the seizure of Basil, Alexius ordered a formal round-up of all adherents of Bogomilism. The prisons were thereupon filled to overflowing with them. Many recanted in fear of torture and burning; but the majority remained steadfast. To distinguish the genuine Orthodox from those who pretended to be Orthodox in order to save their lives, Alexius resorted to another ruse: he ordered all to be burned, but those who professed to be Orthodox were given the choice of a pyre upon which a large cross had been affixed. Those then who chose this particular pyre, were released as having proved their Orthodoxy. The rest were burned or otherwise punished. Basil, although every at-

---

6. Anna Comnena, *op. cit.*, book XV, p. 413, 414.

7. Anna Comnena (*op. cit.*, *book* XV, p. 413) definitely states that the episcopal throne of Constantinople was at the time occupied "by that most blessed of patriarchs, Lord Nicholas, the Grammarian", i. e., Nicholas III, who held the post from 1084 to 1111. But this must be one of her rather frequent slips of memory, for the date does not fit the period of persecution. Moreover, she herself relates the event as having taken place immediately before the death of Alexius.

tempt had been made to induce him to recant, fearlessly went to his death and died like a true martyr.

Simultaneously with the persecution of the Bogomils in Constantinople, similar measures were adopted throughout the Empire. But the persecution served only to further the dissemination of the teaching, as may be learned from the *Life of St Hilarion of Moglen*[8] written by the Bulgarian Patriarch Euthemius (1375-93). Hilarion was consecrated bishop of his diocese during the term of office of Eustatius, archbishop of Ohrid, in the fourth decade of the twelfth century. The *Life*, which unfortunately is a late production, and being closely modelled upon the current hagiographical models, does not inspire full confidence as to the accuracy of its narrative, informs us that Hilarion found his diocese to have been settled predominantly by Manichees, Armenians (Paulicians) and Bogomils.[9] He instantly undertook to combat these formidable opponents of Orthodoxy, and is represented as a valiant and doughty disputant with the leaders of the groups. In fact, the greater part of the *Life* is taken up with the recital of his arguments. Although at first he is said to have been threatened by his foes with bodily injury, the good bishop in the end is represented, as could be expected from so edifying a work, as having won a brilliant victory over them. Indeed it is affirmed that when even Emperor Manuel I Comnenus (1143-80) began flirting with the heresy, Hilarion's "dogmatic words" recalled him to Orthodoxy.[10] The emperor is then said to have written the bishop, encouraging him in his work of uprooting the Bogomilian heresy. Needless to say that the whole episode regarding Manuel's supposed vaccilation in relation to Orthodoxy bears every mark of legendary fabrication.

There is some evidence that Bogomilism continued as an important factor in other parts of the Empire as well. In 1143, a Synod of Constantinople, presided over by Patriarch Michael II (1143-46), condemned as Bogomils two "pseudobishops", Clement of Sassi and Leontius of Babbis.[11] The next year, a similar synod condemned monk Niphon

8. Kalužniacki, E., *Werke des Patriarchen von Bulgarien, Euthymius*. Wien, 1901, p. 27-58.
9. *Ibid.*, p. 33.
10. *Ibid.*, p. 52.
11. Thalloczy, *Acta res Albaniae*, I., no. 85.

on account of the same heresy,[12] and in 1147 even a patriarch of Constantinople, Cosmas, was deposed because of his adherence to Niphon's teaching.

The tragic confusion into which the Empire was plunged after the death of Emperor Manuel I Comnenus (1180) was quickly taken advantage of by the Bulgarians. During the minority of Manuel's son, Alexius II, the regency was in the hands of the boy's mother, the beautiful Mary of Antioch. As usual, many ambitious men tried to win her favor, and in turn when she did choose one of them, they plotted a revolt against his rule. Out of the turmoil, Andronicus I Comnenus (1183-85) emerged as victor and made himself emperor. But his cruel rule soon disgusted the populace. In 1185 there occurred a revolt, which ended in an atrocious murder of Andronicus and the elevation to the throne of Isaac II Angelus (1185-95). Bulgarians seized this opportunity to secure freedom from the galling Byzantine yoke, and organized a revolt in 1186. This time the immediate occasion of the revolt was furnished by the tax unwisely levied for the purpose of securing money for the marriage festivities of Emperor Isaac. The uprising centered in the north-eastern Bulgaria, and was headed by two brothers, Theodore and John Asen, descendents of the old Bulgarian tsars, whose possessions lay in the vicinity of the village of Trnovo, "the place of thorns". They summoned representatives to a meeting in the chapel of St. Demetrius which they had built on their estates, and by a pious fraud of affirming that the saint to whom the chapel had been dedicated had forsaken his post as the guardian of Thessalonica and had come to serve in a similar capacity in his new home, inspired confidence in the success of the revolt they were plotting. The superstitious nobles were persuaded to believe that under St. Demetrius' protection, Bulgaria would regain her lost independence. Always ready to take up arms against the Greeks, the nobles joined the intrepid leaders, and soon the revolt extended even south of the Balkan range. Both Slavs and Wallachians were to be found in the ranks of the revolters. Emperor Isaac II sent an army against the insurgents, but its leader, General Alexius Branas, betrayed his master and had himself proclaimed emperor at Hadrianople. Although Branas was

---

12. *Ibid.*, no. 86.

killed in an effort to take Constantinople, the Bulgarians
in the meantime were able to occupy the territory between
the Danube and the Balkan mountains. To signify the restoration of the former Bulgarian Empire after 167 years
of Greek supremacy, the brothers Theodore and Asen had
themselves crowned tsars, at which time the former, "the
renegade and evil slave" as Michael Acominatus, the archbishop of Athens, calls him, assumed the name of Peter.

Although the Greek domination was externally overthrown, internally the Greek spirit retaining unquestioned
supremacy. Legal concepts, the Byzantine administrative
procedure, finances, military organization, all remained as
before. The tsar's court and its etiquette was also modelled
in strict accord with the imperial example. The church
likewise showed no marked change in its internal life; it
never regained its former position as a leader of the Bulgarian national life until in the time of the Turkish domination, and before the rule of the Phanariots, the venal
bishops appointed by the ecumenical patriarchate, became
dominant. The rôle of leadership passed over to the monks
of Mount Athos.

Since the archepiscopal see of Ohrid, though historically a Bulgarian see, had been entirely dominated by
Greek hierarchy from the middle of the eleventh century,
and hence was generally and rightly regarded as an instrument of the Byzantine government, the new rulers decided
to restore the former autocephalous Bulgarian national
church. Moreover, they felt the need of an ecclesiastical
sanction of their revolt and of their assumption of the imperial dignity, which the Ohrid archbishop or the ecumenical
patriarch could not be reasonably expected to grant. Therefore, the rulers constrained the Greek bishop of Vidin to
ordain, with the assistance of two other Greek bishops, a
Bulgarian priest, Basil by name, as archbishop of Bulgaria
(1185). Basil assumed jurisdiction over the entire reconquered territory, the eparchies of which had hitherto been
governed by Constantinople (through the metropolitan of
Silistria) or by Ohrid. The bishops of these eparchies were
compelled to renounce obedience to their former superiors,
and to acknowledge Basil as their spiritual chief. Since
they were Greeks, it was only by constraint that they were
forced to do so. The archbishop of Ohrid, the learned

Demetrius Khomatianus, relates that the unlucky bishop of
Vidin who had been instrumental in ordaining Basil to his
high post, for some reason later refused to acknowledge
him as his superior and in consequence suffered the penalty
of decapitation. His courageous loyalty to his canonical
superior—if such really were the case—points to a belated
repentance on his part for his share in the uncanonical consecration of Basil. Gradually, all Greek bishops were replaced by Bulgarian. As could be expected, Constantinople
refused to acknowledge either Peter and Asen as tsars or
Basil as archbishop.

This situation lasted till the reign of the youngest of
the Asen brothers, Kaloyan (1196-1207), who succeeded his
elder brothers after they both had been murdered. He was
a fierce and unscrupulous warrior, but along with it a surprisingly adroit diplomat. Emperor Alexius III Angelus
(1195-1203), having his hands full with various revolters
within the Empire, was willing temporarily to come to
terms with Kaloyan, thus giving the latter an opportunity
to strengthen his power over the Second or as it was commonly called the Trnovo Bulgarian Empire. Kaloyan
utilized his opportunity by securing for himself recognition
from the only quarter where his efforts were likely to prove
successful—from the Roman curia. At any rate, he rightly
surmised that he could not obtain like favors from Constantinople.

His desire for legal recognition drove Kaloyan to negotiate with Pope Innocent III (1198-1216). At first his embassy, sent to Rome in 1199 to request the tsarist crown for
their master, was unable to secure passage through the
countries controlled by Hungary or the Byzantine Empire.
But finally, when the Serbian Grand-Zhupan Stephen, the
son of Stephen Nemanya, was driven by a similar desire for
recognition to negotiate with Pope Innocent, Kaloyan's
representatives were permitted to reach Rome by way of
the Serbian lands.

Pope Innocent eagerly grasped the opportunity to recover Serbia and Bulgaria for his jurisdiction. Probably
late in 1199 he sent to Kaloyan a Greek archpriest from
Brindisi, Dominic by name, to open negotiations with the
Bulgarian ruler regarding the submission of the Bulgarian
church to himself. It is an eloquent evidence of the sorry

state of the Slavic culture of the Bulgarians that the pope labored under the impression that he was dealing with Wallachians, a conclusion which he apparently had derived from the title used by Kaloyan—*Imperator Bulgarorum et Blachorum*. Innocent, apparently ignorant of the racial origins of the Bulgarians, and treating the Wallachians as descendants of Dacian Romans, strove to appeal to Kaloyan's supposed Roman origins and antecedents. The shrewd Bulgarian did not trouble to explain to the pope his mistake, but exploited it to his advantage as much as he could, actually referring to Italy as *patria nostra, a qua descendimus*.[13]

The negotiations were long-drawn-out. At first Kaloyan distrusted Dominic on account of his Greek nationality, and imprisoned him as a possible impostor. It was not until two years later that the Bulgarian ruler assured himself of the genuineness of Dominic's credentials, freed him, and accepted as authentic the letter he had brought from Innocent. In it the pope promised, if Kaloyan were to profess his adherence to the Latin faith before Dominic, to send him papal legates who would carry on further negotiations. In this preliminary skirmish the pope carefully addressed Kaloyan merely as a *nobilis vir*, avoiding any formal title whatsoever.

Returning to Rome (1202), Dominic brought letters from Kaloyan and Basil. Both suppliants professed their submission to the pope, the former requesting in return "the rank which our ancient emperors possessed", the latter, who styled himself in his letter as *archiepiscopus Sanctitatis vestrae et pastor de Zagora*",[14] recognition of his rank.

But Innocent did not seem to be in any hurry to answer. Growing impatient at the pope's delay, Kaloyan sent to Rome, in July, 1203, an embassy with Archbishop Basil himself at the head. In the letter carried by this delegation, Kaloyan stated quite truthfully that the Byzantine emperor and the Constantinopolitan patriarch had offered him (in the Spring of the same year) a full and absolute recognition of the political and ecclesiastical independence of Bulgaria. Nevertheless—Kaloyan continued—he determined to carry

---

13. See letter of Kaloyan to Innocent in Theiner, A., *Vetera monumenta Slavorum meridionalium*, Romae, 1863, 1863, I, No. 26, p. 15.

14. Theiner, A., *op. cit.*, I, No. 27 and 28, pp. 16-17.

on his negotiations with the pope, preferring to receive the desired rank for himself and his archbishop from the apostolic see.

The surprisingly radical change in the attitude of the Byzantine state and church may be easily understood when one recalls that at the time the boats of the Venetians transporting the valiant Western barons forming the body of the Fourth Crusade were swarming in the Sea of Marmora. They had come to help the blinded and deposed Emperor Isaac II to regain his throne, which had been usurped by Alexius III. The latter therefore found himself in dire straits. It is no wonder that he was willing to seek aid even at the Bulgarian court.

The intervention of the Crusaders in the inner politics of the Byzantine Empire resulted in its conquest by its erstwhile would-be allies. In April, 1204, the Latins took Constantinople after a stiff fight with the Greek forces, and set up the Latin Empire of Romania. The fall of Constantinople was a signal to Kaloyan for a general attack upon the imperial territories. Finding no great opposition, he quickly and easily conquered Macedonia to the boundaries of Albania, including Ohrid. Thus the Ohrid archepiscopal see was once more included in the Bulgarian empire.

In the meantime, Kaloyan's embassy was on its way to Rome. Basil himself did not reach that destination, for he had been detained at Dyrrhachium and threatened with violence—to be thrown into the sea—by the local Greeks if he should insist on continuing his journey. On the advice of the archdeacon and other local Latin clergy,[15] he returned home, while his companions pressed on to Rome.

But a month after the embassy had left Kaloyan's court, the papal legate, John de Casamaris, arrived at Trnovo. He had started out from Rome in December, 1202, but having had commissions in Bosnia and Hungary, had been greatly delayed on the way. He did not bring the imperial crown, however, although he did bring a pallium for Archbishop Basil; but he had no instructions regarding ordaining him to the office. The pope demanded from Kaloyan a sworn promise ever to remain faithful, along with the entire nation, to the Holy See. Moreover, Pope Innocent notified him that according to the papal registers, Bulgarian rulers

---

15. Thalloczy et. al. *Acta res Albaniae*, I, No. 128, dated after Sept. 8, 1203.

were wont to receive a royal, not an imperial, crown from the popes; the legate was instructed to verify the matter in the Bulgarian registers. As for Basil, the papal emissary delivered to him, on September 8, 1203, the pallium and therewith granted him, in the name of his master, the title of primate of Bulgaria—although not that of patriarch. Basil was likewise required to give solemn promises "to be faithful and obedient to the blessed Peter, and the holy and apostolic Roman see and my lord, Pope Innocent as well as his catholic successors".[16] Both Kaloyan and Basil signed the sworn statements demanded of them, by which the Bulgarian dominions and church were subjected to the Roman See.[17]

Having successfully accomplished his mission, John de Casamaris started on his return journey toward the end of 1203. Kaloyan sent to Innocent another letter in which he thanked the pope for the pallium granted to Basil, but requested that the latter be made patriarch, and that the Bulgarian church be made fully autocephalous by having the right to choose and ordain its own patriarchs and to prepare its own chrysm. Moreover, Kaloyan requested an imperial, not a royal, crown for himself. He concluded his appeal by repeating his solemn promise of perpetual obedience to the Holy See made not only on his own behalf, but also on behalf of his successors and of the entire Bulgarian nation.

Finally, in March, 1204, another papal legate, Cardinal-priest Leo, was sent to Bulgaria to crown Kaloyan. He did not reach Trnovo till October, for he had been detained by the Hungarian King Henry. This enemy of Kaloyan was at war with Bulgaria on account of some territory Henry had occupied. Having learned of the object of Leo's journey, he attempted to dissuade the pope from granting Kaloyan the crown on the ground that the latter was a usurper. The pope felt it necessary to adopt strict measures against Henry, threatening him with excommunication unless he release Leo instantly. Thereupon, the Hungarian king yielded. After the legate reached Kaloyan's court, he consecrated Basil as "Primate of all Bulgaria and Wallachia" (Nov. 7) and raised the bishops of Preslav and Velbuzhd

16. Theiner, A., op. cit., No. 51, p. 32.
17. Ibid., No. 43, p. 27.

to the rank of archbishops.[18]   Four bishops completed the
hierarchical organization.   The next day, the cardinal
solemnly annointed Kaloyan as king, placed the royal crown
sent by Innocent upon his head and a sceptre in his hand.
Moreover, he delivered to Kaloyan a banner from the pope
"with which to lead the hosts into battle" and granted him
the right to coin money with his own effigy.

In the papal letter delivered to Kaloyan by Leo, Innocent replied to the king's request that the title of primate
granted to Basil was almost the same as that of patriarch.
He granted the primate the right to crown the king, and
to prepare the chrysm.   The primate was to be elected and
consecrated by the Bulgarian bishops themselves, but before assuming office, had to secure the papal pallium. Hence,
to all intents and purposes, the Bulgarian primate was
autonomous; consequently, Kaloyan established the practice of calling him patriarch.   As for Kaloyan himself, although he had not received all he had asked for, he promptly
began to call himself emperor or tsar.   Taking advantage
of the ambiguity attaching to the translation of the Latin
word *rex,* which had formerly been equivalent to the original meaning of βασιλεύς, he continued to use the title
tsar.

The ecclesiastical union with Rome was a purely political act.   It had no perceptible consequences upon the inner
life of the Bulgarian church.   Although we have but little
information concerning the matter, yet it is certain that no
important change occurred either in the doctrinal or the
administrative relations.

After having gained the substance of his demands from
the pope, Kaloyan proceeded to take up arms against the
Latin conquerors of the Byzantine Empire.   The Greeks of
Thrace who had at first been satisfied to recognize Renier
de Trit in his new capacity as the Duke of Philippopolis,
changed their minds as time went on and besought Kaloyan
to help them overthrow the new master.   When he accepted
the invitation and invaded Thrace, they greeted him as their
deliverer, and enthusiastically supported his cause.   At the
battle of Hadrianople (April 15, 1205), Kaloyan utterly defeated Emperor Baldwin who along with Count Louis of
Blois had set out to succor his vassal, the Duke of Phil-

---

18.   Theiner, A., *op. cit.*, I, Nos. 40 and 41, pp. 23-25.

ippopolis, and took the Latin emperor prisoner.   Louis of
Blois was killed.   Pope Innocent, as suzerain of both Baldwin and Kaloyan, demanded of the latter that he set the
emperor free.[19]   Kaloyan not only refused to comply with
the pope's request but treated his emissaries with scant
courtesy.   In fact, Nicetas reports that the desertion of the
fickle Greeks of Thrace to the Latins infuriated Kaloyan
to such an extent that he ordered unlucky Baldwin's hands
and feet cut off and his trunk hurled into a ravine (1206).
Baldwin's successor, Henry, incensed at the ignominious
end of his predecessor, undertook an energetic campaign
against the Bulgarian tsar.   But Kaloyan, allied with the
emperor of Nicaea, Theodore I Lascaris, invested Salonica.
In vain did the pope threaten him with an alliance of the
Latins with the Hungarians in order to dissuade him from
his attack upon the crusaders.[20]   King Boniface of Salonica
perished in a Bulgarian ambush.   The war was finally
terminated by the secret assassination of Kaloyan ordered
by his Cuman ally (Oct., 1207).   Persistent rumors associated the name of Kaloyan's wife with his assassination, and
her speedy marriage to the usurper of the throne, Boril, lent
color to the charge.

As has already been mentioned, Kaloyan's conquest of
Macedonia comprised even the town of Ohrid.   He was
therefore confronted with the problem of coordinating the
powers of the two autocephalous archepiscopal sees—Ohrid
and Trnovo—with each other.   He finally decided not to
subordinate one to the other, but to retain both archdioceses
in their standings at the time of the conquest.   He could not
subordinate the archbishop of Trnovo to Ohrid because
Trnovo was his capital, its archbishop had been granted the
title of primate by the pope and was in communion with
Rome, while the Ohrid see was not.   But it was not feasible
to subject Ohrid to the jurisdiction of Trnovo, either; for
the former's tradition went back to Tsar Samuel, and the
Macedonian Bulgarians felt closely attached to it for historical reasons.

Nevertheless, Kaloyan resolved to convert the Ohrid
see from a Greek institution into a Bulgarian one.   It seems
that he left the Greek archbishop in an undisturbed exer-

19.   Theiner, A., *op. cit.*, I, No. 64, p. 42.
20.   *Ibid.*, I., No. 68, p. 44.

8

cise of his authority, but substituted in a larger number of cases Bulgarian for Greek bishops. These in turn filled the parochial vacancies with Bulgarian priests. Moreover, Kaloyan naturally granted preferential treatment and support to the Trnovo see, to the detriment of the Ohrid interests.

After Kaloyan's death (1207), the throne was usurped by the son of Kaloyan's sister, Boril, who promptly married his uncle's widow to secure a semblance of legitimacy for himself. The rightful successor, John Asen II, the son of Asen I, was forced along with his brother, Alexander, to seek refuge in Russia. Nevertheless, the usurper was not able to conserve the unity of the territory left by Kaloyan: two of his relatives succeeded in wresting from him parts of it. One of these, Strez, conquered Macedonia, including Ohrid. Thus the archepiscopal see of Ohrid once more became supreme in its own independent territory. But parts of this archdiocese fell under the domination of the Latin Empire, and Catholic bishops were installed there.

Boril's insecure position was further aggravated by the opposition of the Bogomils within his realm; they appear to have refused to acknowledge his claims to the throne on account of his illegal seizure of it. They comprised a considerable portion of the population, and ever since the time of the Greek domination had earned for themselves the reputation of fearless patriots. Although we have no positive information regarding the matter, it seems probable that the first Asenites adopted a policy of toleration and conciliation toward the Bogomils. Boril, however, decided to persecute them. It is also possible that Pope Innocent III urged Boril to undertake the persecution because he himself was at the time waging a relentless crusade against the Cathari and the Albigenses in the West. This supposition rests upon the fact that the pope sent a cardinal to Boril with a message the purport of which is not known. Boril could thus not only gain the good will of the pope by persecuting his own political enemies, but could at the same time enlist for himself the sympathy of the Orthodox clergy.

Boril therefore issued a call for a Council which was to be composed of "all archpriests, priests, monks, nobles, and many from the rest of the nation", and ordered seizure of the Bogomils all over the land. The Council met at

Trnovo in February, 1211, and was conducted under the presidency of the tsar. Its decrees are extant.[21] It condemned many heresies, Bogomilian among them, and decreed strict persecution of their adherents. The punishments ranged from exile to imprisonment.

But contrary to his expectation, these harsh measures made Boril's position still worse. The two princes, John Asen and Alexander, having gained the aid of some Russian prince, invaded the territory of Vidin. The neighborhood of this city was, according to a fourteenth century testimony, settled by Bogomils. With their help, for in consequence of the persecution they gladly joined the invaders, Vidin and the surrounding territory was quickly seized by the two princes. Boril was constrained to seek peace with the Latins in order to secure Hungarian aid; then, with the help of the latter, he was able to reconquer Vidin. Nevertheless, after King Andrew II of Hungary went on a crusading expedition to Palestine (1217), John Asen and Alexander renewed their invasion of Boril's dominions. When the latter's adherents betrayed his cause, Boril sought refuge in flight, but was caught and by the order of the victors was blinded (1218).

The new tsar, the elder of the brothers, who assumed the title of John Asen II (1218-1241), succeeded to a sorry inheritance. He was, however, an able ruler and diplomat as well as a good warrior. Thanks to his energy, the Bulgarian Empire became for a time the strongest power in the Balkans. He entered into friendly relations with the weak Latin Emperor Robert, as well as the Serbian King Stephen the First-Crowned, and the Despot of Epirus, Theodore I Angelus. He married a daughter of the Hungarian King Andrew, and received with her as dowry the lands which Andrew had conquered from Boril.

The fortunes of the Latin Empire of Romania were growing steadily worse. Under the incompetent rule of Robert, and after his death (1228) under that of his eleven-year-old son, Baldwin II (1228-61), the Empire was gradually losing territory to the Byzantines. The Emperor of Nicaea, John Ducas Vatatzes (1222-54), little by little reconquered almost all Latin possessions in Asia Minor, and Despot Theodore I Angelus of Epirus was even more suc-

---

21. Popruzhenko, M. G., *Sinodik tsarya Borila.* Sofia, 1928.

cessful in his attacks upon the Latin Kingdom of Salonica. He conquered most of Macedonia, including Salonica, and Albania, thus building a vigorous Greek state on the ruins of the Latin kingdom. In 1223 he was crowned emperor by the archbishop of Ohrid, Demetrius Khomatianus, whose ecclesiastical authority was now supreme in Theodore's dominions. The various princes who governed the numerous territories of the Latin Empire began to feel apprehensive of the ominous signs of decay, and decided to urge a defensive alliance with Bulgaria. It was to take the form of marriage of Baldwin with John Asen's daughter Helena. John Asen was eager for such union which would afford him an opportunity to exercise a dominant influence at Constantinople. But the scheme was wrecked on the determined opposition of the Latin clergy who regarded the Bulgarian tsar as an unreliable subject of Rome and a protector of the Bogomils. The matter was referred to Rome for decision, where the marriage plan was summarily rejected. Instead, John de Brienne, the ex-king of Jerusalem, was appointed regent during Baldwin's minority.

In spite of this rebuff, John Asen managed to rise to great power. When he was treacherously attacked by Emperor Theodore Angelus of Epirus, he was not only able to defend himself, but actually completely defeated his foe's army in the battle of Klokotnitse (1230), took Theodore prisoner and had him blinded. Thereupon, he quickly and easily extended his sway over the extensive realms of his erstwhile rival. Ultimately, his domains exceeded in extent Kaloyan's territory, and he thus became the mightiest ruler in the Balkans. The archepiscopal see of Ohrid was once more included within the boundaries of Bulgaria. A still extant inscription which John Asen placed in the church of the Forty Martyrs in Trnovo, bears witness to the pride which he felt in this remarkable extension of his power.

Such phenomenal success was not without effect upon the Emperor of Nicaea, John Ducas Vatatzes, who now zealously sought the friendship of the Bulgarian ruler. He offered him an alliance with himself for the purpose of driving the Latins out of the Empire. Asen saw therein his opportunity to strike a good bargain with the emperor: he demanded, in return for this alliance, a formal acknowledgment of his imperial title and of the primate of Bulgaria as head of an autocephalous church. Consequently, as early as 1232, in a formal agreement, the archbishop of Trnovo acknowledged the ecumenical patriarch as his chief, thus deserting the papal allegiance. This was the first step toward raising the archbishopric to the rank of patriarchate. That the Greeks were aware of this secret intention on the part of the Bulgarian tsar is apparent from a letter written by the patriarchal exarch of Epirus to John Asen, in an endeavor to dissuade him from such a plan. In 1234 the treaty between the emperor of Nicaea and the Bulgarian tsar was concluded at Gallipoli and was guaranted by the marriage celebrated at Lampsacus, between Asen's daughter, Helena, and John Vatatzes' son, Theodore Lascaris. Thereupon John Asen's imperial rank was formally acknowledged. At the same time, Asen requested that the Trnovo archbishop be raised to the rank of patriarch. After some deliberation, even this request was granted. Patriarch Germanos II (1222-1240) along with many hierarchs and hegumens from Mt. Athos held a council at Lampsacus during the summer of 1235, and there, with the written consent of the remaining three eastern patriarchs and with the imperial and synodical approval, granted the patriarchal rank to Archbishop Joachim II.[22] Besides, several prominent Bulgarian bishops were raised to the metropolitan rank. Nevertheless, the granting of the patriarchal rank to Joachim did not carry with it the full equality of the Bulgarian patriarch with the four historic patriarchates. In fact, the Bulgarian chief remained definitely subordinated to the ecumenical patriarch, whose name he was obliged to recite in the liturgy before all others. According to the assertion made later by the Constantinopolitan patriarch Callistos, Patriarch Germanos had even imposed a yearly payment upon the Bulgarian patriarchate, and had subjected the Bulgarian patriarch to the juridical power of Constantinople.

Thus Bulgaria once more came to possess two autocephalous churches: the patriarchate of Trnovo and the archbishopric of Ohrid. But the latter, although not formally deprived of its autocephaly, lost much of its prestige and power. Its former eparchies in Epirus had been transferred to the jurisdiction of the ecumenical patriarchate and were

22. Georgii Acropolitae *Annales*, Migne, *PG.*, v. 140, c. 1057.

administered by a patriarchal exarch. The patriarch of
Trnovo of course retained hegemony within the Bulgarian
church, although historically that rôle belonged to Ohrid.
Thus the latter see practically became subordinate to
Trnovo, although canonically no change had been made in
the status of the two. The archbishop of Ohrid was obliged
to recite the name of his more successful Bulgarian rival
in the liturgy, a practice which has been always regarded
as an acknowledgment of dependence. Indeed it is possible that he was constrained even to pay a nominal contri-
bution to his more fortunate rival.

The falling away of the Bulgarian church from papal
jurisdiction greatly angered Pope Gregory IX (1227-41).
He appealed to John Asen to withdraw from his alliance
with Emperor John Vatatzes and to order a return of his
church to the papal obedience. When the tsar turned a deaf
ear to these appeals, Gregory empowered the Hungarian
archbishop of Kalocz to excommunicate him (1236).

The danger threatening from Hungary, which was no
longer ruled by the friendly Andrew II who had died in
1235, but by his son, Béla IV (1235-70), was sufficiently
grave to induce John Asen to withdraw from his alliance
with Emperor John Vatatzes and to begin negotiations
with the pope. Moreover, John Asen was not slow to realize that it would not be to his advantage to help strengthen
the Empire of Nicaea too much; hence he not only broke
his treaty with Vatatzes, but even went so far as to transfer
his support to the Latins. Greatly angered, the emperor
declared a war against his former ally. This brought about
a prompt change in the policy of the Bulgarian tsar. Having learned that an infectious disease had carried away his
wife, his eldest son, as well as Patriarch Joachim, John Asen
professed to see in the calamity a sure sign of divine dis-
pleasure with his unfaithfulness to the Greeks and once
more resumed his alliance with Vatatzes.

This second rupture with the Roman See incensed
Pope Gregory IX to the extent of ordering, in January,
1238, the Hungarian prelates to preach a crusade against
the disobedient Bulgarians. He appealed to King Béla IV
to become the leader of the expedition. But the Hungarian
king, whose territories had been invaded by the wild hordes
of the Cumans who in turn had been driven westward by

the Mongols, had no desire to assume the rôle of a papal defender. Consequently, John Asen was able to retain his conquests and his rank undisturbed. He died in 1241, having brought his country to a state of power such as it had not enjoyed for a long time.

After his death, the throne of Bulgaria passed to his nine-year-old son, Kaliman I (1241-46). The government was of course in the hands of a regency. In 1245 Pope Innocent IV (1243-54) wrote to Kaliman in an effort to induce him to renew the union with Rome.[23] But nothing came of it.

Kaliman died, probably of poisoning, in 1246. He was succeeded by his half-brother, Michael II, then a boy of eight. His mother, Irene, sister of the Despot of Epirus, Demetrius, assumed the leading position in the regency. She exerted her influence in favor of subversion of the traditional pro-imperial policies of Bulgaria. Under her leadership, the country became pro-Epirean. The consequences of this ill-advised step were swift and tragic. Emperor John Vatatzes immediately took up arms against Irene, and in a successful campaign conquered all of Thrace and of northern Macedonia. Besides taking these Bulgarian territories, he also conquered Epirus, and Despot Demetrius was obliged to acknowledge Vatatzes as his suzeraign. Thus the gains of John Asen II were again lost to the Greeks. Soon after the weak Michael II, who vainly sought to recover at least a part of his patrimony, was assassinated by his cousin, Kaliman, in 1256.

Out of the chaos which succeeded this foul deed emerged as tsar the leader of the nobles, Constantine (1257-77), who claimed descent from the Serbian Stephen Nemanya. He had to engage in long wars with many rivals before he became generally acknowledged. In order to strengthen his position, he divorced his wife and married a daughter of Theodore II Lascaris. But even then he lost a great deal of his territory to the strongest of his rivals, Jacob Svetislav.

Feeling the need of support in his none too secure position, Tsar Constantine was driven to seek the help of the

---

23. Potthast, *Regesta pontificum Romanorum*, Berlin, 1874, nos. 11606 and 11613.

Byzantine Emperor, Michael VIII Palaeologus (1259-82), who had expelled the Latins from Constantinople in 1261 and had reestablished his rule in the old capital of the Byzantine Empire. The emperor needed allies against the forces of the Latins who sought to reconquer the lost territories; hence, he was glad to make alliance with the Bulgarians. Michael's greatest danger arose when Charles of Anjou, King of Naples, revived the project of restoring the Latin Empire (1267), after Baldwin II had surrendered to him his title to it. The Byzantine emperor then sought to ward off the threatening danger by negotiating with the pope for ecclesiastical reunion. Although the move was a bit of politic stalling in order to gain time, yet the clergy and the populace became alarmed and opposed it most energetically. As for his own dominions, Michael employed force to suppress the disaffection. But since the Orthodox churches of Serbia and Bulgaria also felt affected by the measure and loudly protested against it, Michael dealt them a most unexpected blow. In 1272 by a special chrysobull he transferred to the archepiscopal see of Ohrid all the privileges which had been granted the defunct Justiniana Prima by Emperor Justinian and confirmed anew the privileges granted the former see by Emperor Basil II; in other words, he officially identified the ancient defunct see of Justiniana Prima with Ohrid, and assured Ohrid all the historic privileges possessed by both. By this astounding measure the archbishopric of Pech and the patriarchate of Trnovo which had been created out of the territory of one or the other of the older sees, were summarily deprived of their canonical rights and privileges, and were merged with the archbishopric of Ohrid.

As far as the negotiations for reunion of the Greek and Latin churches were concerned, a Council was called to Lyons (1274) where the questions on which the two parties were at variance were to be settled. Michael's emissaries at the Council, headed by Patriarch Joseph I and the imperial logothete George Acropolite, acknowledged the jurisdiction of Pope Gregory X over the patriarchate of Constantinople and included in the submission the dioceses of Pech and Trnovo as parts of the archepiscopal see of Ohrid. This inclusion they justified on the ground that the two national patriarchates had been established without the

papal consent and as such were uncanonical. The legitimacy
of Ohrid was based upon its identification with the see of
Justiniana Prima founded by Justinian I with the consent
of Pope Vigilius I. In spite of this elaborate legal juggling,
the pope appears to have taken no steps to subjugate the
two Slavic sees to his jurisdiction.

The union of the patriarchate of Constantinople with
Rome, a measure dictated by sheer political necessity, was
intensely unpopular among the Orthodox people everywhere. The emperor found himself under the necessity of
persecuting his own subjects as "schismatics". The Bulgarian ruler discerned in this circumstance his opportunity
to place himself at the head of an opposition movement,
not only in behalf of his own people, but of the dissatisfied
masses of the Empire as well. These latter were headed
by the sister of the emperor, Eulogia, who entered into
secret negotiations with Tsar Constantine, who was her
son-in-law, having married her daughter Maria. After Tsar
Constantine had broken his leg and became thus incapacitat-
ed for the duties of government, Maria virtually became
the ruler of Bulgaria. Then the two women, mother and
daughter, were able to cooperate effectively in thwarting
Emperor Michael's ecclesiastical policy. But Maria became
extremely unpopular in Bulgaria on account of her cruel
and crafty character. Opposition to her rule within the
country as well as the danger threatening from Michael
compelled her finally, in 1267, to make peace with Constantinople. Patriarch Ignatius of Trnovo, who had been
pronounced deposed on account of his opposition to the
union, by the unionist ecumenical patriarch, John Beccus
(1275-82), was constrained to appear before the latter and
to make his submission to the Roman curia. This was done
in the presence of the General of the Franciscan Order,
Jerome of Ascoli, who later became Pope Nicholas IV
(1288-92).[24] But as usual, submission extorted by political
necessities was neither sincere nor of long duration. After
Emperor Michael's death in 1282 the union with Rome
lapsed, although for that matter the Bulgarian rulers had
for a long time not observed its terms. At the instigation
of Helena, the zealous Roman Catholic Serbian queen-
dowager, Pope Nicholas IV wrote to the Bulgarian Tsar

24. Theiner, A., *Monumenta historica Hungariae*, Romae, 1859, I, no. 609.

George Terteri I as well as to the Bulgarian patriarch (1291) regarding reunion, but without any result.[25]

The history of the succeeding forty years presents no outstanding events as far as the church is concerned. Politically, the period was very unstable, due to the kaleidoscopic changes on the throne brought about by the rivalries of families of the Terterites and the Asens. The battle of Velbuzhd (1330) between the Byzantino-Bulgarian forces and Serbia resulted in the victory of the latter. This success of the Serbian arms definitely secured hegemony in the Balkans for Serbia, and Bulgaria from that time lost its leading position. This period of disasters and confusion was at last arrested with the elevation to the throne of John Alexander (1331-71), who was able to restore stability to Bulgaria and to gain advantage for his country from the tragic disorders prevalent in the Empire during the struggle for supremacy between Emperor John V Palaeologus and John VI Cantacuzene.

During the disastrous civil war in the Empire which broke out between the adherents of the former Grand Domestic, John Cantacuzene, who had been proclaimed (1342) co-emperor with the young John V, and the partisans of the regent, Anne of Savoy, John's mother, the Serbs and the Bulgarians saw their opportunity to extend their dominions. It was particularly the Serbian ruler, Stephen Dushan, who profited by these disorders. He conquered almost all Greek territory in the Balkans, and in 1346 had himself crowned Emperor of the Serbs and the Greeks. At the same time he elevated the archbishop of Pech, Joannicius II, to the rank of patriarch.

The inner state of the Bulgarian church during the reign of John Alexander was not encouraging. It shared the general character of the Byzantine church of the period, the most outstanding feature of which was a form of mysticism known as hesychasm. This movement had much in common with Western mysticism of the type of Tauler and of Meister Eckhardt. It originated with Gregory the Sinaite, who stressed as the goal of perfect monastic life a state of mystical ecstacy which he called theory, in distinction from the life of asceticism which he regarded as merely preparatory for the life of mystical vision, and which

<hr>

25. *Ibid.*, n. 608.

he called practice. Having settled at Mount Athos, Gregory gathered about him a considerable number of disciples, among whom his biographer, Callistos, later patriarch of Constantinople, mentions many Bulgarians and Serbians. The hesychasts gave themselves to the mystical ecstacy of the vision of what they fondly regarded as "the transfiguration light" which had shone about Jesus on the Mount of Transfiguration (identified by them with Mount Tabor). The teachings of Gregory found their chief opponent in the Western-influenced Calabrian monk, Barlaam, who ridiculed them and sought to discredit them by pointing out their similarities with certain features of Bogomilism and Messalianism. The chief defender and exponent of hesychasm arose in Gregory Palamas, later archbishop of Salonica. His championship of the doctrine of the "uncreated light" finally won its acceptance at the Council of Constantinople held in 1351. The teachings of Barlaam and his associates were there condemned and their adherents were excommunicated.

Hesychasm soon penetrated into Bulgaria, where Theodosius of Trnovo (d. c. 1367 or 68), a disciple of Gregory the Sinaite, became its most celebrated exponent. On his frequent peregrinations from one monastery to another, Theodosius met Gregory the Sinaite and became his devoted disciple. After the latter's death, Theodosius visited Mount Athos and became acquainted with the mode of life of the hesychasts there. In the end, when Theodosius settled in Bulgaria, Tsar John Alexander gave the group of disciples which had gathered about him an extensive tract of land on a hill about two hours' distance south of Trnovo, where they established a monastic community. It is said that the community consisted of fifty members.

In spite of his retired manner of life, Theodosius soon acquired a wide and truly important influence in the religious life of the country. He took lead in the struggle between the power-loving ecumenical patriarch, Callistos I (1350-63), and the Bulgarian patriarch Simeon, in which he upheld the cause of the former—a strange proceeding from the nationalistic point of view! The Bulgarian patriarch sought to make himself fully independent of the overlordship of the Constantinopolitan see. He therefore dropped the latter's name from the liturgy and no longer applied for

the chrysm to him. Patriarch Callistos naturally protested
against this revolt on the part of the head of the Bulgarian
church. But the most remarkable feature of the affair is
that Theodosius and his collaborator Romanus took sides
with the ecumenical patriarch, because the latter was a
distinguished member of the hesychast party. Ignoring
their own patriarch, they turned directly to Constantinople,
professing readiness to support the cause of Callistos. This
is an eloquent proof of the *esprit de corps* of the hesychast
party which overrode even the nationalistic interests.

The effort of the Trnovo patriarch to gain complete
independence from his ecumenical superior may be linked
with the policy of the tsar as well as with the fact that the
times afforded a favorable opportunity for such revolt.
The Bulgarian tsar claimed the title of "emperor of the
Bulgarians and the Greeks", and as such did not wish to be
outdone by the upstart Serbian Stephen Dushan who had
just then assumed the imperial title and raised his archbishop to the rank of patriarch. For that reason he desired
to see his own patriarch possess the same independence as
the Serbian had assumed. The very success of the Serbians
in their venture encouraged the spirit of revolt in the Bulgarians.

In the *Life of Theodosius* written by Patriarch Callistos,
the Bulgarian mystic is represented as the sole leader in the
struggle against the heresies which were troubling the life
of the Bulgarian church. The Bulgarian patriarch is treated
as a person of no account. Theodosius alone is given credit
for the calling of the first council to deal with the heresies
and is depicted as playing a predominant rôle in the organization of the second council. This is undoubtedly a gross
exaggeration of the facts. No one but the patriarch or the
tsar had the right to call councils. Hence, such a gathering could not have been held without an active co-operation
of the patriarch. Especially since this dignitary was on
bad terms with Theodosius it is not possible to imagine that
he would have voluntarily relinquished his rights to his
opponent. The primary credit for the councils must be
given to the patriarch, despite Callistos' assertion to the
contrary.

There were abundant reasons for holding the councils
against the various anti-ecclesiastical movements. The com-

mon people were living in misery and squalor which the church did nothing to alleviate. On the contrary, the church was but too often among the oppressors. Moreover, the hierarchy strove to extend still further its privileges and was not interested in improving the miserable lot of the people. The barren mysticism of the hesychasts was not calculated to improve the social and economic misery, either. Thus the laity were left a prey to superstition and to anti-ecclesiastical movements.

The Bogomils exerted a wide and potent influence by their propaganda, and several other sectarian movements shared popularity with them. A certain monk, Theodoret by name, came from Constantinople and preached the anti-hesychast doctrines of Barlaam, and was accused of some heathen practices besides. More stir was caused by two monks, Lazarus and Cyril surnamed Barefooted, who had been expelled from Mt. Athos on account of their adherence to the Bogomil tenets. Bogomilism had spread to the Holy Mountain, according to a story, from Salonica, where a pious nun, Irene by name, had infected her monastic visitors with the virus of this vigorous anti-ecclesiastical teaching. She enjoyed great fame on account of her piety and benevolence and many monks from Mt. Athos resorted to her for that reason. When the adherents of Bogomilism were discovered to have penetrated even the hallowed retreats of the Holy Mountain, among those who were expelled were the two above-mentioned monks who took refuge in Bulgaria. They came to Trnovo where Lazarus is said to have divested himself of clothes and to have preached the necessity of emasculation. These features would indicate Messalian influence. Cyril opposed the worship of icons and of the cross, claimed to have visions, and taught that husbands and wives should separate. In general, therefore, the character of the teaching of these two monks bore likeness to Bogomilism. Another popular preacher of an opposite tendency, Theodosius by name, gathered large crowds of people about him, formed a band of followers of them, and walking about the villages and the country-side, often naked, taught them to indulge in orgiastic excesses. Thus both the ascetic and the orgiastic forms of religious enthusiasm met! But similar situation existed several centuries later for instance among the Russian sect of Khlysti, who often indulged in unrestricted promiscuous orgies, and the closely related Skoptsy, who reacted in the opposite fashion and practiced emasculation. The Adamites who existed in Bohemia in the first half of the fifteenth century also walked naked and practiced immorality.

These various religious irregularities finally led to the calling of two councils for the purpose of restoring order. As already said, the *Life of Theodosius* gives chief credit for the councils to the leader of the Bulgarian hesychasts. But we have already seen that such could not have been the case. The Bulgarian patriarch Simeon, who had moral stamina enough to carry on a long struggle for ecclesiastical independence with the ecumenical patriarch, undoubtedly possessed sufficient energy to take resolute measures for the suppression of the various disturbers who were troubling his church. At any rate, in 1350 a council was convened under the presidency of the tsar, and strict measures were passed against the Bogomils and other anti-ecclesiastical movements. It may be freely conceded that Theodosius might have taken a leading part in the denunciation of these sectaries and in the defence of Orthodoxy. The two monastic disturbers of peace, Lazarus and Cyril, were tried; the former abjured his views, but the latter along with his adherent Stephen remained steadfast; they were branded on the face and banished from the country.

Nevertheless, the measures taken at the council did not put a stop to the religious dissensions. To the previously existing troubles was added a curious Judaising movement initiated by the Jews resident in Bulgaria. They were emboldened to launch their propaganda trusting in the protection of their mighty former co-religionist, the tsaritsa. The aging John Alexander had fallen in love with a Jewess, and having compelled his wife, Theodora, the daughter of Bessarab of Wallachia, to retire to a cloister, married the Jewish charmer. She of course found it necessary to submit to the rite of baptism in which she assumed the name of Theodora. But she must have remained at heart loyal to her own people. At any rate, that is what they thought of her. The second council which convened c. 1360 dealt, therefore, in addition to the Bogomils, with the Judaisers. All doctrines at variance with Orthodoxy were anathematized and the leaders of the anti-ecclesiastical groups were banished. The rights of the Jews were limited and three leaders of the Judaising party were put to death.

In the struggle between Callistos and Simeon, the mystics gained the final victory. It appears not to have come till in the days of Patriarch Euthemius, who was a disciple of Theodosius. But then the Bulgarian patriarch acquiesced in his position of subordination to Constantinople.

In spite of the expansion of Serbia and Bulgaria, a most dangerous enemy had appeared on the horizon who was destined to destroy both the Greek and the Slavic powers of the Balkans: the Ottoman Turks. Their emir, Orkhan (1326-57), had been given Emperor John Cantacuzene's daughter, Theodora, in marriage in consideration of the help rendered John by the Turks in his struggle with the party of John V and his mother Anne of Savoy (1344). In 1349 Cantacuzene called upon his son-in-law once more to aid him against Tsar Stephen Dushan who was besieging Salonica.

The Turks, thus given an idea of the sorry state of the Byzantine Empire, profited by their opportunity to the full. From that time Thrace, Bulgaria, and Serbia were never free from their periodic invasions. After the forced retirement of John Cantacuzene to Mt. Athos (1355), Orkhan became openly hostile to the Empire. In 1356, thirty thousand Turks, under the leadership of his two sons, Sulaiman and Murad, crossed the straits of the Dardanelles and settled permanently in Europe. From that time they became a lasting and ever increasing menace to the Balkan powers and the Empire.

In view of the grave danger threatening from the Turks, it was supremely unwise on the part of Tsar John Alexander to divide his territory. Nevertheless, spurred by his love of his second wife and wishing to reserve for her son, John Shishman, the bulk of his dominions, he deprived the only surviving son of his first marriage, John Sracimir, of the succession, and assigned him merely the territory of Vidin. This was done before 1360. Besides, a strip of coast-land in the northeastern part of Bulgaria was likewise torn away from John Alexander's dominions and was set up as an independent despotate under Dobrotić (hence

it is known to this day as Dobruja). Consequently, almost
the whole littoral of the Black Sea passed out of the tsar's
hands. Ecclesiastically, this region became subject to
Constantinople.

Still greater weakening of the Slavic hegemony in the
Balkans occurred after the death of the mighty Serbian
tsar, Stephen Dushan (1355). His territories were torn
apart into a number of small principalities, ruled by his dis-
united and mutually jealous epigones. In their separate
weakness, they could no more effectively withstand the onward rush of the consolidated Turkish power than could a
flock of magpies withstand the attack of an eagle.

The new Turkish sultan, Murad I (1359-89), is numbered among the mightiest of Turkish warriors. He soon
attacked John Alexander, and in 1363 conquered the important Thracian capital, Hadrianople, which he made, two
years later, the new capital of his empire. Thereupon the
center of Turkish power shifted to Europe. Moreover, the
ambitious and insatiable Hungarian king of the Anjou
dynasty, Louis I (1342-82), casting covetous eyes upon the
weakly protected region of John Sracimir, invaded and conquered Vidin in 1365. Sracimir's father, John Alexander,
was in no position to come to his son's aid. Thus Vidin
passed to Hungary as a special banate, ruled by Dionysius,
formerly the voyevod of Transylvania. Louis wrote the
pope asking him for two thousand monks to Catholicize the
conquered territory. The pope sent him eight friars who
had been preaching in Bosnia. With the help of the military, these Franciscans obtained, according to their report,
an astonishing success in their missionary endeavors. In
fifty days they converted one-third of the total number of
the inhabitants. The populace, which was largely Bogomil,
was quickly constrained to accept Roman Catholicism. But
this success was quickly undone when Vidin was retaken
by the Bulgars. Thereupon, five of the friars were put to
death and many of the converts were reclaimed.

But the greatest calamity for Bulgaria was the defeat
which the armies of John Alexander suffered at the hands
of the Turkish army. Beginning with 1369, the Turks sys-
tematically attacked the Bulgarian territory. The loss of
Philippopolis was a serious blow to the power of John
Alexander. In 1371 the defeat of the Serbian armies at the

battle on the Maritsa was, according to Jireček, "the beginning of the Turkish domination over the southern Slavs".[26] John Alexander died before this signal defeat of the Serbs (Feb. 17, 1371), at which time Bulgaria was but a shadow of what it had been earlier in his reign.

The remaining territory of Bulgaria was divided into three parts: the largest share was inherited by John Shishman, the son of John Alexander's second wife. The Vidin territory, reconquered from the Hungarians in 1370, was restored to Sracimir at the price of his acknowledgment of Hungarian suzerainty. Finally, the third part, the strip along the Black Sea, remained in the hands of Dobrotić. But the worst feature of this unstatesmanlike division was that the three rulers were so criminally short-sighted in their policies as to prey upon each other's territories and thus to weaken themselves. Sracimir, when Shishman was obliged to acknowledge Sultan Murad's overlordship after the battle on the Maritsa, invaded Shishman's dominions and occupied Sredets (Sofia). Moreover, he removed the church of his dominions from the jurisdiction of the Trnovo patriarch and submitted it directly to the rule of Constantinople. This may have been done with the active encouragement of the ecumenical patriarch. At any rate, in 1381, the metropolitan of Vidin, loyal to Trnovo, was deposed, his place being taken by an appointee of Constantinople, Cassian. Thus both Bulgaria and Serbia, on account of internal petty rivalries and lack of a strong commanding personality, were utterly unable to withstand the Turkish encroachments.

In spite of the threatening political situation, the cultural life of Bulgaria was heightened to a feverish degree. The chief credit for the literary revival is due to the disciple of Theodosius of Trnovo, Euthymius, who later became Bulgarian patriarch (1375-93). He was of course a hesychast. We derive our knowledge of his life from the *Eulogy* written by his relative and disciple, Gregory Tsamblak, although this source suffers from all the defects usually met with in hagiographical writings. It is apparent that he used Callistos' *Life of Theodosius of Trnovo* not only as a literary example but as a literary quarry, actually incorporating portions of it in his own work.

---

26. Jireček, K., *Geschichte der Serben*, Gotha, 1911, I, p. 438.

It seems that Euthymius came of a prominent Bulgarian family. He chose the monastic life early, becoming some time later a disciple of Theodosius of Trnovo. Tsamblak asserts that he even accompanied his master to Constantinople when Theodosius went there to see his one-time school-fellow, Patriarch Callistos (1365). After Theodosius' death which occurred c. 1367 or 68, Euthymius resorted to Mt. Athos where he gave himself to rigorous asceticism including even a voluntary imposition of absolute silence upon himself. He soon won the admiration of his fellow hesychasts. After having been exiled from Mt. Athos by an order of Emperor John V because he could not produce the treasure which a fellow monk denounced him as possessing, he returned to Bulgaria and settled near Trnovo in a cave (1370). According to Tsamblak, he busied himself with the translation and correction of Church-Slavonic liturgical and other religious books. Soon a monastery, named in honor of the Holy Trinity, was founded near Euthymius' cave, and an important school of Slavic literature came into existence there. This school was founded with the aid and possibly under the direction of Euthymius.

After the death of Patriarch Joannicius II, most likely between 1375 and 1378, Euthymius was chosen to fill the vacancy on the patriarchal throne, although the details of the event are not known. He soon became known as a zealous opponent of all laxity in monastic life and of the anti-ecclesiastical movements, chiefly Bogomilism. But his fame rests *par excellence* upon his literary activity.[27] Tsar John Shishman, who was a patron of arts and literature, eagerly supported all cultural movements. With the active encouragement of the ruler as well as of the patriarch, Bulgarian literature experienced a new revival and blossomed out in unparalleled luxuriance. The work comprised partly revision of the existing Church-Slavonic works, partly original compositions. Probably Euthymius wished to carry through such a thoroughgoing revision of the Church-Slavonic texts in ecclesiastical use as was undertaken almost three centuries later by Patriarch Nikon of Moscow— with the tragic result of giving rise to the Great Schism.

---

27. Kalužniacki, E., *Werke des Patriarchen von Bulgarien, Euthymius.* Wien, 1901.

But besides this work of revision, the school produced original compositions. Euthymius himself composed *Lives* of John of Rilo, of Paraskeva, of Philotheos, of Hilarion of Moglen, and *Eulogies* of Emperor Constantine and Helena, of Michael of Potuka, and of the martyr Nedela; finally, he also wrote a *History of the Rebuilding of the Church of Jerusalem,* and many other works. Moreover, he translated much from Greek. The most important of these translations were some ancient liturgies. Nevertheless, it must be conceded that the work of the whole literary band was not characterized by any startling originality; it followed slavishly the Greek models not only as to the form but often even in respect to the content.

The literary school founded by Euthymius survived the downfall of the Bulgarian Empire. Among his literary collaborators the most important were Dionysius, Joasaph the metropolitan of Vidin, Cyprian who later became metropolitan of Kiev, and Gregory Tsamblak who played an important rôle in the history of the church of Russia. Thanks to the labors of this devoted band, the Bulgarian cultural life outlived the catastrophe of the political life of Bulgaria.

Euthymius also helped the hesychast movement to gain complete victory in Bulgaria. In the struggle which his predecessors in the patriarchal office had waged with the see of Constantinople over the matter of complete autocephaly of the Bulgarian church, Euthymius, as could be expected from a disciple of Theodosius, yielded to the demands of the ecumenical patriarchate. By his orders, the name of the ecumenical patriarch and other eastern patriarchs were recited in the liturgy before his own.

But the days of Bulgarian political independence were numbered. The Turks were determined to extend their dominion over the entire peninsula. In 1382 the important city of Sredets (modern Sofia) was taken by them, and the possession of this key city opened the way to the Danube. In 1386 Sultan Murad conquered Nish which was a part of the territory of the Serbian Prince Lazar. John Sracimir of Vidin was constrained to acknowledge the Turkish overlordship. With the fall of Salonica in 1387, the whole region of Macedonia to Albania passed into the hands of the Turks.

As for John Shishman, he retained his throne only at the good will of Murad, who imposed heavy duties upon him but did not judge the time expedient to occupy his lands. Under the leadership of the Serbian Prince Lazar, the Christian princes of the Balkans at last realized the immense danger threatening them, and a group of Serbian princes with the aid of the Croatian band organized themselves for a determined struggle with the Turks. Murad, supported by contingents of his various Balkan vassals, met them in battle of Kosovo Polye. During the decisive battle which occurred there on June 15, 1389, a Serbian noble, Milosh Kobilich, found his way into Murad's tent and murdered him there. But the sultan's oldest son, Beyazid, instantly assumed command of the army and caused the Christians such a bloody defeat that from that time Slavic Christian power in the Balkans was utterly broken.

Beyazid showed himself even a more terrible foe of the Slavs than his father had been. Because of his swift marches and blows, he received the surname of Ilderim, the Lightning. Serbian territories were soon in his power, and then came the turn of Bulgaria.

Tsar John Shishman had not taken a direct part in the battle of Kosovo Polye, although he had joined the league against Murad. Nevertheless, when in mortal terror for his throne he began negotiations with the Hungarian court for support against the Turks, at the cost of accepting Hungarian overlordship, the blow fell. Beyazid invaded Bulgaria in 1393, and after investing the Bulgarian capital for three months, took it on July 17.

The fall of Trnovo is described by Gregory Tsamblak in the *Life of Euthymius* in terms which leave no doubt of their rhetorical exaggeration. Nevertheless, the Turks undoubtedly wrought terrible havoc in the conquered city. They destroyed the palaces of the tsar, pulled down churches, converted the cathedral into a mosque and other churches were given over to secular uses. Since the tsar had left Trnovo before the siege had begun and had found refuge in Nicopolis, Patriarch Euthymius became the chief representative of the people. He secured from Beyazid a promise that the lives of the inhabitants would be spared. This promise was granted, but as soon as Beyazid himself left the city, the military governor gathered the representative citizens in a church and had them cut down in cold blood. Patriarch Euthymius himself was sentenced to death, but his sentence was in the last moment changed to exile and imprisonment. He was dispatched to Macedonia where he possibly soon afterwards died.[28] The terrible suffering endured by the populace induced many to accept Islam. Shishman held out against a capture for some time, but finally surrendered. He was imprisoned in Philippopolis, but after two years was put to death. One of his sons, Alexander, accepted Islam and received an appointment under the Turks.

The loss of political independence involved the Bulgarian church in the loss of its autocephaly. The exact details are not known, the only fact that seems clear being that the ecumenical patriarch Anthony IV (1389-97) appointed, in 1394, the Wallachian metropolitan Jeremiah as a temporary administrator of the Trnovo see. Jeremiah's nomination to the Wallachian diocese had met with such strenuous protest on the part of his subjects that he was glad to go to Trnovo, where he arrived in 1395. Whether the Bulgarians themselves, discouraged and leaderless, followed the example of Vidin, Dobruja, and Wallachia, all of which were already administered by the ecumenical patriarchate, and voluntarily submitted to Constantinople, or whether the ecumenical patriarch saw in the chaotic conditions following the imprisonment of Euthymius his opportunity to enlarge his jurisdiction by downright seizure of the see, is not known. In spite of the fact that Bulgarian writers are inclined to interpret the event in the latter sense, it seems that under the circumstances the subjection of the Bulgarian church to the jurisdiction of Constantinople was on the whole beneficial to it. In 1402 Trnovo see had a metropolitan fully subordinated to the ecumenical patriarchate and despite the loss of the patriarchal rank and autocephaly did not seem to protest against the situation. The new archbishop bore the title of "exarch of all Bulgaria" and appears to have been fully independent as far as his functions within his exarchate were concerned. Nevertheless, the Bulgarian church ceased to be autocephalous and retained only autonomy. At first the exarch ranked fifth in the scale of

28. Kalužniacki estimates that Euthymius' death took place between 1396 and 1419; *op. cit.*, p. xxv.

dignity in the list of Constantinopolitan hierarchs, but later was relegated to the tenth place. The peaceful acceptance of the situation on the part of the Bulgarian church may have been the result of the pro-Constantinopolitan policy of Euthymius which prepared the way, or of the faith in the invincible character of the Byzantine Empire which inspired the Bulgarians with hope to which they could hitch their own aspirations for recovery of political independence.

THE RISE AND FALL OF THE
SERBIAN CHURCH

The work begun by St. Sava was ably continued by his successors. During the long term of office of Archbishop Arsenius (1233-63), quiet but solid progress was made in establishing and strengthening the work. But nothing of great importance is reported regarding his incumbency. To be sure, the period was disturbed and the country suffered great ruin and loss of life during the Mongolian invasion of 1242; at that time many churches were burned or otherwise destroyed. It was most likely then that the archepiscopal see was transferred from Zhicha to Pech, which was farther inland and therefore safer, although even after Arsenius' time some archbishops continued to live at the former place. The reason for the removal, as given by Jireček[1] was the destruction of the Zhicha monastery during the invasion of the country by Bulgarians and Cumans in 1253; Novaković,[2] however, regards the new delineation of the boundary line, which placed Zhicha too near the frontier, as the true cause of the removal. At any rate, whenever the final removal took place, the see was ultimately located at Pech and ever since retained that honor.

The century which followed the death of Vladislav (1243 to 1331) was characterized by almost monotonous revolts of the heirs to the throne against their fathers. Vladislav's successor was his brother, Stephen Urosh I (1243-76). Although Serbian chroniclers bestowed upon him the title "Great", it is difficult to see how he merited it. As a matter of fact he lacked the qualities which had made his father a notable figure in history, and was on the whole quite a mediocre and commonplace individual.

He married a French princess, Helena, whom some historians regard, without sufficient evidence, as a daughter of the one-time Latin Emperor Baldwin II. On her account Urosh manifested a favorable leaning toward the

---

1. Jireček, K., *op. cit.*, I, p. 314.
2. *Glas*, 80 (1909) p. 4.

Roman Church.   Although she was and remained a faithful
adherent of the Roman communion, even Daniel, the archepiscopal historian, praises her for her keen mind, goodness
of heart, and genuine religious zeal and piety.   She became
not only a patroness and benefactress of the Latin foundations in Serbia, but likewise exercised a potent pro-Catholic influence upon her husband and through him upon the
state policy.   Helena restored several cities destroyed by
the Mongols and restored or founded a number of Roman
Catholic churches and monasteries.   She long survived her
husband, having died in 1314 after a life of singular beneficence and piety.

The Orthodox church keenly felt the danger implicit
in the indulgent attitude of the king toward the zealous
and fervent religious activity of his Catholic wife.   After
Arsenius' death, the archepiscopal see was filled by the
brother of the king, the youngest son of Stephen the First-
Crowned, Sava II (1263-c. 1272).   Following in the foot-
steps of his famous sainted uncle, Sava I, he became a monk
of the Khilandar monastery, where he received his education
in the "theological academy".   After having returned from
a pilgrimage to the Holy Land, he was chosen hegumen of
the monastery.   From this position he was called to the
post of the bishop of Ston in Hum (which was later known
as Herzegovina) where it devolved upon him to wage a stiff
fight against the expansionist policy of the Latin church
and the propaganda of the Bogomils. After Arsenius' death,
he was called to succeed him as archbishop of Serbia.   He
exerted a considerable influence in counteracting the sway
of Helena over her husband and in his struggle against the
preponderant Roman Catholic propaganda; he especially
combatted the efforts of the archbishop of Dubrovnik. Sava
rivaled the activity of Queen Helena in restoring many
churches and monasteries ruined during the Bulgaro-Cuman
invasion of 1253.   He also compiled the most ancient
known text of the Nomocanon.   He died c. 1272, and was
later proclaimed a saint by the Serbian church.

Sava was succeeded in the archepiscopal office by his
one-time fellow-monk at Khilandar and companion on his
Palestinian pilgrimage, Joannicius I (1272-76), who was
nominated to the office by the king.   Having succeeded
Sava in the dignity of hegumen at Khilandar, he was later

called to fill the post of archimandrite of Studenitsa. During Joannicius' term of office, the Serbian church was stirred to a high pitch of patriotic and religious fervor by the treacherous action of Emperor Michael VIII Palaeologus. Fearing an invasion of his territories by Charles I of Anjou, king of Naples, who championed the cause of the defunct Latin Empire of Romania after its last ruler, Baldwin II, had surrendered to him his claim to it, Michael entered into negotiations with the pope for reunion of the Eastern and Western churches, hoping thus to save his Empire. These pourparlers led to the calling of the unionist Council of Lyons (1274), where Michael, in order to revenge himself upon the churches of Serbia and Bulgaria for their stubborn opposition to his unionist policies, repudiated his recognition of their autocephalous status and affected to treat them as subject to Ohrid, which in turn he identified with the defunct see of Justiniana Prima. In such way he proceeded to treat the Serbian and Bulgarian churches as mere eparchies of Ohrid, and hence as involved in the unionistic acts of the Council of Lyons. This crafty action of Emperor Michael aroused the nationalistic pride of the Serbs who scornfully repudiated any such interpretation of the status of their church with the concomitant deductions.

As archbishop, Joannicius was greatly beloved by King Urosh, whom in turn he loyally supported. After Urosh had been deprived of his throne by his son Dragutin, Joannicius voluntarily followed the defeated king into exile in Hum, where he soon died.

Stephen Urosh's son, Stephen Dragutin, had been impatiently waiting for his chance to ascend the throne; when his father's long and peaceful reign became too irksome to Dragutin, and Urosh showed himself unwilling to entrust any part of his dominions to his son, he, with the military aid afforded him by his brother-in-law, the dissolute Hungarian king, Ladislav IV the Cuman (1272-90), rose up in revolt against Urosh and defeated his army in the battle of Gatske Polye (1276) in Hum and seized the throne for himself. Urosh was exiled, and died in 1282 in a Durazzo prison.

Stephen Dragutin's short reign (1276-81) was not particularly remarkable for any outstanding accomplishment. Along with the king of Hungary and other allies,

Dragutin attempted an unsuccessful attack upon the Byzantine Empire. The project resulted in the loss of some Serbian territory on the southern border. This lack of success, combined possibly with an infirmity which partially disqualified him for the strenuously active duties of a Balkan ruler—for he was lame—induced him, in 1281, to bow to the will of the opposition party organized by his younger brother, Stephen Milutin, and to abdicate his throne in favor of the latter. Dragutin himself retained the rule of the territories of Sirmia (with Belgrade), Machva, and Bosnia, which his Hungarian wife had received as her dowry when she had married him.

As could be expected of a son of Queen Helena, Dragutin was favorably disposed toward the Roman church. While he ruled Serbia, his obvious leanings toward the pro-Latin policy brought Archbishop Daniel I into an active conflict with his royal master, which ended in the deposition of the latter. After he had abdicated the Serbian throne, Dragutin was actually brought over into the bosom of the Roman Catholic church by the clever maneuvers of Pope Nicholas IV. True to the type of genuine neophytes, Dragutin henceforth zealously furthered the interests of his adopted faith. In Bosnia, which was ruled by his son-in-law, Stephen Kotroman, he undertook a persecution of the Bogomils who were very numerous there, and called for that purpose Franciscan friars into the country. Nevertheless, he was not successful in his missionary activity; he died in 1316, after years of rigorous asceticism which included sleeping in a grave filled with thorns and sharp stones, as monk Theoctistus, having assumed the monastic habit shortly before his death.

King Stephen Urosh II surnamed Milutin (1281-1321) made his reign a memorable epoch in the history of his country, and made Serbia of primary political importance in the Balkans. During his reign the Serbian dominions were not only considerably extended by means of wars and advantageous marriages, but also greatly gained in wealth. The source of the unprecedented wealth Serbia then enjoyed was found in silver mining which was greatly developed by the middle of the thirteenth century, especially by German miners who had been attracted to Serbia. Milutin's palace at Skoplye is described as of almost bar-

baric splendor, showy with massive gold and silver orna-
ments. The royal robes were heavy with pearls and spark-
ling jewels.

As for his personal character, King Milutin is depicted
by his Serbian contemporaries as a pious and generous
prince, a ruler of great statesmanship and valor, while the
Greek writers regard him as a coarse profligate and a barbarian. Probably both were right. Being richer than any
of his predecessors, Milutin found it comparatively easy
to gain fame for himself on account of his generosity. He
was regarded as the most munificent patron of monasteries
and churches. He did not build new monasteries, but repaired and endowed old and ruined ones, and transformed
small and poorly endowed foundations into well-endowed
houses. Proportionately, he renewed and endowed more
monasteries in the territories conquered from the Byzantine
Empire than those located in old Serbia. His pious generosity was not confined to his dominions alone, but extended to Byzantine monasteries, to Mt. Athos, where he
had rebuilt the famous Serbian cultural center, the monastery of Khilandar, to Salonica, to Palestine, to Constantinople itself, where he had built a church and a hos-
pital, and even to Italy.[3] According to a tradition, Milutin
made a vow that for every year he would remain on the
throne he would build a church.[4] Whether or not the tradition has a historical basis, it at least illustrates the popular reputation in which Milutin was held by later gener-
ations. No wonder that in spite of the unedifying story of
the four marriages of this Henry VIII of the Balkans he
was soon proclaimed a saint. Dante, however, thought
otherwise of him, and placed him among the evil kings for
counterfeiting the coins of Venice.[5]

In spite of his many benefactions by which the church
was greatly enriched, Milutin, like another Emperor Leo
VI the Wise, became entangled in acrimonious struggle
with his clergy on account of his four marriages. After he
had divorced his first wife, daughter of Duke John of
Neopatras, he desired to marry Elizabeth, daughter of the
Hungarian King Stephen V, formerly a Roman Catholic

---

3. Yanich-Hankey, *op. cit.*, p. 51-52.
4. *Ibid.*, p. 52.
5. *Divine Comedy*, Paradise, Canto XIX, 140-141.

nun. Archbishop Jacob (1286-92) strenuously opposed this
match on the ground that the marriage fell within the
prohibited degrees, the bride being a sister of Dragutin's
wife, Catherine. When the marriage took place despite the
archbishop's prohibition, Jacob pronounced the ceremony
uncanonical and forbade any mention of the Queen in the
liturgy. The bold archbishop, be it said to Milutin's honor,
retained his office in spite of his courageous stand. Soon
after, however, Milutin divorced Elizabeth and married his
third wife, Anna, daughter of the Bulgarian Tsar George
Terteri I.

The growing power and importance of King Milutin
was not without its effect upon Emperor Andronicus II
Palaeologus (1282-1328), who desired to strengthen his
position by an alliance with a strong and comparatively
wealthy ruler like the Serbian king. He therefore proposed
a treaty of alliance with him, to be sealed by marriage with
the Emperor's widowed sister. Milutin, who was tired of
Anna, was quite willing to accept the flattering proposal.
His father-in-law, George Terteri, had been deposed and
hence the marriage with Anna had no longer any political
value for Milutin. On the other hand, a matrimonial
alliance with the imperial family had potentialities of the
greatest magnitude—possibly even a union of Serbia with
the Empire—under a ruler who could be a Serb as well as
a Byzantine. But unfortunately there were difficulties in
the way: the canon law quite definitely forbade fourth marriage. Nevertheless, casuistry was not invented by the
Jesuits, and Byzantine lawyers were equal to the demand
made upon their ingenuity. They declared the second and
third marriages of Milutin null and void on the ground
that they had been contracted during the life-time of his
first wife. Thus legally Milutin was declared to have been
married only once. Hence having dismissed Anna (1299),
Milutin was free and ready to marry the Byzantine bride.
But this lady now developed scruples about the legality of
such marriage, or possibly about the advisability of marrying such notorious rake as the Falstaffian bridegroom. But
this did not terminate the affair: Andronicus, nothing
daunted, offered Milutin his only daughter, Simonis, who
was then not quite six years old! The Serbian king, who
was older than the bride's father, consented to the new

match in spite of the horrified opposition to it on the part of the ecumenical patriarch and Milutin's pious mother, Queen Dowager Helena. Nevertheless, the marriage soon took place.

The schemes cherished by Milutin regarding the possibility of uniting the Empire with his own territories came to naught when Simonis in course of time failed to bear her husband an heir. She abhorred her new and to her barbarous country as cordially as she did her uncouth and aged husband, and spent most of her time in Constantinople. But failing an heir borne by Simonis, Milutin had to relinquish his dream of a Serbo-Byzantine Empire ruled by his son. Simonis' loathing of her marriage reached such a pitch that she wished to become a nun. After her husband's death, she actually carried out her wish.

Having failed in the objective of his bizarre marital adventure, Milutin turned his attention to another project which bid fair to bring him to the desired goal of uniting the Empire with his own lands. In 1307 Milutin entered into negotiations with the titular emperor of the Latin Empire, Charles of Valois, brother of the French King Philip IV the Fair, offering him an alliance the object of which was an attack upon Andronicus' dominions.[6] While this scheme was being considered at the French court, Milutin entered into negotiations with the papacy regarding ecclesiastical reunion—a necessary preliminary to the French alliance. The papacy had long been interested in Serbia, hoping that through Queen Dowager Helena the entire country might ultimately be won to papal jurisdiction, for it must be remembered that there already existed six Roman Catholic episcopal sees within the realm. Popes Nicholas IV (1288) and Benedict XI (1303) had initiated the program of winning Serbia to Roman Catholicism,[7] and the policy was continued by the first French pope of the period of "the Babylonian captivity", Clement V (1305-14), who wrote Milutin a letter recommending the archbishop of Antivari to his good graces and addressing the King as his *carissimo in Christo filio*.[8] Clement was therefore more than pleased when the Serbian king ap-

---

6. Thalloczy, *Acta res Albaniae*, I, nos. 588-89.
7. Theiner, A., *Monumenta historica Hungariae*, I, Nos. 581, 653.
8. Theiner, A., *Mon. Slav. merid.*, I, No. 176, p. 124.

proached him with a cautious inquiry as to the terms of admission into the Roman church to be required of him in case he should decide to join it. Pope Clement replied in 1308, submitting to the opportunist Serbian king a tolerably full creed, and demanding as the condition of Milutin's admission the acceptance of the *Filioque* clause, the acknowledgment of the pope as the vicar of Christ and as the successor of Peter, possessing the right to bind and loose, and finally assent to the primacy of the Roman See.[9] But the French court was dilatory about committing itself to the project suggested by Milutin and finally the negotiations broke down; thereupon, the zeal of Milutin for the Roman church also cooled and the correspondence with the papacy was dropped.

In spite of these various political intrigues which involved Milutin in flirting with the Roman church and hence caused the Serbian archbishop a certain amount of uneasiness or even anxiety, the king was as a rule on excellent terms with the church. He held Archbishop Nicodemus (1316-24) in high esteem "as his own brother", and welcomed his cooperation in the political life of the country. Even when Nicodemus had been hegumen of Khilandar, before he had become archbishop, Milutin employed him on a political mission to the court of Constantinople. In return, the church loyally supported the king, who soon after his death despite his fourth marriage came to occupy in its regard the place of *svety kral*—the saintly king.

Milutin's illegitimate son, Stephen, who, following the well-established tradition of Serbian heirs-presumptive, had revolted against his father with the intention of seizing the throne for himself, was defeated by his father, supposedly blinded, and exiled to Constantinople. But later Archbishop Nicodemus was instrumental in reconciling Milutin with his rebellious son, and the latter was recalled. After Milutin's death (1321), when serious disturbances about the succession broke out among the rival claimants, Nicodemus steadily supported the cause of Stephen against those of Constantine, another natural son of Milutin who had been designated as his successor during the period of Stephen's disgrace, and of his cousin Vladislav, the son of Dragutin, to whom his father had reserved the throne at

9. *Ibid.*, I, No. 181, pp. 127-30.

the time of his abdication in Milutin's favor. Stephen, who claimed to have miraculously regained his sight, finally prevailed against his rivals, thanks to the support of the church. Thereupon, Nicodemus crowned him king (1321). That Stephen possessed the robust virtues characteristic of the Balkan rulers in common with others, may be judged from the manner in which he disposed of his rivals: Vladislav was exiled to Hungary, and Constantine was nailed to a cross and then sawn asunder.

In order to strengthen his somewhat defective title to the throne, Stephen assumed the family name of Urosh, and also sought support in allying himself with some outside power by marriage. With that in view, being a widower, he sought the hand (1323) of a faithful adherent of the Roman Catholic church, Blanche, daughter of Philip of Taranto. In order to gain her hand, he was willing to accept Roman Catholicism. Pope John XXII sent Bishop Bertrand of Brindisi to carry out the provisions of the treaty of religious union accepted by Stephen, and also granted the king a certificate annulling his illegitimacy. Considering the fact that Stephen had gained his throne largely by the aid of the church, his action manifested a base form of opportunism as well as ingratitude. Fortunately, the marriage negotiations in the end broke down and in 1236 Stephen married a Greek princess, Maria Palaeologa; with this marriage the pro-Roman policy was abandoned. Henceforth, Stephen remained loyal to the Orthodox church, although he did not shower it with as munificent gifts as his predecessor had done. Stephen built only one monastery (1330), the important establishment at Dechany, from which he has been known in history as Stephen Urosh III Dechansky.

His reign (1321-31) coincides with the greater part of the term of office of one of the most outstanding archbishops of mediaeval Serbia, Daniel or Danilo II (1324-38). Born of a noble family, Daniel had served at Milutin's court as royal secretary before he became a monk. Eventually he found his way to Khilandar, and as most of his predecessors in the archepiscopal office, became hegumen of this famous Serbian establishment. It was during this time that Daniel began the composition of that important, even though patriotically heavily biased and abjectly servile, source of

Serbian history, entitled *Genealogy of the Serbian Kings and Archbishops,* which placed him in the ranks of cultural leaders of his people; this work was continued by some anonymous writer or writers after Daniel's death. Then at the request of King Milutin, Daniel returned to Serbia and became bishop of Banya, later being associated with Archbishop Sava III as coadjutor and administrator of the archdiocese. When Nicodemus became archbishop, Daniel's services were apparently no longer needed and he was given a bishopric in Hum, but later resumed his direction of the Khilandar monastery. With his monastic community, he acted as an intermediary between Stephen, then exiled to Constantinople on account of his revolt against Milutin, and finally, with the help of Archbishop Nicodemus, brought about a reconciliation between the father and the son. After Nicodemus' death (1324), Daniel was called to the highest office in the gift of the Serbian church.

As archbishop, Daniel II became remarkable for his zeal in the discharge of his duties, staunchly opposing the pro-Roman policy of the king during the period of the latter's wooing of Blanche. Moreover, Daniel won great fame as an outstanding writer, being credited with having written "a large number of works". In spite of the rather low level of Serbian culture at the time, which fell far beneath that of their Greek or Latin neighbors, Daniel belonged to the chosen few who in themselves gave promise of an indigenous culture which was to come. The archbishop remained a cultural force and encouraged others to labor in behalf of Serbian letters and arts during the reign of the three greatest mediaeval Serbian kings, Milutin, Stephen Dechansky, and Stephen Dushan. Besides his administrative and literary labors, he is credited with the building and repair of some thirty churches and monasteries. He likewise took a most active part in the political life of the country, and exercised a potent influence upon the rulers. No important decision was taken, especially by Stephen Dechansky and Stephen Dushan, without the archbishop's knowledge and advice.

The growing power of Serbia naturally evoked envy and resentment on the part of that other great Slavic power in the Balkans, Bulgaria. Hence, the Bulgarian Tsar Michael decided to put an end to the growing hegemony of

Serbia by force of arms. He therefore entered into an
alliance with the Empire, the object of which was an invasion of the Serbian territory. But Stephen learned in
time of the plot, and hurried his forces toward his eastern
boundary to intercept the invading army. At Velbuzhd, the
present-day Bulgarian city of Kustendil, the two armies
met, and on June 28, 1330, a decisive battle took place there.
The Bulgarians were utterly defeated, Tsar Michael losing his life in the engagement. His ally, the Byzantine
Emperor Andronicus II, having learned of the defeat, quickly withdrew his armies from the southern border of the
Serbian territory where he had planned to deliver his attack.

The victory of Velbuzhd raised Serbia to the rank of
the dominant power in the Balkans. Had King Stephen
united Bulgaria with his own land at the time, when he well
could have done so, the history of southern Slavs would
most likely have been spared the instances of isolated im-
potence and of fratricidal wars for which it is unhappily
noted. But he contented himself merely with making Bulgaria a Serbian dependency, permitting it to exercise
autonomy. His mild policy excited disaffection among
the nobles in Serbia, which led to the usual revolt of the
heir presumptive against his father. The twenty-two-year-
old son of Stephen, also named Stephen and later surnamed
Dushan, placed himself at the head of the nobles dissatisfied
with the weak policy of the king, and raised a standard of
revolt in the zhupa of Zeta which he governed. He succeeded in defeating the loyalist army and in capturing his
father, who was then declared deposed. Thereupon, Archbishop Daniel crowned the young Stephen king (Sept. 8,
1331). Stephen Dechansky was strangled two months
later, certainly with the connivance, if not by the order, of
the young ruler. It is possible that young Stephen's surname, Dushan, was derived from the word for strangling
or throttling—*dushiti*—which would be an eloquent re-
minder to the mighty ruler of the manner in which he had
gained the throne.

From the political point of view, Stephen Dushan
(1331-56) was the greatest of the Serbian mediaeval rulers.
During his reign, the Serbian state as well as the church
attained the summit of their respective power and influence.

10

Dushan revived the project of King Milutin of making himself master of the Byzantine Empire, and this dream dictated his policy throughout his reign. Although he was not a really great statesman or organizer, he had the means and the energy to seize the opportunity offered in the weakness and disorganization of the Byzantine Empire, and thus to build up the power of his own realm. In the first place, by marrying the sister of the Bulgarian Tsar John Alexander, Dushan succeeded in retaining Bulgaria as his dependency. Furthermore, because of the pressure exerted upon him by the warlike party which had placed him on the throne, Dushan immediately invaded the imperial territory, and with the aid of a turn-coat Byzantine general, Sergiannos, he conquered a great part of Macedonia, and even laid siege to Salonica. But the threatened invasion of his own territory by the Hungarian King, Charles Robert, induced him to accept the terms of peace offered him by Emperor Andronicus III (1334) by which Dushan retained the northern regions of Macedonia and returned the southern. Thereupon, he turned his arms against the Hungarian king who had in the meantime invaded Rascia. Again he was victorious, and annexed a great part of Machva to his possessions. Between 1336 and 1340 he conquered the Angevin possessions in Albania except Durazzo, and northern Epirus as far as Joannina.

When Emperor Andronicus III died in 1341, a civil war broke out between the two regents of the boy-emperor, John V, John Cantacuzene, and the dowager-empress, Anne of Savoy. During the trying period of anarchy which ensued, Dushan was able to fish most successfully in the muddy waters of the Byzantine Empire. In the wars that broke out between John Cantacuzene, who in 1342 yielded to the importunate requests of his friends and had himself crowned co-emperor, and the partisans of Anne and John V, Dushan joined one or another camp as advantage dictated. Ultimately, the Serbian king conquered all of Macedonia with the exception of Salonica, and all of Epirus. Albania had been a part of his possessions for some time. When he finally incorporated within his dominions even the important city of Seres (1345) he came to regard himself as the true successor of Andronicus III in place of the woman and the small boy (Anne with John V) or the usurper (John

Cantacuzene), who fought for the possession of the Byzantine throne.

Consequently, in 1345 Dushan determined formally to assume the imperial title, and proclaimed himself "Tsar of the Serbians and the Greeks" or in Greek "Emperor of Serbia and Romania". But in order to be crowned properly, he had to secure patriarchal cooperation, since in accordance with Byzantine legal notions no one but a patriarch could crown an emperor. But any thought of securing the services of the Ecumenical Patriarch John XIV (1334-47), the strong partisan of Anne and John V, was out of the question. Hence, some other means of solving the difficulty had to be found. But since patriarchs who might be induced to grant Dushan's claims were not plentiful, he determined to create one of his own.

The Great Council held in Skoplye (the ancient see of Justiniana Prima) in April, 1346, was attended, besides Dushan's own archbishops of Pech and Ohrid—Joannicius II and Nicholas—and the Greek metropolitans and bishops from the territory recently conquered from the Empire, also by the Bulgarian Patriarch Simeon and the representatives of the Athos monasteries. This assembly found it advisable to bow to the will of the mighty Serbian ruler and to raise the rank of the autocephalous Serbian archbishopric of Pech to that of patriarchate, and elected Archbishop Joannicius II, (1337-54) formerly Dushan's logothete, the first patriarch. A little later, on April 16, the Council acclaimed the Serbian kingdom an empire, and the newly-created Serbian patriarch thereupon crowned Dushan with a tiara as a true successor of Constantine, his wife an empress, and their son a king. At the same time the double-headed Byzantine eagle was introduced as the emblem of the new empire. Although the action had the support of the two autocephalous sees within Dushan's territories—Pech and Ohrid—and of the patriarch of Bulgaria, it was done without the approval of the ecumenical patriarch. Nevertheless, for a period of seven years thereafter the last-named dignitary saw no reason to protest.

The establishment of the Serbian patriarchate entailed the proclaiming of Pech as the patriarchal see, in spite of the fact that historically the see of Ohrid had a much better claim to that distinction. It must be remembered that

prior to the Greek conquest of Bulgaria (1018) Ohrid actually held the rank of patriarchate. But the reason for preferring Pech is obvious: Pech was a Serbian national see,
while Ohrid had soon after the Greek conquest become a
Greek see and had retained that character ever since. Nevertheless, even though Pech had been raised to a patriarchate,
Ohrid was not deprived of its independence; on the contrary, Dushan not only confirmed its privileges, but the
famous *Code of Laws of Tsar Dushan* even extended them, so
that it then possessed a greater measure of self-government
than it had enjoyed before. Along with the raising of the
rank of Pech, the chief bishoprics were raised to the rank
of metropolitanates.

Since the Byzantine Empire was torn by internal dissensions between the two imperial rivals, for Emperor John
V Palaeologus refused to recognize John VI Cantacuzene
as co-emperor, Dushan was able to continue his conquests
practically undisturbed; in 1349 he added Thessaly to his
possessions. It was his policy in conquered territories in-
habited by a non-Serbian population not to change the ac-
customed forms of government but to leave the governmental system largely as he had found it. In spite of this
policy, however, the adding of new Greek territories involved Dushan in difficulties with the ecumenical patriarch:
because of the doubtful loyalty of the Greek bishops of
the newly acquired territory, Dushan finally decided to
drive them out of their sees (1351) and to substitute Serbian bishops for them. But the latter were placed under
the jurisdiction of the Pech patriarchate.

It seems that it was now that Patriarch Joannicius assumed the title of "Patriarch of the Serbs and the Greeks",
which his successor, Sava, also bore. It was this action,
which seemed to suggest that the Serbian patriarch aimed
to usurp the place of the ecumenical patriarch just as his
imperial master intended to do in regard to the Byzantine
rulers, which prompted the ecumenical patriarch to take
vigorous measures against the Serbian church and state.
This circumstance also explains the fact why it was
not until the term of office of Patriarch Callistos I of Constantinople (1350-54) that the adverse action was taken.
Previous patriarchs, John XIV (1334-47), in whose time

the Serbian patriarchate had been set up and Isidore I (1347-50), his successor, had raised no protest against the establishment or the canonicity of the Pech patriarchate. But Callistos, whom Emperor John Cantacuzene had raised to the patriarchal throne in 1350, two years later anathematized the Serbian Patriarch Joannicius II and the whole Serbian church, Emperor Stephen Dushan and the whole Serbian nation. The reason given for this action specified that it was on account of "the rank and the cities". This phrase, in the light of the above explanation, must be understood to refer to Dushan's assumption of the title of emperor of the Serbians and the Greeks, as well as Joannicius' assumption of the title of patriarch of the Serbians and the Greeks, and the transfer of ecclesiastical jurisdiction over the newly conquered Greek territories to the patriarchate of Pech. One of Callistos' successors, Patriarch Philotheos (1364-76), reaffirmed the condemnation and specified the same reasons (1371).

Dushan's title to fame rests not only on his unprecedented success in conquering imperial territory, but also on his work as legislator. *The Code of Stephen Dushan*[10] reveals a great deal that is of interest in the study of ecclesiastical conditions of the time. It was adopted by a council (1349) composed of "the illustrious Patriarch Lord Joannicius and all the hierarchs and clergy, great and small, and by me, the Orthodox Tsar Stephen, and all nobility of my tsardom, both great and small".[11]

In this celebrated *Code,* the spiritual freedom of the church and the duties and privileges of the hierarchy and the clergy were confirmed and defined. The entire church was subject to the tsar, the patriarch, the logothete, and no one else.[12] The patriarch as well as bishops possessed jurisdiction in matters reserved for them. But when a prisoner escaped from the patriarchal court to the tsar's or vice versa, he was granted the right of asylum at the place to which he had escaped.[13] Legislation against selling of ecclesiastical offices on the part of the patriarch or the tsar was quite strict: whoever should be found appointing metropolitans, bishops, or hegumens by means of simony, was to be

---

10. Novaković, S., *Zakonik Stefana Dushana.* Beograd, 1898.
11. *Ibid.,* p. 6.
12. *Ibid.,* p. 25.
13. *Ibid.,* art. 113.

anathematized.[14] But this provision apparently had passed through many revisions; the Mt. Athos text changes the punishment for simony from anathema to deprivation of office for him who was guilty of simony and also for those he had appointed.

In spiritual matters, all men must obey their bishops. If a man transgressed against the episcopal prerogatives, whether wittingly or unwittingly, he must make proper amends; otherwise, he was liable to excommunication.[15] Spiritual matters were reserved for the episcopal court; laymen exercising jurisdiction in these reserved cases were to be fined three hundred gulden (perpers, ὑπέρπυρον).[16] Defamation of a bishop, monk, or priest was punishable by a fine of one hundred gulden. In a case of murder of one of these ecclesiastical persons, the perpetrator of the crime was to be put to death by hanging.[17]

As for the monastic dignitaries, the hegumens were appointed by the tsar, but it was specified that they could not be appointed without the consent of the church, which seems to mean that the tsar could not appoint them of his own will contrary to the wish of the church.[18] But once appointed, they had charge over the entire establishment: the buildings, horses, mares, sheep, and everything else.[19] Moreover, the hegumens were enjoined to reside in the monastery over which they presided, and had to rule their monastic community in accordance with the established rules. They were bound in important cases to seek advice of the elders of the monastery. All monasteries were to be governed by uniform rules.[20]

Monastic legislation occupies a good deal of space in the *Code*. In the first place, no one could enter a monastery or a convent without an explicit permission of his or her bishop.[21] But for some reason not clearly specified, those born in villages belonging to a monastery could not join that monastery but had to go to some other district.[22] This

---

14. Art. 13.
15. Art. 4.
16. Art. 12.
17. Art. 95.
18. Art. 14.
19. Art. 35.
20. Art. 15.
21. Art. 196.
22. Art. 18.

was possibly done in order to prevent the monk from keeping in too close touch with his own family. That some monks and nuns actually were in the habit of leaving their monasteries and living at home is to be inferred from the enactment which forbade such practice.[23] If the monk abandoned his vows, he was to be imprisoned until he returned to his obedience.[24] Monasteries were granted various exemptions and privileges: they were free from the ordinary duty of conveying the goods of the tsar when he was making his usual rounds.[25] The horses of the tsarist transport must not be quartered upon monastery stables or monastic villages.[26] Monks were taken under special protection of the law in cases of molestation.[27] On the other hand, it was the duty of monasteries possessing at least one thousand houses to support fifty monks.[28] Moreover, the monasteries served in a fashion as relief stations: they were charged with the duty of relieving the poor in accordance with the stipulations of the founders. Wherever the monastery authorities failed in this duty, they were to be deprived of their office.[29]

As for the churches within the dominion of the tsar, all were freed from all kinds of duties.[30] They were subject to the two "great churches", namely the patriarchal churches of Pech and Ohrid.[31] But the Greek monasteries had been granted full autonomy and were exempt from patriarchal jurisdiction. Whoever should demolish a church, was to be put to death.[32] Landowners were free to erect private chapels on their estates, such foundations not being subject to the tsarist or patriarchal jurisdiction. The patron had the right to nominate for priest a candidate of his own choice and to demand from the local bishop his consecration. In such cases, bishop had jurisdiction only over spiritual matters[33] in connection with the private chapel.

It appears that there were priests in the country who

23. Art. 17.
24. Art. 19.
25. Art. 23.
26. Art. 38.
27. Art. 30.
28. Art. 16.
29. Art. 28.
30. Art. 26.
31. Art. 27.
32. Art. 130.
33. Art. 45.

had not received ordination at the hands of the eparchial
bishops. This is clear from the provision that bishops were
to ordain priests for all parishes, and such clergy as had
not been ordained in the canonical manner were to be driven
out.[34] The cleric caught in receiving bribes was to suffer
corporal punishment and was to be expelled.[35] Priests were
ordinarily supported from the produce of the glebe attached
to the parish. In such cases, although their ordinary status
as serfs was not actually changed, they owed their master
no service for the use of the glebe, and were in effect free.
In cases however where no glebe was attached to the church,
the priest was entitled to the use of three fields for which
he owed his master no service. But for any fields beyond
that extent he had to render service just like any other serf.[36]
The master was duty-bound to protect the priest in his
right to the above-specified living. In case the master failed to do so, the priest could complain to his bishop; if the
master failed to heed the admonitions of the bishop, the
priest was free to leave his master.[37]

Ever since the days of St. Sava the church had exerted
itself to stamp out the pagan marriage rites and to impose
upon the people the convention of the Christian marriage
rites. This is clearly reflected in Stephen's *Code*. It was
ordered that the marriage ceremony must be performed
either by a bishop or by a cleric appointed by him.[38] Moreover, marriage had to be solemnized in a church.[39] When a
"half-believer" (a heretic not specifically defined) married
an Orthodox woman, he must receive baptism; if he refused, he was to be deprived of his wife and children and a
part of his property was taken from him for their support.[40]

The intolerant zeal of the dominant Orthodox church
is reflected in the legislation regarding the Roman Catholics
and other non-Orthodox or heretical groups. Roman Catholicism, uniformly referred to as the "Latin heresy", was
indeed and of necessity tolerated in regions where its adherents formed the majority of the population as well as
among the foreign settlers—the numerous German miners

34. Art. 11.
35. Art. 24.
36. Art. 31.
37. Art. 65.
38. Art. 2.
39. Art. 3.
40. Art. 9.

and the merchants. But any proselytism was strictly forbidden. If a "Christian" (i. e. an Orthodox) should adopt "the azymite rite", he was to be exhorted to return to "Christianity". If he refused, he was to be punished in accordance with the provisions of the holy fathers.[41] These provisions were specified in another redaction of this article as confiscation of property and exile; the proselytizing Latin clergy were to be imprisoned and their church confiscated. Moreover, to prevent the "Latin heresy" from spreading from the infected foci—the cities and market places—the patriarch was instructed to appoint special archpriests for such places to instruct those who had fallen into the heresy in order to regain them to the true faith.[42] A Roman Catholic priest who converted "Christians" to the "Latin faith" was to be punished.[43] That these provisions did not apply to Roman Catholics living in the land but only to those who had fallen away from Orthodoxy by adopting the "Latin faith" may be clearly inferred from the provision ordering a mixed jury to try cases between Orthodox Serbians and foreign merchants. Such juries were to consist of equal numbers of Serbians and of the nationals of the foreign party.[44]

Heresy, especially Bogomilism which was known in Serbia under the designation of the Babun faith, was still extant, as the pertinent legislation proves. A heretic found living among the Orthodox population was to be branded on the face and exiled. Anyone affording him an asylum was to suffer the same punishment. This of course obviously referred only to the native Serbian heretics. Specifically against the Bogomils the *Code* decreed that whoever should preach "the Babun doctrine", if a noble, must pay one hundred gulden; if a commoner, twelve gulden, but in addition must receive a flogging.[45] Apparently, Bogomilism was upheld by the nobles to some extent. Such then in brief was the ecclesiastical legislation codified by Stephen Dushan's legal advisers.

Patriarch Joannicius II died in 1354, being followed

---

41.   Art. 6.
42.   Art. 7.
43.   Art. 8.
44.   Art. 153.
45.   Art. 85.

two years later by Emperor Stephen Dushan[46]—both out
of communion with the patriarchate of Constantinople. After the death of Dushan, then only 48 years old, a rapid
decline of the Serbian empire set in. Had he lived and carried out his project of conquering Constantinople—an undertaking by no means impossible—who knows whether
the Turkish conquest of the Balkans would have taken
place?

Under the nineteen-year old son of Dushan, Stephen
Urosh V (1356-66), the Serbian empire almost immediately fell apart into separate principalities ruled by selfish and
ambitious princes who were apparently capable of but two
thoughts: to perpetuate their power in their own families
and to prey upon the territories of their neighbors. The
young feeble tsar was unable to preserve even an appearance of central authority with the result that Dushan's
empire was soon to fall piecemeal to its powerful and well-
organized neighbors, the Turks.

The Turkish danger, which threatened the Byzantine
Empire as well as the Serbian and Bulgarian territories,
showed Emperor John V Palaeologus, who became sole
emperor after John Cantecuzene's abdication in 1355, the wisdom of opposing a united front to the common danger.
Hence, he took the initiative in an attempt to negotiate an
alliance with Stephen Urosh; but in order to conclude such
defensive alliance, it was necessary first to secure ecclesiastical pacification between the Constantinopolitan and the
Serbian patriarchates. Consequently, in the summer of
1363 John sent Patriarch Callistos, the hierarch who had
proclaimed the anathema against the Serbian church in
1352, to the widow of Emperor Dushan, then nun Elizabeth,
living at a convent in Seres. Through her John hoped to
gain access to the youthful Tsar Urosh and to win him for
his design of a united attack upon the Turks. The unlucky Callistos, to whom the task must have been particularly distasteful, loyally obeyed the command of his master,
but before any results could be secured, he sickened at Seres
and died. Emperor John did not repeat his attempt, and
thus a wise, constructive scheme which could not but benefit
the Christian cause in the Balkans, had it been consummated, was allowed to fall in abeyance.

46. Cf. Miklosich, F., *Monumenta Serbica*, CXL.

The insensate rivalry of the Serbian princelings brought about the downfall of Stephen Urosh V in 1366. One of the Serbian despots, the cup-bearer and "guardian" of the young tsar, Vukashin, whose territories adjoined the Danube, consumed by a desire for extending his power and lands, rose up in revolt against Urosh, drove him from the throne, and himself assumed the tsarist crown and extended his sway over the lands which had been ruled by the dispossessed young tsar. He then rewarded his brother, John Uglyesha, who had aided him in the revolt, with a despotate comprising the territories round Seres, which were largely Greek in population.

Despot John Uglyesha wisely took steps to restore his diminutive dominion to the ecclesiastical jurisdiction of the ecumenical patriarch, from whom they had been wrested by Dushan and on account of which Callistos had laid an anathema upon all Serbia. Uglyesha first took care to establish himself firmly in his rule. Since his Greek subjects felt restive under the sentence of excommunication pronounced upon them, without their fault, and hence exerted a strong pressure in the direction of a pacific policy, Uglyesha judged it expedient to make peace with the ecumenical patriarch. In March, 1368, he sent his representatives to the new patriarch, Philotheos (1364-76), humbly beseeching him to remove the sentence resting upon his people and offering to restore all eparchies within his land to his jurisdiction.[47] Nevertheless, the proposed restoration was not consummated till 1371,[48] when Emperor John had returned from his Western trip where he had sought aid against the Turks and even had accepted church union with the Latins to accomplish his purpose. Thereupon, the excommunication of John Uglyesha's territories was repealed and he with his people was restored to communion.[49] This action, of course, did not extend to the rest of the Serbian lands, which remained ecclesiastically estranged for four years longer.

The first of the disasters which ultimately were to put an end to the mediaeval Serbian empire overtook Tsar

---

47. Miklosich, F., *Monumenta Serbica*, CLXII; Miklosich-Müller, *Acta Patr. Const.*, I, 562-63.
48. Miklosich, F., *op. cit.*, 171, p. 182.
49. *Ibid.*, No. 169, p. 181.

Vukashin in 1371. The alarming progress of the Turks in Thrace, where they had made Hadrianople the center of their domains, led Vukashin to resolve upon an attempt to check them. Foolishly supposing that his and John Uglyesha's armies would suffice for the task, he invaded Thrace beyond Philippopolis. There on the River Maritsa a greatly inferior Turkish force surprised them and so thoroughly defeated them that the Christian armies were almost wiped out. Both Vukashin and John Uglyesha perished in the struggle, the former by the hand of his own servant. Macedonia purchased its autonomy only at the price of a yearly tribute and of military service to be rendered to the Turks.

The perilous dignity of Serbian tsardom now passed to Lazar Hrebelyanovich, who wisely assumed the modestly diminished title of "Prince" instead of the imperial title so proudly borne by Stephen Dushan. The disastrous defeat on the Maritsa thoroughly alarmed the new bearer of the Serbian supreme authority—whatever that was worth— and showed him the folly of disunion of Christian forces in the face of a relentless and powerful enemy. When therefore an occasion arose to terminate the ecclesiastical schism which had blocked the possibility of cooperation between Serbia and the feeble Empire, he did not hesitate to show himself eager to take advantage of it. The Serbian monks living on Mt. Athos experienced many and serious hardships on account of the excommunication resting upon the whole Serbian church. Spurred by the sorry plight of his monastic confraternity, an old Serbian monk of the Holy Mountain, Isaiah by name, journeyed to Lazar's court and presenting the case to the prince, gained him quickly for the project of ecclesiastical reconciliation with the Greeks. A council was called to discuss the question which, commissioning Isaiah to go to Constantinople, empowered him to offer submission of the Serbian church to the patriarch. Isaiah reached the Byzantine capital in 1375 and presented the Serbian request for reunion both to Emperor John V and to Patriarch Philotheos. The offer was gladly accepted in view of its obvious political advantages to both parties, and the desired reconciliation was effected. But alas! circumstances were soon to prove that it came too late! Nevertheless, the patriarchal representatives were dispatched to the Serbian capital, Prizren, where they solemnly revoked the anathema laid upon Tsar Stephen Dushan, Patriarchs Joannicius II and Sava IV, Tsar Stephen Urosh V, and all Serbians who had died during the schism. Thereupon, the Serbian church was restored to communion with the ecumenical patriarchate on the following terms: the autocephaly of the Serbian church was fully acknowledged, and its rank as patriarchate was confirmed; the only proviso made was to the effect that in case the Serbians should ever in the future conquer Greek territory, the metropolitans resident there should not be displaced by Serbians. As circumstances were shortly to prove, the fears of any future Serbian aggression were grotesquely superfluous!

The steady, relentless onward march of the Turkish armies presaged the inevitable collision between them and the Serbian forces. When in 1386 Nish was conquered by the Turks, Prince Lazar was forced to conclude an ignominious peace with them by a promise of tribute and of auxiliary troops. Thereupon, he decided to make a desperate test of his fortune; allying himself with his neighbors, Tsar John Shishman of Bulgaria and Prince Mirchea of Wallachia, the powerful Bosnian King Stephen I Tvrtko, and even the Croatian ban, Lazar took the field against Sultan Murad's armies. The decisive battle, the subject of numberless popular Serbian ballads and elegies for centuries afterwards, was fought at Kosovo Polye—the Field of Blackbirds, on June 15, 1389—the fatal *Vidov Dan,* St. Vitus' Day. In spite of the valor of the Christian armies who learned to cooperate but too late, and in spite of the assassination of Murad by a noble Serb, Milosh Kobilich, Murad's son, Beyazid, who thereupon assumed command of the Turkish forces, all but completely annihilated the armies of the Balkan league. Prince Lazar was taken prisoner and beheaded in the tent in which the dying Murad lay.

The battle of Kosovo Polye sounded the death knell of Serbian independence. Although the greatly diminished Serbian principality survived the tragic defeat of 1389 by another seventy years, the legendary estimate of the meaning of Kosovo Polye as a symbol of the loss of national freedom had much to justify it. *Vidov Dan* from that time forth was mournfully commemorated throughout the Serbian lands as the day on which free Serbia had died, and when finally the dream of Greater Serbia was realized after

the World War by the unification of the Serbians, Monte-
negrins, Croatians, and the Slovenes, the Constitution
effecting the unification was purposely proclaimed on the *Vidov
Dan* to symbolize the undoing of the defeat suffered 528
years previously.

Sultan Beyazid I recognized the youthful son of Prince
Lazar, Stephen Lazarevich (1389-1427), as the ruler of the
greatly diminished Serbian principality, on condition of being given Lazar's daughter in marriage, of an annual tribute, and of military service. King Tvrtko of Bosnia likewise retained his royal crown, and even added Dalmatia
and Croatia to his already extensive territories. Other
smaller fry among the Serbian princelings continued their
rule. But with most of these Serbian despots it was but a
shadow of their former independent power. Stephen
Lazarevich found it prudent to adopt a Turcophil policy,
and his contingent of troops struck the decisive blow on
the Turkish side in the defeat of Emperor Sigismund's motley armies in the battle of Nicopolis in 1396. He assisted
his master Beyazid even in expeditions against other Serbian princes. It is sad to relate that despite these tragic
circumstances in which the Serbians found themselves, the
princes had not learned to pool their resources against their
common enemy. George Brankovich, a nephew of Stephen
Lazarevich, dissatisfied with his lordship of the territory
of Prishtina, rose up against Stephen to grasp from him
the shadowy semblance of power. Their armies met at the
ill-fated Kosovo Polye (1403), but the battle resulting
largely in a draw, the rivals accepted the *status quo ante*. But
this was not the last time such shameful internecine and
fratricidal wars were waged! Stephen was obliged to go to
war with his brother Vlkan and once again with George
Brankovich. But despite all, he retained his power to the
end of his life.

Stephen Lazarevich was a person of pronounced cultural, especially literary, tastes, and converted his court
into a busy literary center. He was himself an author, and
encouraged translations from Greek to be made by the literary men he had gathered about him. He likewise supported art, and founded the magnificent monastery of Manassia.

Toward the end of his life, having preserved his unstable throne by rare diplomacy and faithful service to the

various Turkish sultans, Stephen Lazarevich decided to appeal to Hungary for protection of his realm. He recognized Emperor Sigismund as his overlord, and obtained confirmation of George Brankovich, who had so often striven to supplant him, as his successor. He died in 1427.

Despot George Brankovich (1427-56) proved himself a shrewd diplomat and *real-politiker*. His policy was consistently and unchivalrously pro-Turkish. In order to appease Murad II who demanded from him the surrender of Serbia, he promised the sultan the hand of his daughter Maria with some Serbian territory as her dowry, an annual tribute, military aid, and abandonment of any connection with Hungary. On these terms he retained his precarious throne which was secure to him only so long as the sultan regarded a tributary state more profitable to himself than an annexed one.

But even then George Brankovich was not permitted to reign in peace: the wrath of the sultan was aroused over the despot's erection of a strong fortress at Semendria,— the present Smederevo—on the southern bank of the Danube, and by his surrender of Belgrade to the Hungarians. The latter action was prompted by the despot's desire to secure for himself the aid of Hungary. Murad invaded Serbia, laid siege to Semendria, to which George had moved his capital from Krushevats, and before Brankovich could secure Hungarian aid, took it (1439). Thereupon, he occupied almost all of Serbia, which thus became a Turkish province. George Brankovich fled and took refuge at various places, ending finally in Dubrovnik.

Hungary now took fright at the perilous contiguity of the Turkish boundary. Allying himself with various neighboring rulers equally threatened, and securing as the leader of the expedition a man who became the most famous Turkokiller, the Roumanian general John Hunyadi, the Hungarian King Vladislav I undertook a crusading expedition across the Danube. The invasion was successful, and Murad was compelled to sign an ignominious treaty of peace at Szegedin (1444). Among other provisions, it was stipulated that Brankovich was to be restored to his despotate of the whole of Serbia, although he had to pay half its annual revenue to Murad.

From that time on, George Brankovich judged it expedient to pursue a policy of opposition to the various attempts made by Hungary against the Turks in order to retain the sultan's favor. When by the advice of the papal legate, Cardinal Julian Cesarini, Vladislav I decided to break the treaty so recently agreed upon and treacherously to attack Murad once more, Brankovich refused to join in the treachery. The expedition was most disastrously defeated at Varna (1444). Despot George likewise pursued the policy of armed neutrality during the expedition which ended in the rout of the Christian forces in the third battle of the Kosovo Polye (1448), at which time he even took Hunyadi prisoner, only to relinquish him to Hungary later.

In spite of his cautious and from the point of view of the Hungarians craven policy, the despot did not prevent a Turkish attack upon his territories. Sultan Mohammed II who ascended the throne in 1451, after having taken Constantinople in 1453, decided that the moment to annex Serbia had come. He sent an ultimatum to George Brankovich, ordering him to surrender his country to him. The Serbian despot did not obey, and with the aid of Hungary was able to withstand the Turkish invasion for the rest of his life (1456).

Even the sorry remnant of George Brankovich's one time possessions gave rise to criminal intrigues among his heirs. The despot's successor, his youngest son Lazar, probably poisoned his mother Irene with whom he was supposed to divide the rule. His sister, the former wife of Sultan Murad, together with her brother took refuge at the court of Mohammed. But Lazar III did not rule long. He died in 1458. By his direction, his daughter married Stephen Tomashevich of Bosnia, and the latter, with the help of the Hungarian King Matthias Corvinus, assumed the rule over Lazar's diminutive realm. But the Serbs of Semendria revolted against him because of his reputation for zeal in behalf of Roman Catholicism and of his pro-Hungarian policy, preferring to submit to Mohammed II. Hence, they opened the gates of Semendria to the Turks. By 1459 Serbia, with the exception of Belgrade, became a Turkish pashalik.

Thereupon, the church became the heart of Serbian nationalism—a function which it performed till the recovery of autonomy in the beginning of the nineteenth century. The patriarch in a way assumed the headship of the nation. Orthodoxy became synonymous with the Serbian nationality so that those Serbs who had accepted Islam were regarded as lost to the nation, and as having become Turks. It was this strong sense of the national character of the Orthodox church as much as loyalty to the faith of their fathers which accounts for the fidelity and heroic steadfastness with which Serbians upheld their faith despite the horrible and often inhuman persecution by the Turks.

BOGOMILISM IN BOSNIA AND HUM

During the reign of the mighty organizer of the independent Serbian state, Grand-Zhupan Stephen Nemanya (1168-95), Bogomilism became an issue in the internal politics of Rascia. Nemanya well understood the anti-governmental tendencies of the movement and discerned in it a danger to his power. He proclaimed the Orthodox rite to be the religion of the state, although he greatly exerted himself to keep on good terms with the Roman Catholic West, the good-will of which was essential to him. Bogomilism, which entered his territory at an unknown date and gained a considerable power, opposed his centralizing ecclesiastical, political, and social policy. When he brought a proposal of suppressing the movement before a Council, he found that many nobles were staunch adherents of the movement and opposed to any persecuting measures against it. It was not until after stormy scenes had occurred that the Council agreed to exterminate Bogomilism by force of arms. The sect rose up in defense of its faith, and Nemanya was forced to conduct a crusade against it. The armed uprising of the Bogomils collapsed after they had suffered serious losses. Thereupon, large numbers of the sectaries took refuge in the neighboring territories, Bosnia and Hum, although some remained, adopting the "protective coloration" of outward acceptance of Orthodoxy.

That Bogomilism actually survived in Serbia is manifest from the fact that Tsar Stephen Dushan (1331-55) inserted a paragraph[1] in his famous *Law Code* (1349-54) according to which any one preaching Bogomilism—known in Serbia under the name of the Babun movement—was to be fined in accordance with his means.

From Serbia, Bogomilism penetrated into the territory then known as Hum, but since 1448 generally designated as Herzegovina, i. e. the Land of the Herzog, as the territory of "the Duke of St. Sava" came to be known. This territory was ruled in the days of Stephen Nemanya by his

---

1. Novaković, St., *op. cit.*, par. 85, p. 67.

younger brother, Miroslav, who was at enmity with Stephen. It was for that reason that he befriended the Bogomils expelled from Serbia. Moreover, Miroslav had been carrying on a bitter feud with the ecclesiastical superior of the country, the archbishop of Spalato, a creature of the Hungarian king Béla III. To spite him, he refused to permit the archbishop to settle a Roman Catholic bishop in, the country and favored the Orthodox and the Patarenes, as the Bogomils came to be called both in Hum and in Bosnia. When Pope Alexander III (1159-81) sent his legate, Subdeacon Theobald, to Dalmatia in 1180,[2] the Bogomils must have become fairly numerous in the country, Miroslav himself having joined them, for Theobald placed the land under an interdict. When this measure proved ineffective, the pope appealed to the Hungarian-Croatian King, Béla III (1173-1196), who was the suzerain of both Hum and Bosnia, to force Miroslav to restore to the church the alienated property. How the matter ended is not known; but by 1199 Miroslav was no longer living.

Bosnia, the principality north of Hum, was ruled at the time by an able, energetic and ambitious ruler, Ban Kulin (1168-1204), who in spite of his acknowledgment of a nominal suzerainty of Hungary, possessed very extensive independent powers. His reign of thirty-six years is the brightest period of Bosnian history. Merchants of the wealthy and cultured Dubrovnik (Ragusa) planted their commercial enterprises throughout the banship,—a commercial treaty between them and Kulin being the earliest known Bosnian document (1189)—and opened silver mines which had been unworked since the days of the Romans. The Saxon miners were encouraged to settle in the country and enriched it by their industry. After their expulsion from Serbia, Bogomils found refuge in Kulin's territory, and were well received by him. They in fact found increased favor with the ban as time went on, because such policy seemed advantageous to Kulin from the political point of view.

Since Kulin strove to make his country entirely independent of any foreign domination, a policy of "splendid isolation" seemed wise. In 1120 Bosnia had voluntarily submitted to the rule of the Hungarian King Koloman—as

2. Jaffé, *Regesta*, II, No. 13694, p. 364.

Croatia (1102) and Dalmatia (1105) had done—but in 1166 the country had been conquered by the Byzantine Emperor Manuel I Comnenus, and the Hungarian overlordship had temporarily lapsed. After Manuel's death (1180), Hungary had renewed its pretentions to the overlordship, and although Ban Kulin had acknowledged the relationship nominally, his whole policy was directed toward complete independence. Hungary, on the other hand, desired to convert its nominal overlordship into an actual rule. Kulin, therefore, found it necessary to orient his policy in relation to the designs of the Hungarian King, Béla III. A religion opposed as much to Roman Catholicism as it was to Eastern Orthodoxy seemed to afford—as was often the case in the East—the needed support of the national policy of independence. Hence Kulin's friendly attitude toward the Patarenes.

The Hungarian expansionist policy received an unexpected aid from the Roman curia. In 1191 the much transferred bishopric of Bosnia once more changed hands, this time passing from the jurisdiction of Dubrovnik to that of the archbishop of Spalato. The occupant of the Spalato see at the time was a Magyar, Archbishop Peter—the same against whom Miroslav of Hum had striven—who was ready to use his spiritual authority in behalf of the secular interests of the Hungarian king. Because of the very cordial and close relations between the papacy and Béla III, the transfer of ecclesiastical jurisdiction involved a considerable political danger to Bosnia, hence greatly perturbing Ban Kulin. In order to ward off the danger threatening his independence from the papal-Hungarian quarter, the ban adopted an anti-Roman policy. In this he was encouraged by his sister, the widow of Miroslav of Hum, who lived at Kulin's court after her husband's death. Hence, in 1198 or 1199, Kulin with his wife, his sister, many relatives, and with more than 10,000 of his subjects joined the Patarene movement. At least that was the assertion which Kulin's enemy, Vlkan, the self-styled "prince of Dioclea and Dalmatia", made to Pope Innocent III, in 1199.[3] In consequence, Patarenism in course of time not only became the dominant religion in Bosnia, but spread into the neighboring countries of Croatia, Slavonia, Hungary, and Dalmatia. Arch-

---

3. Theiner, A., *Monumenta Slavorum merid.*, I. no. x, p. 6.

deacon Thomas of Spalato records in his *Historia Salonita-tum pontificum* (1266) that the sect established itself even in Spalato, the seat of the archbishop. It was led by two brothers, Matthew and Aristodius, goldsmiths by trade, who had adopted the Patarene doctrine during their sojourn in Bosnia.[4] The destruction of Zara by the Crusaders in 1202 was justified by the chronicler on the ground that the city had become heretical.

Although Vlkan did not mention the heresy by name, the pope seems to have had no doubts about its nature. On October 11, 1200,[5] he turned to the successor of Béla III, King Henry I (1196-1205), with the demand that he, as Kulin's overlord, force the latter to drive the heretics whom he designated as Patarenes out of his dominions. If Kulin should refuse, Henry was to invade the country and drive the Bosnian ban out along with the Patarenes. In other words, the pope exhorted the Hungarian king to undertake a crusade against Bosnia. As Klaić remarks, "thus began a cruel war against the Bosnian Patarenes which lasted two and half centuries, and finally culminated in the acceptance, on their part, of the Mohammedan faith and in becoming Turks, rather than to submit to the Roman See".[6]

The policy which Kulin had adopted to ward off the danger of Hungarian interference thus proved the direct occasion of it. Henry, who dreamed of extending his rule not only over Bosnia, but over Serbia and Bulgaria as well, gladly fell in with the suggestion of the pope who on his part wished to bring the whole Balkan peninsula back to the jurisdiction of the Holy See. Thus by posing as a defender of the faith, Henry could further his own expansionist schemes, although he himself was being cleverly used as an instrument of an equally ambitious papal policy.

Realizing the folly of resisting Henry's demand for abjuring Patarenism, Kulin diplomatically yielded. He offered in his behalf the rather lame excuse that he had regarded the Patarenes as good orthodox Christians and offered to send a Patarene delegation to Rome to explain to the pope their way of life, abjuring at the same time any

    4. Thomae archidiaconi, *Historia Salonitana*, cap. 24; in Klaić, V., *Poviest Bosne*, p. 58, footnote 8.
    5. Theiner, A., *opus cit.*, I, no. xx, p. 12-13.
    6. Klaić, Vjek., *Povjest Hrvata*, Zagreb, 1899, vol. I, p. 188.

errors of which they might be found guilty. The pope professed himself satisfied with the offer.[7] Kulin actually sent, in 1202, the archbishop of Dubrovnik, and Archdeacon Marinus of the same city, together with some Patarene representatives, to Rome; of course he must have known what the result would be. He therefore at the same time requested that the pope send his own legates to investigate the religious situation in Bosnia. Innocent appointed as his representatives the archbishop of Spalato, Bernard, already well known for his zeal in persecuting the Patarenes of Spalato and Trogir, and his own court chaplain, John de Casamaris. They were to learn the true state of the Bosnian church and bring the Patarenes into the bosom of the Catholic church.[8]

What measures John de Casamaris adopted to carry out his mission is not known; but they were successful. At a meeting held on April 6, 1203, at "Bolino Poili", identified with Byelopolye (White Field) by the river Bosna, in the presence of the papal legate John and Archdeacon Marinus of Dubrovnik, Ban Kulin, along with many representative Patarenes, abjured his schism in behalf of himself and the monastic communities[9]. They all swore faithful adherence to the Roman church, acknowledging it their mother and the head of the church universal; furthermore they promised to introduce altars and crosses into their places of worship, and to read the Old Testament besides the New; they likewise assented to accept Catholic priests and to observe the holy days and other church services in accordance with the usage of the Roman church: to adopt confessionals and the penitential system; to communicate at least seven times a year, that is, on Christmas, Easter, Pentecost, the Birth of Apostles Peter and Paul, the Assumption of the Virgin, her Birthday, and the All-Saints Day; and to observe canonical fasting. They obligated themselves not to admit any "Manichee" or other heretics into the membership of their monasteries, to keep women apart from men in their monasteries, and finally not to arrogate solely to themselves the name of Christians. Moreover, they promised to receive faith-

---

7. Theiner, A., *op. cit.*, I, no. xxv, p. 15.
8. *Ibid.*, I, no. xxv, p. 15.
9. Who are designated "*priores illorum hominum, qui haetenus singulariter Christiani nominis prerogativa sumus.*" Theiner, A., *op. cit.*, I, no. 35, p. 20.

fully whatever else the Roman church should impose upon them.[10]

This agreement, signed by their representatives as well as the ban, became binding upon the entire Patarene monastic community in Bosnia. To give it more solemnity, the papal legate, Ban Kulin, and two representatives of the Patarene community repaired to the court of King Henry and there solemnly promised before the king, the archbishop of Kolocz, the bishop of Pécz and many other dignitaries to observe faithfully the agreement of Byelopolye. In case of its nonobservance, Kulin was pledged to forfeit 1,000 silver marks. Moreover, to prove his sincerity, he and his wife undertook to restore a church, as the oldest extant Bosnian inscription testifies. Thus Pope Innocent triumphed in Bosnia without any bloodshed. As the most important historian of the Bogomil movement, Franjo Rački remarks, the church "did not find in Kulin a Bosnian Raimond, nor in King Henry a Simon Montford".[11]

In order to make the victory more secure, the papal legate, John, suggested in his letter to the pope dated June, 1203[12] that beside the one "moribund" bishopric existing in Bosnia, three or four others should be erected. Moreover, he urged the pope to appoint "Latins" as bishops rather than Slavs. But the suggestions were not carried out, because Hungary was secretly opposing any move that would strengthen Bosnia.

In the meantime, the Patarene movement continued to flourish, for no serious effort had been made to exterminate it. The agreement of Byelopolye was but a measure to ward off the danger threatening Kulin from the pope and the Hungarian king, and as soon as the danger was past, any attempt to enforce the agreement was abandoned. Innocent was in no position to give attention to Bosnian affairs; he was fully occupied with the Fourth and the Albigensian Crusades. Moreover, after his death (1216) his successor, Pope Honorius III (1216-27), was more than occupied with the "Hohenstauffen eaglet", Emperor Frederick II. Hungary, on the other hand, during the reign of

---

10. The document is to be found in Theiner, A., *op. cit.*, I, no. 35, p. 20.
11. Rački, Franjo: *Bogomili i Patareni*, in *Rad jugoslovenske akademije znanosti i umjetnosti*, Zagreb, Kniga VI (1869) p. 144.
12. Theiner, A., *op. cit.*, I, no. 34, p. 19.

King Andrew II (1205-35) was passing through difficult times of internal disorder, which culminated in the granting of the Golden Bull of 1222, whereby the nobles gained from the king many important privileges which lessened the power of centralized authority and led to feudal decentralization. Under such circumstances, Bosnia was left undisturbed. Kulin, doubtless, kept his word as far as he personally was concerned, but the provisions regarding the persecution of the Patarenes were not enforced.

This situation remained essentially unchanged under the successor of Kulin, Ban Stephen (1204-32). Although he himself was apparently a zealous adherent of the Roman church, he did not prevent the Patarenes from re-establishing their organization during his reign. They grew powerful not only in Bosnia, but gained strength in Croatia as well. In Hum even the ruler of the country, Peter, was a Patarene.

It was not till 1221 that measures to deal with Patarenism were revived. Pope Honorius III (1216-27) who freely acknowledged the gravity of the situation, appointed in that year his court chaplain, Subdeacon Acontius, as his legate apostolic for Bosnia and Hungary. He received unlimited power to deal with the situation as he saw fit. He was to call upon the Hungarian king and clergy to conduct a crusade against the Patarenes and their supporters. Besides, the pope wrote directly to King Andrew, the archbishop of Gran, and the rest of the Hungarian prelates, requesting them to aid his legate in any way possible. But the whole project came to naught: King Andrew, as has already been stated, had his hands full trying to deal with a revolt of his nobles, and succeeded in preventing a civil war only by granting the "Golden Bull" (1222).

Thereupon the archbishop of Kalocz, Ugrin (1219-41), came forward with an offer to organize an expedition against the Bosnian Patarenes, provided the Bosnian bishopric as well as Usora and Soli, the northern territories bordering upon Hungary, were placed under his jurisdiction.[13] To this Pope Honorius agreed in 1225. But the archbishop did not find it easy to carry out his promises. He enlisted the services of John, son of Emperor Isaac Comnenus and of Margaret, the sister of the Hungarian

---

13. *Ibid.*, I. Nos. 118, 119.

King Andrew. John consented to lead the crusade, and
even accepted from Ugrin 200 silver marks toward the project. But that was the last anyone heard of the crusade,
for John did nothing more. Pope Honorius wrote him on
January 15, 1227, remonstrating with him, but to no effect.
After Honorius' death later in the same year the whole
crusading project was abandoned.

Encouraged by the ineffectiveness of the measures
adopted against them, Bosnian Patarenes now felt strong
enough to assume the offensive. In 1232 their power was
so great that they succeeded in driving the ban, Kulin's son
Stephen, from the throne, mistrusting him on account of
his Roman Catholicism, and elevated to it their own partisan, Matthew Ninoslav (1232-50). He was a Patarene by
birth and education. The deposed Ban Stephen and his son
Sebislav succeeded, with King Andrew's aid, in retaining
for themselves a small part of their patrimony, a territory
known as Usora. Thus in the third decade of the thirteenth
century, Bosnia became once more a Patarene country *par
excellence,* for the ban, the nobles, even the bishop, and the
majority of the population were numbered among the adherents of the Patarene movement. In fact, Patarenism
became the faith of all Bosnian patriots who sought to preserve their national independence from the encroachments
of Hungary.

This extraordinary state of affairs stirred the curia to
renewed activity: the Holy See was then occupied by
Gregory IX (1227-41) who was known for his zeal in ex-
terminating the French Cathari. He now proceeded with
the same zeal against the Bosnian Patarenes. In 1232 he
ordered his legate in Hungary, Cardinal Jacob, bishop of
Penestrino, to investigate the religious conditions in Bosnia.

Cardinal Jacob found the Bosnian Catholic church in
an unbelievably sorry plight: not only were the great majority of the inhabitants Patarenes, but so were likewise most
of the nobles, with the relative of the ban, Uban Priyezda,
at their head. The pope later said that only the expelled
Sebislav, son of the former Ban Stephen, had remained faithful to Roman Catholicism, and had been "among the nobles
of the Bosnian bishopric like a lily among thorns". Even
the Roman Catholic bishop "fell into the senseless heretical
teaching", i. e., became a Patarene, excusing himself on

the ground that he had joined the sect "ex simplicitate",[14] having regarded the Patarenes as orthodox Christians. Jacob learned further that the archbishop of Dubrovnik had known of the "heresy" of the Bosnian bishop, but had regarded it with indifference.

Indignant at the situation he had found, Jacob punished the archbishop of Dubrovnik by transferring the jurisdiction over the bishopric of Bosnia to the more reliable and more zealous Hungarian archbishop of Kalocz, Ugrin, who thus succeeded in his schemes of securing it without having led a crusade against the Bosnians. The luckless bishop of Bosnia, after having abjured the heresy, was later by the order of the pope deposed from his office. Jacob succeeded even in his chief task, namely, in securing the conversion of the ban. Following the politic example of the illustrious Kulin, Matthew Ninoslav abjured the faith in which he had been born and brought up and accepted Roman Catholicism.[15] His example was followed by Uban Priyezda and other Bosnian nobles. This was done for reasons of policy, in order to put a stop to the depredations of the Croatian Herzog Koloman (1226-41), son of the Hungarian King Andrew, who posing as a defender of the faith, had annexed much of the Bosnian border territory to his own.

In place of the deposed bishop, Jacob filled the see in 1233 by appointing to it a Dominican monk, John, a Westphalian German. In order to prove his zeal for the newly adopted faith, Ban Ninoslav gave the Dominicans a considerable amount of land throughout the banship, the nobles following suit. Moreover, he took measures against the Patarenes: he deprived any noble who refused to accept Roman Catholicism of his lands, or his villages, or any other possession. This led to a strenuous opposition on the part of the disaffected nobles. Thereupon, Ninoslav appealed to Rome for help. The pope besought for him the aid of the Croatian Koloman—which was like asking a fox to guard a hen-coop—and took Bosnia under the protection of St. Peter.

Having successfully accomplished his mission, Cardinal Jacob left the country. But before the year was out,

14. *Ibid.*, I, No. 192, dated June 3, 1233.
15. *Ibid.*, I, No. 200, dated Oct. 10, 1233.

disquieting rumors regarding an alarming growth of
Patarenism again began to reach the pope. It appeared
that Bosnia once more swarmed with the sectaries, and it
was even rumored that the movement had extended to
Slavonia for the first time. In 1234 Gregory wrote that
"the number of the perfidious had so increased in Bosnia
and the neighboring provinces that the whole land, like a
trackless desert, was mourning and languishing".[16] Matthew
Ninoslav was accused of having availed himself of the military strength of the Patarenes, in which case it surely had
not been for an expedition against them. It was thus evident that the submissive attitude of the ban during Jacob's
stay in the country had been merely a ruse.

King Andrew of Hungary commissioned his son, Koloman of Croatia, to lead the crusade, and at once ceded
Bosnia to him as a reward for the services. The pope confirmed this grant in 1235.[17] By this act, Ban Matthew
Ninoslav was deprived of his office.

Highly incensed, the pope now determined upon a crusade against Bosnia: he called upon the Croatian Herzog,
Koloman, ordering him to suppress the heresy in Slavonia,
and upon King Andrew II of Hungary to invade Bosnia.
Moreover, he wrote to the Bosnian bishop, John, and to the
bishop of Zagreb, Stephen II, promising all who should join
the crusade the same indulgences as were granted to the crusaders to the Holy Land.

King Andrew of Hungary commissioned his son, Koloman of Croatia, to lead the crusade, and at once ceded
Bosnia to him as a reward for the services. The pope confirmed this grant in 1235.[17] By this act, Ban Matthew
Ninoslav was deprived of his office.

The war against heretical Bosnia broke out in 1234
and lasted five years. The crusading army was led by Koloman himself, accompanied by the Bosnian bishop, John. At
first the invading armies had no success. Ban Matthew
Ninoslav with his Bosniacs, firmly united in defense of
their national independence, was so uniformly victorious
that even Bishop John despaired of ever occupying his see
again. But the luck of the crusaders changed in the summer of 1236 when their forces were augmented by the accession of Prince Sebislav of Usora, the son of the deposed
Ban Stephen, who thus hoped to regain his patrimony.
With his help, Koloman finally gained victory over Matthew Ninoslav early in 1237 and penetrated as far as
Patarene-ruled Hum. Thereupon, the Patarenes were every-

16. *Ibid.*, I, No. 207, dated Feb. 13, 1234.
17. *Ibid.*, I., No. 229, (Aug., 1235).

where hunted down and subjected to cruel tortures. Bishop John, who had either resigned or had died during the war, was succeeded by another Dominican monk, Pons by name, who annexed Hum to his Bosnian diocese. The archbishop of Kalocz sent Dominicans into the country to help Bishop Pons bring the erring into the bosom of the true church, and to build churches and monasteries. Moreover, the archbishop built several fortresses in Bosnia "for the protection of the Bosnian church and faith and the extermination of heresy".[18]

But the rule of Koloman over Bosnia did not last long. As soon as the crusading army withdrew, Matthew Ninoslav in the autumn of 1239 rose up against the new rulers. Hungary was busy elsewhere, unable to give Bosnia any attention. Thus Matthew Ninoslav regained his banship, and to strengthen his position entered into an alliance with Dubrovnik (March, 1240). In 1241, Hungary was invaded by the Mongols and terribly ravaged. The archbishop of Kalocz, Ugrin, the great persecutor of the Patarenes, fell in the disastrous battle of Muhi (1241), along with one hundred thousand other Magyars. It required much time before King Béla IV (1235-70) was able to repair the damage done, and in the meantime the Balkans were free from the threat of his invasion. Hence Matthew Ninoslav, with the support of the Patarenes, became firmly established on his throne.

It was not till 1244 that the Patarenes again called down fire upon themselves: in that year King Béla IV of Hungary complained to the pope that heresy in Bosnia had strongly increased and that the Catholic church had but few upholders there. The pope was induced to sponsor another crusade against Bosnia, which he entrusted, in 1246, to the Kalocz archbishop, granting him at the same time the right to take away from the heretics their lands, to be awarded to zealous Catholics. This expedition was in preparation between 1246-48, but we have no information as to whether or not it was ever actually carried out. Béla was at war with the Austrian Archduke Frederick II, and could not spare the necessary time or men for the Bosnian crusade. Moreover, his eastern boundaries were constantly threatened by the Mongols. Thus both Matthew Nino-

18. *Ibid.*, I., No. 372, dated August, 1246.

slav and the Patarenes were left in peace. The latter now
consciously strove to make their church the national church
of Bosnia, and came near to realizing their goal. They were
well organized, and had a resident *ded,* or bishop. Pope
Innocent IV in his letter of September, 1247,[19] complained
that the Bosnian church "had totally lapsed into heresy".

Unfortunately for the Patarenes, the bright prospects
for the establishment of a Patarene national church were
utterly frustrated by the death of Ban Matthew Ninoslav
in 1250. The date marks the beginning of a period of
decadence which proved greatly detrimental to the country's prosperity as well as to the aspirations of the Patarenes. Matthew Ninoslav's heirs began to quarrel about the
succession, and the prevailing anarchy gave rise to bitter
feuds between the Catholics and the Patarenes. As a result, King Béla IV of Hungary invaded Bosnia (1254) and
easily subjugated it as well as Hum. In order to insure for
himself a permanent hold on it, he divided the country into two parts, the southern of which—Bosnia proper—was
left to be governed by native bans, who for political reasons
adhered to Roman Catholicism. The northern parts—Soli
and Usora—were ruled by Magyar appointees. Later, this
region was combined with certain northern Serbian territories to form the banat of Machva, and was ruled by the
son-in-law of the king of Hungary, the Russian Prince
Rostislav. Along with Bosnia, it formed an advance post
of Hungary in the Balkans.

During the reign of the dissolute King Ladislav IV the
Cuman (1272-90), Hungary was in a sad state of disorder.
The king led a merry life with his Cuman companions and
left the cares of the government to others. During this
period the royal court was more pagan than Christian.
Thus the Catholic church in Bosnia was left without its
natural defender. It was with the purpose of stimulating
the king to a resumption of a pro-Catholic policy that the
pope sent a legate to Ladislav's court (1279); the king
promised to exterminate the heresy[20] and actually gave orders for a renewal of persecution. But as a matter of fact,
nothing was done.

In 1282 Bosnia as well as the territory of Machva

19. *Ibid.,* I., No. 382.
20. *Ibid.,* I., No. 556.

passed to the rule of the brother-in-law of the Hungarian
King Ladislav IV, the one time king of Serbia, Stephen
Dragutin (1282-1316).   The clever policy of pope Nicholas
IV (1288-92) brought him into the Catholic church and in
consequence Dragutin and his lands were placed under the
protection of St. Peter.   Thereupon Dragutin, with the
fierce zeal of a genuine neophyte, adopted a policy of persecuting the Patarenes, at the same time requesting the
pope to send him Franciscan friars from Croatia who could
speak the vernacular to help him in the task of converting
the masses.   Two such friars were sent and charged with
the *inquisitionis officium*.   In spite of this however, demands
of practical politics obliged Dragutin to give the Patarenes
what was due to their strength: there is evidence to the
effect that in his counsels there sat besides the Roman Catholic and Eastern Orthodox dignitaries also the Patarene
ded Miroslav.[21]   Thus on the whole the campaign against
the Patarenes had made but scanty progress.

The successor of Stephen Dragutin who died in 1316
was Mladen II Shubich, who since 1312 had been ruling
over Croatia and Dalmatia, and in 1314 became master of
all Bosnia.   Thus under this powerful ruler not only all
Bosnia was reunited, but was linked with Croatia and
Dalmatia in a temporary personal union. However, Mladen's
power was exercised under Magyar suzerainty.   Mladen
had some friendly relations with Pope John XXII.   In 1319
the pope granted him a dispensation to marry a daughter
of the Count of Ortenberg to whom he was related by blood
relationship within the prohibited degrees.[22]   But the Hungarian King, Charles Robert of Anjou (1309-42) looked
with disfavor upon the growing might of Mladen, who was
becoming too dangerous, and invading his territory upon
some flimsy pretext, took him prisoner and kept him in con-
finement till his death.

King Charles then appointed his protegé, Stephen
Kotromanich, as ban of Bosnia (1322-53), with whom be-
gins a period of comparative prosperity.   In 1325 Stephen
annexed Hum and a considerable stretch of the Dalmatian
coast to his dominions.   He was a member of the Orthodox
church; nevertheless, he found it expedient to show himself

21.   Miklosich, *Monumenta Serbica*, p. 69.
22.   Theiner, A., *Mon. Slav. mer.*, I., No. 192, p. 135.

friendly toward the papal curia. Moreover, he was related through his wife, Elizabeth, daughter of the former Serbian king Stephen Dragutin and his Hungarian wife, to Charles Robert of Hungary. Hence he found it politic to preserve that mighty ruler's good will. As a subordinate governor of Bosnia during Mladen Shubich's reign, Stephen Kotromanich had earned Mladen's praise for his vigorous measures against the Patarenes; but upon becoming ban of Bosnia, he grew lukewarm in the matter. Pope John XXII therefore lost no time in encouraging him to undertake the project of extermination of heresy: in 1325 he sent to Bosnia a Franciscan inquisitor, Fabian, and wrote to King Charles Robert as well as to Ban Stephen Kotromanich and his wife Elizabeth to give Fabian any aid they could. But Fabian's mission shared the fate of most of the previous similar attempts; the Hungarian king found it impossible to render him any material help, and Stephen also was fully aware of the difficulty of taking any strenuous measures against the Patarenes who constituted the majority of his people. Moreover, Fabian's authority was doggedly resisted by the Dominicans, who claimed the *officium inquisitionis* for themselves. The fact was that some time before, in 1327, Innocent VI had written to the priors of the Dominicans in Hungary exhorting them to preach a crusade against all heretics in Transylvania, Bosnia, and Slavonia, promising such crusaders the same indulgences as were granted to those embarking on an expedition to the Holy Land.[23] There existed, therefore, a conflict of authority over the office of the Bosnian inquisitor, which was not resolved until the papal court rendered two decisions in favor of the Order of St. Francis; Fabian could thereupon proceed with his work. But even then the endeavors of the good father had but meagre success because Ban Stephen was far more interested in establishing his dynasty upon the throne of Bosnia, Usora, Soli, and Hum, and in extending his territories, than in quarreling with his Patarene subjects over matters of religion.

After the accession of Pope Benedict XII (1334-42), the matter was resumed with renewed zeal. In 1339 Benedict dispatched to Ban Stephen the Minister General of the Franciscan Order, Brother Gerald. He found the Bosnian

---

23. *Ibid.*, I., No. 314, p. 233-34.

ban hesitant about any measures which were likely to cause disaffection among his Patarene subjects. Stephen frankly confessed that their political strength was such that it must be seriously counted with. Moreover, there was the further danger that persecution of the Patarenes might result, at their instigation, in an interference in Bosnian internal affairs, of the powerful and very ambitious Serbian ruler, Tsar Stephen Dushan (1331-56). This was a real danger, for Dushan dreamed of uniting all Balkan Slavs with the Greeks of the moribund Empire into a single imperial dominion. His plans actually involved the conquest of Bosnia and Hum, for the latter, it is well to remember, had been taken from Serbia by Stephen Kotromanich in 1325. Gerald found it necessary to be lavish with promises of material aid, which were confirmed by Pope Benedict, who appealed for aid in behalf of Stephen to the Hungarian King Charles[24], in order to predispose the cautious ban to the plan. At any rate, the pressure exerted upon Ban Stephen, combined with the promises made him, resulted in his joining, in 1340, of the Roman Catholic Church. Many nobles and lesser subjects followed his example. As all neophytes, Stephen then sought to prove his zeal for the new faith by exerting himself valiantly in its behalf: besides the existing bishopric of Bosnia, two others were created, so that the three bishops were able to supervise their dioceses with greater care. Ban Stephen granted the bishops a tithe from the provinces of Usora and Soli and from the southern part of the country, for the upkeep of the churches. He wrote to the pope for more friars and priests "who knew the Slavic language or could at least learn it", and exerted himself in behalf of unification of ecclesiastical jurisdiction in the hands of the Franciscans. No wonder, therefore, that when Pope Clement VI wrote him in 1346, he addressed him as his *dilecto filio*.[25]

With such effective support on the part of the ban, Bishop Peregrinus was able to report a large number of accessions, Patarenes among the rest, to the membership of the true church. The same success had crowned similar efforts at Dubrovnik. Unfortunately, this remarkable period of restoration of Catholicism came to an end in 1353 with

24. Theiner, A., *Monumenta historica Hungariae*, I., No. 951
25. Theiner, A., *Mon. Slav. mer.*, I., No. 282, p. 216.

the death of Ban Stephen, which was followed three years later by that of Bishop Peregrinus. Nevertheless, the Patarenes were quite successful in retaining the loyalty of the great masses of people who identified the cause of nationalism with that of the Patarene church: the latter came to be regarded more than ever as the national faith, and for the first time received the name of "the Bosnian church".

Stephen Kotromanich was succeeded by his nephew, the mighty Stephen Tvrtko I (1353-91). He was the greatest ruler Bosnia produced. After overcoming dangers threatening from Hungary as well as from the revolt of his own powerful magnates, he rose to the rank of the first king of Bosnia, having assumed in 1376 the title of "King of Serbia, Bosnia, the Maritime Provinces and the Western Lands", for he had secured from the hard-pressed Despot Lazar Hrebelyanovich a large part of Serbian territory in consideration of military aid against the latter's unruly rivals and subjects. The magnificent coronation ceremony of Tvrtko was performed on the grave of St Sava at Mileshevo. In 1390 he reached the peak of his success by becoming King of Croatia and Dalmatia, thus consolidating under his scepter a vast Slavic territory. But being an Orthodox, the Catholic church did not find in him an ever-ready help in time of trouble. He was tolerant toward the Patarenes, for he needed their help toward realizing his aspiration of securing the grandiloquent royal title which he assumed in 1376. Profiting by the disunion of Serbia and the weakened condition which the defeat of the Serbians at the hands of the Turks in the Battle on the Maritsa entailed, Tvrtko became the strongest of the rulers of the Serbian lands. Thanks to his tolerance, the Patarenes enjoyed civil equality with the other two confessions of Bosnia.

This period of respite resulted in a considerable spread of Patarenism and in zealous missionary work on their part. Pope Innocent VI (1352-62) viewed the situation in Bosnia with such alarm that he granted the bishop of Bosnia, Peter, the right to ask the aid of the secular arm in the exercise of his duties as inquisitor.[26] Pope Urban V (1362-70) regarded Bosnia as the cesspool of all heresy of all parts of the world.[27] That this heresy was freely disseminated in sur-

26. *Ibid.*, I., No. 327, p. 240.
27. Theiner, A., *Mon. Hung.*, II. p. 91.

rounding regions is evident from Pope Urban's strict orders, issued to the archbishops of Spalato and Dubrovnik, to excommunicate all who would be found to give shelter or aid to any of the Bosnian heretics, and to prohibit all intercourse with them.[28] Despite this measure, the Italian Patarenes freely visited Bosnia, and their Slavic confreres were by no means rare in Italy.

Stephen I Tvrtko survived the crushing Serbian defeat of Kosovo Polye. He had been an ally of the heroic Prince Lazar Hrebelyanovich, but instead of sharing the latter's fate, his power and territory were greatly extended. Unfortunately, he died the next year, and with his death the process of disintegration of his kingdom set in.

Tvrtko was followed by his younger brother or cousin, Stephen Dabisha (1391-95), who however was not able to retain the gains which had been made by his predecessor. In 1393 he was forced to surrender to the Hungarian King Sigismund (1387-1437) the lands of Croatia and Dalmatia, and even to acknowledge him as his own overlord and grant him the right to occupy the Bosnian throne after his own death. The latter provision, however, remained a dead letter; for after Stephen's death in 1395, his widow, Helena Gruba, ruled the land in behalf of her minor son, Tvrtko, till 1398. But in reality the country was governed by all-powerful magnates who regarded themselves as independent of all central authority.

In the end, Bosnia did not escape the fate which had overtaken the rest of the Serbian lands. In 1398 it was invaded for the second time by the Turks who left in their wake the customary ruin and devastation. Thereupon the magnates thought it expedient to depose Queen Helena, displacing her by Stephen Ostoya (1398-1404, 1408-1418), who was probably a natural son of King Tvrtko I. He was but a puppet in the hands of the most powerful of the nobles, voyevod Hrvoye Vukchich, "the Bosnian king-maker". But when Ostoya betrayed an intention of emancipating himself from the tutelage of his all-puissant subject by acknowledging King Sigismund as his suzerain, Hrvoye called together an assembly of nobles and had the recalcitrant royal marionette deposed (1404).

---

28. Theiner, A., *Mon. Slav. mer.*, I., No. 366, p. 265.

Thereupon, the domineering king-maker elevated to the throne another *roi fainéant* in the person of the legitimate son of King Tvrtko, Tvrtko II Tvrtkovich (1404-8). Needless to say that Hrvoye remained the power behind the throne; the king ruled but did not govern. The citizens of Dubrovnik who wrote to Hrvoye that "whatever thou dost command in Bosnia is done", had no illusions as to the identity of the real ruler of Bosnia.

But King Sigismund would not permit himself to be flouted in such a flagrant fashion. He twice invaded Bosnia, and finally in 1408 scored a victory over "the renegade Arians and Manichees". King Tvrtko was taken prisoner, 126 nobles were beheaded, and proud Hrvoye was compelled humbly to sue for pardon. But the nobles of the rocky and inaccessible Hum held out against the Hungarian army and retained their independence. They restored the former ruler, Stephen Ostoya, to the throne (1408-18), but no longer as a vassal of Hungary. Sigismund, who had in the meantime become emperor, finally (1415) sent Tvrtko to recover the land, he himself being too much occupied with the great Council of Constance which had for its chief objective ending of the shameful partition of Christendom among three popes. In this emergency, Stephen Ostoya took the fatal step of calling to his aid the Turks, who indeed expelled the Magyars, but did not thereupon betray any intention to retire from the country. In fact, Sultan Mohammed I appointed, in 1416, his general, Isaac by name, governor of the important district of Vrhbosna, in the very heart of the land, the present district of Sarajevo. Fortunately, Isaac soon died, and his garrison thereupon left Bosnia. Stephen Ostoya died in 1418, and for the brief period of three years the throne was occupied by his son, Stephen Ostoyich (1418-21). Tvrtko II Tvrtkovich thereupon succeeded in wresting it from Stephen's feeble hold and for the second time assumed the royal crown of his father, the mighty Tvrtko I.

Under the reigns of Stephen Ostoya and his son, the Patarene church reached the summit of its power and strength. It had become quite a factor even in the preceding reign. Powerful magnates, among them even the mighty king-maker, Hrvoye Vukchich, who wielded great influence with the court of Naples, and Sandal Hranich who after

Hrvoye's death (1415) became in a manner successor to the latter's power, were adherents of the national religious communion. Under such protection, Patarenes were able to carry on their zealous propaganda in peace. Whole cities adhered to their tenets: for instance, the inhabitants of the important silver mining center of Srebrenitsa "were all of the Bogomil heresy". The domain of that most important center of culture and commerce, Dubrovnik, was honeycombed with Patarenes. They had their own places of refuge in the city, and were granted the privilege of *ius asyli* by the municipality, whereby anyone obtaining refuge in their homes was guaranteed against seizure for his trespass. From a letter sent by the Patarene ded Radomer to the rulers of Dubrovnik (Jan. 8, 1404) it is clear that the Patarene church was legally recognized by the government of that city and that its adherents enjoyed the rights and privileges of full citizenship.

The situation was not much changed when Tvrtko II regained his throne (1421-43), in spite of the fact that the king was a Roman Catholic. Pope Martin V (1417-31), who had been elected by the Council of Constance after that body had summarily deposed all three existing holders of the papal title, was too much occupied with the Husite revolt in Bohemia to give much attention to the matter of conversion of the Patarenes living in the relatively unimportant region of the Balkans. It therefore remained for his successor, Pope Eugenius IV (1431-47), to take some definite steps in this direction. In the first place, Eugenius sent (in 1432) a friar, Jacob de Marchia by name, to Bosnia to revive and reorganize the work of the Franciscan Order. Much was likewise expected from the work of the Council of Basle (begun 1431) among whose tasks not the least had to do with devising means for combating heresy. Although the Husite defiance of papal authority was placed in the forefront of the Council's attention, the Patarenes of Bosnia were by no means forgotten. A Dominican, John Stoykovich of Dubrovnik, who had attracted considerable attention by his efforts to unite the Eastern and Western churches in a common front against the Turks, was commissioned by the Council to induce the Bosnian and Serbian rulers to send their representatives to the Council. But nothing came of his efforts.

The Council thereupon conferred upon Jacob de Marchia full authority as inquisitor for Bosnia. But the good friar's zeal in restoring discipline in his own order outran his discretion to such an extent that he was faced with noncooperation on the part of his subordinates, and in the end found it expedient to retire from the country. In his chagrin, he tried to relieve his wounded pride by casting blame for his failure upon the king by affirming that Tvrtko Tvrtkovich was "no Christian but rather a pagan".

In the meantime the political sky became overcast by ominous clouds threatening severe storm. One of Tvrtko's chief nobles, Sandal Hranich, together with the Serbian Despot, George Brankovich, still bent upon the fatuous and criminally short-sighted policy of self-aggrandizement irrespective of common weal, offered to buy from Sultan Murad II the dominions of Tvrtko. For a good round sum the sultan graciously granted his permission, undoubtedly privately marvelling what fools these Christians be! In this desperate situation Tvrtko found it necessary to seek refuge at the court of Emperor Sigismund (1433), where he remained for three years. In the meantime, his territories were divided between the two noble and at the same time ignoble purchasers: the Serbian despot annexed the Danubian region known as the district of Usora to his dominions, while Sandal Hranich took possession of the southern portion and of a part of what later formed Montenegro. After his death in 1435, his acquisitions passed to his nephew, Stephen Vukchich, who was raised, in 1448, by Emperor Frederick III to the rank of "Duke of St. Sava". His territories then came to be regarded as independent of Bosnia, and since in German he was known under the title of "Herzog", his domains received and have ever since retained the designation of Herzegovina.

But despite the purchase of these lands from the sultan, they were repeatedly harried by invasions of the sultan's armies and also suffered greatly by virtual anarchy. The Turks restored their garrison to Vrhbosna in 1436. Following the example of those who had deprived him of his lands, Tvrtko Tvrtkovich, by paying an enormous sum to the sultan, to whom the Bosnian throne thus became a not inconsiderable source of revenue, recovered his throne. Henceforth, the Bosnian king was obliged to pay the sultan

25,000 ducats annually, and even then found himself no more
than the sultan's vassal. At the same time, to be somewhat
protected against further Turkish encroachments, Tvrtko
entered into an alliance with Hungary, by the terms of
which Jacob de Marchia was to be invited to return to
Bosnia. In spite of his former bitter experience, Jacob accepted the summons, but found the situation disheartening:
according to a letter written to Pope Eugenius (1437), six-
teen Franciscan monasteries and churches had been destroyed by "the most inhuman Turks" during the previous
two years.[29] Unable to accomplish much, he left Bosnia the
next year.

King Tvrtko having been violently put to death by his
subjects in 1443, the Bosnian magnates elected to the throne
Stephen Thomas Ostoyich (1443-61), an illegitimate son
of King Stephen Ostoyich. He completely reversed the religious policy of his predecessors by becoming a persecutor
of the Patarenes. He had been born in that communion, but
upon succeeding to the throne became convinced that the
only way to gain some security against the ever-growing
Turkish menace was to embrace Roman Catholicism. He
not only accepted the Latin rite, but even repudiated his
Patarene wife on account of her plebeian origin, and after
securing from Pope Eugenius IV (1445) a divorce decree
and a dispensation which in some marvellous fashion known
only to popes annulled his illegitimacy,[30] he married Catherine, a daughter of Stephen Vukchich, the Duke of St. Sava.
She too had been brought up a Patarene, but in order to
marry the Bosnian ban embraced Catholicism.[31] Because
of this step, he secured the hearty support of the pope as
well as of the governor of Hungary during the minority of
King Ladislav the Posthumous, the famous warrior John
Hunyadi. The pope even offered Stephen Thomas, through
his legate, Bishop Thomas, the royal crown, which the former prudently declined on the ground that by its acceptance
the sultan's jealousy might be aroused and he might attack his country on that account; later, however, Stephen
Thomas bore the royal title. The example of the ruler in
accepting Catholicism was followed by his brother Radivoy,

29. Theiner, A., *Mon. Slav. mer.*, I., No. 538, p. 375.
30. *Ibid.*, I., No. 555, p. 388.
31. *Ibid.*, I., No. 556, p. 388.

who, together with his wife, passed over to the Roman church. But although such a step appeared politically expedient, the nobility, with rare exceptions of which the conversion of one of the richest and most powerful nobles of Hum, Ivanish Pavlovich, is the most outstanding case, did not follow their ruler's example in any considerable numbers.

Becoming a Catholic, Stephen Thomas afforded the Roman clergy as much support as conditions permitted. Their propaganda had some notable results, yet the Franciscans were forever dissatisfied because the ban did not persecute the Patarenes. They constantly complained to the pope that Stephen Thomas failed to take severe measures against the heretics. The ban sent an envoy to Rome to justify himself on the ground that the policy of leniency toward the Patarenes was absolutely necessary for reasons of state: they were too numerous and powerful. He promised to exile or to put to death anyone who should refuse to accept Roman Catholicism, as soon as such rigorous measures could be resorted to with political impunity. Pope Eugenius, after having ordered his apostolic nuncio to make sure of Stephen Thomas' sincerity, and having been assured by the nuncio on that score, professed himself satisfied.

As a matter of fact, Stephen Thomas rightly judged that it would have been suicidal from the political point of view to provoke the powerful and numerically dominant Patarene constituency to enmity. He knew that they were ready to make a common cause with the Serbian despot, George Brankovich, or even with Sultan Murad II, against him and deprive him of his throne, if necessary. Therefore, for the time being he bided his opportunity.

But in 1446, unfortunately, Stephen Thomas yielded to the pressure exerted upon him: at an assembly of prelates and nobles, convened at Konyitsa, it was decreed with the king's consent that the Patarenes must build no new churches, nor might they repair old ones. Moreover, the Catholic church was assured in the possession of its own property. This decree resulted in a great exodus of the Patarenes.

Pope Nicholas V (1447-55) who succeeded Eugenius, adopted his predecessor's policy regarding Bosnia. The new pope sent a nuncio into Bosnia, an Augustinian, Francis de Lara, who reported that the country was "still polluted by the Manichaean heresy".

The demands constantly made upon Stephen Thomas both from the pope and John Hunyadi finally drove him to carry out his oft-repeated promises of suppressing the Patarenes—an unfortunate decision which brought about tragic results. Aided by the papal nuncio and the Franciscans, he undertook, in 1450, a severe persecution of all who refused to accept Roman Catholicism. Some forty thousand Patarenes, rather than to abjure their faith, took refuge in Herzegovina, governed by the Patarene Duke Stephen Vukchich, while many settled in the neighboring Serbian and Turkish lands where they besought the rulers to invade Bosnia. The act dictated by religious bigotry had fatal and tragic consequences: it weakened Bosnia just when it needed solidarity more than ever, and it drove the powerful Patarene group into an open and determined opposition. It helped the Turks not only because it divided and weakened the Bosniacs, but because the Patarenes actually besought their aid and offered them their services against Stephen Thomas.

Mohammed II the Conqueror girded himself with Osman's sword and thus assumed rule over the Ottoman dominions in 1451. He set his mind inflexibly upon the conquest of the pitiful remnants of the Byzantine Empire, consisting principally of the city of Constantinople. His conquest of that city on May 29, 1453, constitutes an epic to which few events in world's history are comparable. The magnificent Fatieh Mosque—the Mosque of Conquest in Istanbul—commemorates the event, although no special monument was necessary. Having taken Constantinople, Mohammed was free to turn his forces against the remaining vestiges of Christian power in the Slavic Balkans. He found an ally in the Duke of St. Sava who then signed himself "by the grace of God and of the Great Monarch, the Emperor-Emir, Sultan Mohammed, Duke of St. Sava".[32] In 1454 Mohammed conquered Ostrovitsa, and in 1459 Serbia was his.

King Stephen Thomas in this extremity of danger frantically called upon Pope Callistus III (1455-58) for help. The sultan demanded of him (1457) the surrender of

---

32. Miklosich, F., *op. cit.*, p. 460.

four cities along the Danube which would afford him an
easy access to the territory beyond the Save River. But
with papal help a crusade against the Turks was organized
by allied forces of Hungary and Bosnia. Unfortunately,
the death of King Ladislav the Posthumous of Hungary
put an end to this project.

Thereupon, Stephen Thomas sought to compensate
himself for his losses by securing for his son, Stephen
Tomashevich, what little was left of the Serbian despotate.
He arranged his son's marriage with the granddaughter of
George Brankovich, thus securing for him a semblance of
legal claim to the remnant of the Serbian territory which
centered around the stronghold of Semendria. But the inhabitants of that city preferred to turn the keys of the fortress to Sultan Mohammed rather than to permit a Roman
Catholic Hungarian protegé to rule over them. Soon after,
Stephen Thomas was murdered by his son, Stephen Tomashevich and his brother, Radivoy, who, incredible as it may
seem, did not hesitate to perpetrate the crime in order to
secure his shaky throne.

Stephen Tomashevich (1461-63), who thus climbed to
the throne over the corpse of his murdered father, succeeded
to an unenviable inheritance. The populace was fiercely divided by religious fanaticism, and the country was almost
hourly threatened by the great Turkish Conqueror. But
like the man in the legend who, hanging on a breaking
branch over a precipice forgot his danger in reaching for a
few drops of wild honey, the new ruler sent an embassy to
the pope, professing himself a faithful son of the church
and requesting a royal crown for himself. Moreover, he
informed Pope Pius II (1458-64) that Sultan Mohammed
was planning to invade Bosnia in the near future, and peti-
tioned for help from Hungary and Venice without which
he declared his lands could not possibly be saved. He also
reminded the pope that the Turkish sultan would not stop
with the conquest of Bosnia, but would carry his standards
far beyond, even to Rome itself.

Pius complied with Stephen Tomashevich's request,
sending his nuncio to crown the new Bosnian ruler—a ceremony performed for the last time in the presence of the
united aristocracy of Bosnia and Herzegovina. Imbued with
arrogance which under the circumstances was as absurd

as it was pretentious, Stephen assumed the title of "King of Serbia, Bosnia, Hum, Dalmatia, and Croatia"—this at a time when most of these lands were in the hands of great and jealous neighboring powers whom the senseless action must provoke to anger! And so it turned out: King Matthias Corvinus of Hungary, whose aid was absolutely necessary to Bosnia if that country were to withstand Mohammed, felt deeply offended by the papal sanction of the grandiloquent title of the Bosnian king, who seemed thereby to have repudiated the Hungarian suzerainty over Bosnia. Hence, he refused to aid Stephen against Mohammed. In order to appease Matthias' wrath, Stephen had to offer him a great sum of money and surrender to him a part of his territory. But at the obstinate request of the irascible Hungarian king, Stephen added to the follies already committed the almost incredibly foolish promise to refuse the sultan the customary tribute!

Thereupon, fatuously relying upon the preaching of a crusade ordered by the pope, and upon the promised Hungarian aid, the Bosnian king insultingly refused to turn over the payment of the annual tribute to the sultan's emissary sent to collect it, after he had tantalized him by taking him into his treasury and showing him the money ready for the payment. Furious at the affront, Mohammed II instantly determined to invade Bosnia, but was not able to put his plan into execution till 1463.

At the eleventh hour, affrighted at the fierce jinni which his own foolhardiness had conjured, Stephen Tomashevich offered the sultan a truce. Mohammed decided to resort to treachery in order to prevent his rash opponent from securing aid abroad. He professed to accept the terms of the truce, but four days after the departure of the embassy he set out with his army from Hadrianople for Bosnia. So completely was Stephen taken by surprise that Mohammed advanced unopposed until he reached the former capital of the country, the strongly fortified castle of Bobovats. The commander of the castle, Radak by name, a former Patarene forcibly converted to Catholicism, was devoid of loyalty to a régime bent upon persecution of the faith of his fathers, and after a siege of two days surrendered the castle which might have held out for years. With the fall of Bobovats, all seemed lost. The king attempted a flight from the country, hoping to be able to secure Hungarian aid; but he was overtaken by his Turkish pursuers, and surrendered to them upon receiving a written promise that his life should be spared. He was taken to Mohammed who, in the meantime, had conquered the capital, Yayce (the Egg), without a blow. The crestfallen Stephen Tomashevich then himself helped the sultan to complete the conquest of the land by writing, at the latter's bidding, to the captains of the various garrisons, instructing them to open the gates of their castles to the Turkish forces. By the middle of June, 1463, the war was practically over, and Bosnia ceased to exist as an independent country.

Mohammed then turned his attention to Herzegovina. But this mountainous, difficult country withstood the sultan's assaults, and he was forced to return to Constantinople without having accomplished his design. Before he returned, he had the luckless Stephen Tomashevich beheaded in spite of the written promise of immunity granted him in Mohammed's name by the lieutenant who had taken him captive. His skeleton was found and identified in 1888. Many of the relatives of the luckless king were likewise put to death. His wife, Maria, became the wife of a Turkish official. Herzegovina retained its autonomy, if not complete independence, till 1483, when it was finally annexed by Sultan Beyazid II. Of all Serbian lands, ultimately only the little principality of Montenegro retained its freedom.

The Patarenes, who under the last two Bosnian rulers had little cause to regard the government with devotion, revenged themselves in the hour of crisis by direct or passive disloyalty. In many instances they preferred the Turkish rule to the religious persecution they suffered under their own kings, and "the mufti's turban to a cardinal's hat". In fact, so many of the Patarene Bosnian nobles accepted Islam after the conquest of their country, for on that condition the sultan permitted them to retain their lands and to exercise very much the same power over the subject population as they had done before, that Bosnia to this day is strongly Mohammedan. Even the half-brother of Stephen Tomashevich, Sigismund, was among them. Thus the Patarenes, who had long withstood the earnest endeavors of their rulers and the outside powers striving to impose Roman Catholicism upon them, and who had come near making

theirs the national church of Bosnia and Hum, ended by
turning Mussulmans. Hence Bosnia proved in a more dra-
matic fashion than even the rest of the Serbian and Bulgarian lands have done that the religious factor plays a
most important rôle in the history of mankind. As Miller
remarks, Bosnia "is perhaps the best and the saddest example of what boundless mischief religious persecution can
accomplish".[33]

---

33. Miller, W., *Essays on the Latin Orient*, Cambridge, 1921, p. 491.

EPILOGUE

And now casting a glance over the entire period traversed and summarizing the chief characteristics of the process of Byzantinization or Christianization of the Balkan Slavs, the following general conclusions may be offered:

In the first place, Byzantinization and Christianization were two aspects of the same process. Just as in our day the missionary work in the Far East is inextricably bound with westernizing influences, so in the case of evangelization of the Slavs, Byzantine cultural influences were concomitant with the process of Christianization, or vice versa. In this process, the pagan mores of the Slavic peoples, although to some extent retained and perpetuated, and partially assimilated, became a constitutent part of the emergent culture; but on the whole they gave way to the superior Byzantine culture. There was at first a considerable opposition to the process of Christianization, just because it meant the surrender of the ancient Slavic folkways and religion. But later, especially when the new religion was preached to them in their own language, it was generally received by the rulers—freely or by constraint—because of the political and cultural advantages it offered; the common people of necessity followed. With it came Byzantine legal ideas, art and architecture, literature, trade, and everything else which constitutes a distinctive civilization. In course of time, the primitive Slavic culture lingered only among the common people. The educated classes created a literature which was either a direct translation from Greek, or if original, was thoroughly informed by the Byzantine mind. Art and architecture, especially the latter, were likewise essentially following Byzantine models, although certain amount of the native influence is still discernible. With rare exceptions, the Slavs of the Balkans lagged culturally behind the Byzantines of the Empire, their cultural achievements being but a reflex of the higher civilization of the former. In short, it may be said that the Slavs became spiritually assimilated by the Byzantine Empire, despite the

185

fact that they retained their own language and their
political independence. If the Slavs originally conquered
the imperial Danubian provinces, the Byzantine culture in
the end conquered them.

But granting the essentially Byzantine character of
the culture of the Balkan Slavs, they yet managed to make
it truly national. Of course, in a way, even this feature is
genuinely Byzantine. The Orthodoxy of the Empire developed a spirit of submissiveness to the state which frequently degenerated into subservience. The church became
an arm of the government, a department of the caesaropapal
state. In that sense, the church was a national institution,
and in this general characterization, the Byzantine and the
Russian Empires were at one. Wherever else Orthodoxy
became established as the dominant church, it manifested
the same genius for accommodating itself to the needs of
the state. It was for this reason that when Orthodox states
lost their political independence, the church became the
center of their national life and in a sense continued to
function as the national governing body. In some instances,
as in the Turkish empire, the ecclesiastical organization was
actually charged with the civil government of its people.

The only exception worthy of note to the above statement is furnished by the Bogomils-Patarenes. But even
this exception proves the rule. These movements were not
merely religious, and in their later phases certainly were not
primarily religious, but were even more nationalistic than
the Orthodox communion. They represented the nationalistic protest of the native population against the various
foreign conquerors. The Bogomils of Bulgaria were devout
patriots whose revolt against the Byzantine conquest of
their land took a religious form. The astounding success of
the Patarene movement in Bosnia and Hum, where it lacked but little to become a truly national church, can not be
understood on any other ground than the nationalistic. Like
Poland which became bigotedly Roman Catholic to ac-
centuate its resentment against its conquerors, Orthodox
Russia and Lutheran Prussia, or like Ireland whose fervent
Catholicism was formerly due not a little to its hatred of
Protestant England, Bosnia and Hum sought in Patarenism
a unifying force which would weld their peoples into a body
opposed to the political encroachments of Roman Catholic

Hungary and Orthodox Serbia. The Patarene movement is an outstanding example of the political function frequently performed by religious communions.

Finally, as for the quality of the religious life which prevailed in the Balkans, unjustifiably harsh and severe judgments coupled with invidious comparisons are often passed upon it. All such judgments and comparisons rest upon false assumptions of a fixed character of normative Christianity. Viewed from the socio-historical point of view, no such norm of Christianity exists. Each age and each cultural unit adapts Christianity to its own standard of culture, and since levels of culture are not the same with different groups or in successive periods of time, and none of these cultural levels can be said to be absolute, no form of Christianity may claim to be normative. One may only speak of the degree of success which a given historical phase of Christianity attained in serving the needs of its time and generation. What one age or group extols as the ideal Christianity, another denounces as superstition or bigotry. Measured by this relative standard, all that can be said in regard to the Balkan Slavs is that Christianity played an important part in raising the wild pagan Slavic tribes which had invaded the Balkan peninsula to a much higher cultural level than they had occupied before, so that by assimilating the Byzantine culture thus made available to them, they became members of the civilized world of Western Europe. This alone was a service of no mean order. From unorganized barbaric tribes, they were gradually transformed— thanks to the process of Byzantinization-Christianization— into strong national units whose political might often equalled and sometimes excelled that of the Empire. The Turkish conquest of the Balkans, to be sure, arrested their natural cultural development before it came to its fruition; but it never entirely destroyed the cultural heritage of Byzantium which the Slavs had made their own. This culture has survived among them to this day, whether it speaks Bulgarian, Serbian, or modern Greek.

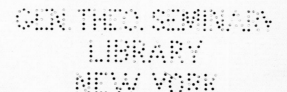
13

SELECTED BIBLIOGRAPHY

I. Sources

Anna Comnena, *Alexias.* In Migne, *PG.,* Vol. CXXXI; translated by Elizabeth A. C. Dawes, *The Alexiad.* London, 1928.

Constantine Porhyrogenitus, *De administrando imperio.* In Migne, *PG.,* Vol. CXIII. Paris, 1864.

Domentiyan, *Zhitie svyatykh serbskykh prosvetitelei, Symeona i Savvy.* Ed. by Cyril Zhivković, Paris, 1858.

Fermendžin, E., *Acta Bosnae, potissimum ecclesiastica.* In *Monumenta spectantia historiam Slavorum meridionalium,* Vol. XXIII. Zagreb, 1892.

Jaffé, P., *Regesta pontificum Romanorum ab condita ecclesia ad annum post Christum natum 1198.* 2d ed., 2 vols. Leipzig, 1885-88.

Jordanes, *Romana et Getica.* Ed. by Theo. Mommsen. In *Monumenta Germaniae historica,* Vol. V, Berlin, 1882. Translated by C. C. Mierow, *The Origin and Deeds of the Goths.* Princeton, 1908.

Kalužniacki, E., *Werke des Patriarchen von Bulgarien, Euthemius.* Wien, 1901.

Liudprand, bp. of Cremona, *Works.* Transl. by F. A. Wright, New York, 1930.

Mansi, J. D., *Sacrorum conciliorum collectio.* 50 vols. Paris, 1901-.

Migne, J. P., *Patrologiae cursus completus. Series Graeca.* 161 vols. Paris, 1857-66; *Series Latina.* 217 vols. Paris, 1878-90.

Miklosich, F. von, *Monumenta Serbica, spectantia historiam Serbiae, Bosnae, Ragusii.* Vindobonae, 1858.

Miklosich, F. von and Müller, J., *Acta et diplomata graeca medii aevi sacra et profana.* Tom. I-II: *Acta patriarchatus Constantinopolitani.* Vindobonae, 1860-62.

Monumenta Germaniae historica. Ed. by G. H. Pertz and others. Hanover and Berlin, 1826-.

Niebuhr, B. G. and others, (editors), *Corpus scriptorum historiae Byzantinae.* 50 vols. Bonn, 1828-97.

Novaković, S., *Zakonik Stefana Dushana, tsara Srpskog, 1394 i 1354.* Beograd, 1898.

Paulus Diaconus, *Historia Longobardorum.* Ed. by L. Bethmann and G. Waitz, in *MGH., Scriptores rerum Longobardorum;* translated by W. J. Foulke, *History of the Longobards.* Philadelphia, 1907.

Popruzhenko, M. G., *Sinodik tsarya Borila.* Sofia, 1928.

Popruzhenko, M. G., *Sv. Kozmy prezvitera Slovo na eretiki.* St. Petersburg, 1907.

Potthast, A., *Regesta pontificum Romanorum inde ab anno 1198 ad annum 1304.* 2 vols. Berlin, 1874-75.

Procopius of Caesarea, *History of the Wars.* Tr. by H. B. Dewing, in *Loeb Classical Library.* 5 vols. London, 1914-.

Šafařík, P. J., *Památky dřevního písemnictví Jihoslovanův.* Praha, 1851.

Thalloczy, L. de, Jireček, C., and Sufflay E. de, *Acta et diplomata res Albaniae mediae aetatis illustrantia.* Vol. I. Vindobonae, 1913.

Theiner, A., *Vetera monumenta historica Hungariam sacram illustrantia.* 2 vols. Romae, 1859-60.

Theiner, A., *Vetera monumenta Slavorum meridionalium.* 2 vols. Romae, 1863.

Teodorov-Balan, A., *Kiril i Metodi,* Vol. I, Sofia, 1920.

Theophanes, *Chronographia.* Ed. by I. Bekker, in *Corpus scriptorum historiae Byzantinae,* Vol. XXXIII. BONN, 1838.

Thomas, archidiaconus Spalatensis, *Historia Salonitanorum pontificum atque Spalatensium.* In *Monumenta historiae Slavorum meridionalium.* Vol. XXVI. Agram, 1894.

Yanich, V., and Hankey, C. P., *Lives of the Serbian Saints.* London, 1921.

Zachariae von Lingenthal, K. E., *Imp. Justiniani Novellae.* Leipzig, 1881-84.

Zigabenus, E., *Panoplia dogmatica.* In Migne, *PG.,* Vol. CXXX.

II. General Works

Bury, J. B., *History of the Later Roman Empire (395-565.)* London, 1923.

Bury, J. B., *History of the Eastern Roman Empire (802-867).* London, 1912.

Bury, J. B., *The Early History of the Slavonic Settlements in Dalmatia, Croatia, and Serbia.* London, 1920.

Cambridge Medieval History, Vol. VII: *The Eastern Roman Empire.* New York, 1923.

Dvorník, F., *Les Slaves, Byzance et Rome au IXe siècle,* Paris, 1926.

Farlati, *Illyricum sacrum.* 8 vols. 1751-1815.

Florinsky, T., *Yuzhnye Slovyane i Vizantiya vo vtoroi chetverti XIV veka.* 2 vols. St. Petersburg, 1882.

Krumbacher, K., *Geschichte der byzantinischen Literatur (527-1453).* 2d ed. Munich, 1897.

Golubinsky, E., *Kratki ocherk istorii pravoslavnykh tserkvei, bolgarskoi, serbskoi, i rumynskoi.* Moscow, 1871.

Murko, M., *Geschichte der aeltesten südslavischen Literaturen.* Leipzig, 1908.

Niederle, L., *Slovanské starožitnosti.* Vols. I-IV. Praha, 1900-24.

Schlumberger, G. L., *L'épopée byzantine à la fin du dixième siècle.* 3 vols. Paris, 1896-29.

Vasiliev, A. A., *History of the Byzantine Empire.* 2 vols. Madison, Wis., 1928-29.

Zeiller, J., *L'empire romain et l'église.* Paris, 1928.

Zeiller, J., *Les origines Chrétiennes dans la province romaine de Dalmatie.* Paris, 1906.

Zeiller, J., *Les origines Chrétiennes dans les provinces Danubiennes.* Paris, 1918.

III. General Works on Bulgaria

Blagoev, N. P., *Besedata na presviter Kozma protiv Bogomilite.* Sofia, 1923.

Blagoev, N. P., *Pravni i sotsialni v'zgledi na Bogomilite.* Sofia, 1919.

B'lgariya 1000 godini, 927-1927. Sofia, 1930.

Gelzer, H., *Der Patriarchat von Achrida.* Leipzig, 1902.

Georghieff, S., *Les Bogomiles et Presbyter Kosma.* Lausanne, 1902.

Hýbl, F., *Dějiny národa bulharského.* 2 vols. Praha, 1930.

Ivanov, Yor., *Bogomilski knigi i legendi.* Sofia, 1925.

Kiselkov, V. S., *Slavyanskite prosvetiteli Kiril i Metodii, zhivot i deinost.* Sofia, 1923.

Klincharov, I. G., *Pop Bogomil i negovo vreme.* Sofia, 1927.

Radchenko, K. F., *Religioznoe i literaturnoe dvizhenie v Bolgarii.*

Runciman, S., *A History of the First Bulgarian Empire.* London, 1930.

Snegarov, I., *Istoriya na Okhridskata arkhiepiskopiya.* Vol. I. Sofia, 1924.

Snopek, F., *Konstantinus-Cyrillus und Methodius, die Slaven-apostel*. Kremsier, 1911.

Snopek, F., *Die Slavenapostel*. Kremsier, 1918.

Tsukhlev, D., *Istoriya na B'lgarskata ts'rkva*. Vol. I. Sofia, 1910.

Undolsky, V. M., *Kliment, episkop slovyenskii*. Moscow, 1896.

Zlatarsky, V. N., *Istoriya na B'lgarskata d'rzhava prez srednite vekove*. Vol. I², Sofia, 1927.

IV.   General Works on Serbia, Bosnia, and Hum

Burković, T. J., *Khilandar u doba Nemanyicha*. Beograd, 1925.

Dimitrijević, St. M., *Istorija Pechske patrijarshije*. Beograd, 1904.

Hudal, A., *Die serbisch-orthodoxe Nationalkirche*. Graz und Leipzig, 1922.

Ilarion, Bishop, *Iz istorije Pechske patrijarshije*. Sr. Karlovtsi, 1931.

Jireček, K. J., *Geschichte der Serben*. 2 vols. Gotha, 1911-18. Vol. 3 published in French under the title: *La civilisation Serbe au moyen age*. Paris, 1920. The entire work in four volumes published only in Serbian, *Istorija Srba*. Beograd, 1923.

Jireček, K. J., *Die Handelstrassen und Bergwerke von Serbien und Bosnien waehrends des Mittelalters*. Prag, 1916.

Klaić, V., *Povjest Bosne*. Zagreb, 1882; also in German, *Geschichte Bosnien von den aeltesten Zeiten bis zum Verfalle des Koenigreiches*. Leipzig, 1885.

Klaić, V., *Povjest Hrvata*. 3 vols. Zagreb, 1899-1911.

Laskaris, M., *Vizantiske printseze u srednjevekovnoj Srbiji*. Beograd, 1926.

Marković, V., *Pravoslavno monashtvo u srednjevekovnoj Srbiji*. Sr. Karlovtsi, 1920.

Miller, W., *Essays on the Latin Orient*. Cambridge, 1921.

Šišić, F. von, *Geschichte der Kroaten*. Vol. I. Zagreb, 1917.

Rački, F., *Bogomili i Patareni*. In *Rad jugoslovenske akademije znanosti i umjetnosti*. Vols. 7, 9, 10. Zagreb, 1869-70.

Stanojević, St., *Istorija srpskoga naroda*. 3d ed. Beograd, 1926.

Stanoyevich, M. S., *Early Jugoslav Literature (1000-1800)*. New York, 1922.

INDEX

Achaia, 2, 3
Alaric, 3
Alexius I Comnenus, Emp.,
  as general, 94
  persecuted the Bogomils, 95-96
  condemned Basil, 97-99
Anastasius the Librarian, 41-42
Anchialus, 2; battle of, 52
Andrew II of Hungary,
  granted the Golden Bull, 163
Andronicus II, Emp.,
  the marriage schemes of
  Milutin, 134-35
Anna Comnena, 95-96
Antae, a Slavic tribe, 4
Antivari
  became an archbishopric, 75-76
Arianism, 3
Arsenius, Archbishop, 89, 129
Asperuch
  founder of the Bulgarian state, 26
Avars, 4
Auxentius, Bishop, 2

Babun faith (i. e., Bogomilism), 147
Baldwin I, Emp.,
  defeated by Kaloyan, 106-07
Baldwin II, Emp.,
  surrendered his title, 114
  mentioned, 129
Barlaam, a monk
  opposed hesychasm, 117
Basil, Archbishop
  consecrated, 101-02, 105
  requested patriarchal
  rank, 102-05, 106
Basil I, Emp.,
  recovered Dubrovnik, 21
  sent missionaries to
  the Croatians, 22
  Christianization of the
  Serbians, 23-24
  seized the throne, 41
  B. and the Bulgarian church, 42

redeemed Slavic priests, 47
  sent them to Bulgaria, 49
Basil II, Emp.,
  subjugated Bulgaria, 71-72
  his ordering of the Bulg.
  church, 91-92
Basil, leader of the Bogomils,
  came to Constantinople, 97
  condemned by Alexius, 98-99
Béla III of Hungary
  ordered to drive out the Bogomils, 158
  wished to conquer Bosnia, 159
Béla IV of Hungary
  his expedition against
  Bosnia, 167
  conquered Bosnia and Hum, 168
Beyazid I, Sultan,
  overthrew Bulgaria, 126-27
  defeated the Balkan league
  at the Kosovo Polye, 152
Bogomil,
  Cosmas' description, 63
Bogomilism,
  its origin, 61-63
  its tenets and organization, 64-67
  expelled from Serbia, 79
  its patriotic character, 94-95
  persecuted under Alexius, 94-99
  spread to Moglen, 99
  its influence in the Empire, 99-100
  its opposition to Tsar Boril, 108-09
  Council of 1211, 109
  spread to Mount Athos, 119
  condemned at two councils, 120
  prohibited in Serbia, 147
  proscribed by Nemanya, 157
  penetrated into Hum, 157-58
Boril, Tsar,
  opposed by the Bogomils, 108
  deprived of his throne, 109
Boris, Khan,
  accepted Christianity, 29, 32
  strove for eccl. independence, 33, 38-43
  revolt against him, 37

193